M000281851

KATIE GALE

A Coast Salish Woman's Life on Oyster Bay

LLYN DE DANAAN

UNIVERSITY OF NEBRASKA PRESS | LINCOLN AND LONDON

Library of Congress
Cataloging-in-Publication Data
De Danaan, Llyn.
Katie Gale: a Coast Salish woman's life
on Oyster bay / LLyn De Danaan.
p. cm.
Includes bibliographical references.
ISBN 978-0-8032-3787-2 (cloth: alk. paper)
1. Gale, Katie. 2. Coast Salish
Indians — Washington (State) — Biography.
3. Indian women — Washington
(State) — Biography. 4. Coast Salish
Indians — Social life and customs. I. Title.
E99.S21D43 2013
979.7004'97940092 — dc23 [B] 2013009237

Set in Garamond Premier by Laura Wellington.
Designed by Nathan Putens.

In fond memory of
Margaret "Midge" Ward, Quileute Nation

Dedicated to
David Whitener (1934–2012), Squaxin Island Tribe,
and Judy Wright (1939–2013), Puyallup Tribe of Indians
Historians and stewards of heritage and legacy
and
All of our grandchildren

Special thanks to Pete Bloomfield

They reserved everything in the salt water and in the creeks and in the rivers and up on the hills, and that is what made the Indians agree to this treaty that was made, because they reserved all of this; they thought they were going to have it all to themselves.

DICK JACKSON, *Duwamish et al. v. United States of America*, U.S. Court of Claims, March 1, 1927

There is no need
For you to give
Back to us
What we already own

TED C. WILLIAMS (Tuscarora),
"Repatriating Ourselves"

Contents

Illustrations

IMAGES

Following page 114

MAPS

KATIE GALE

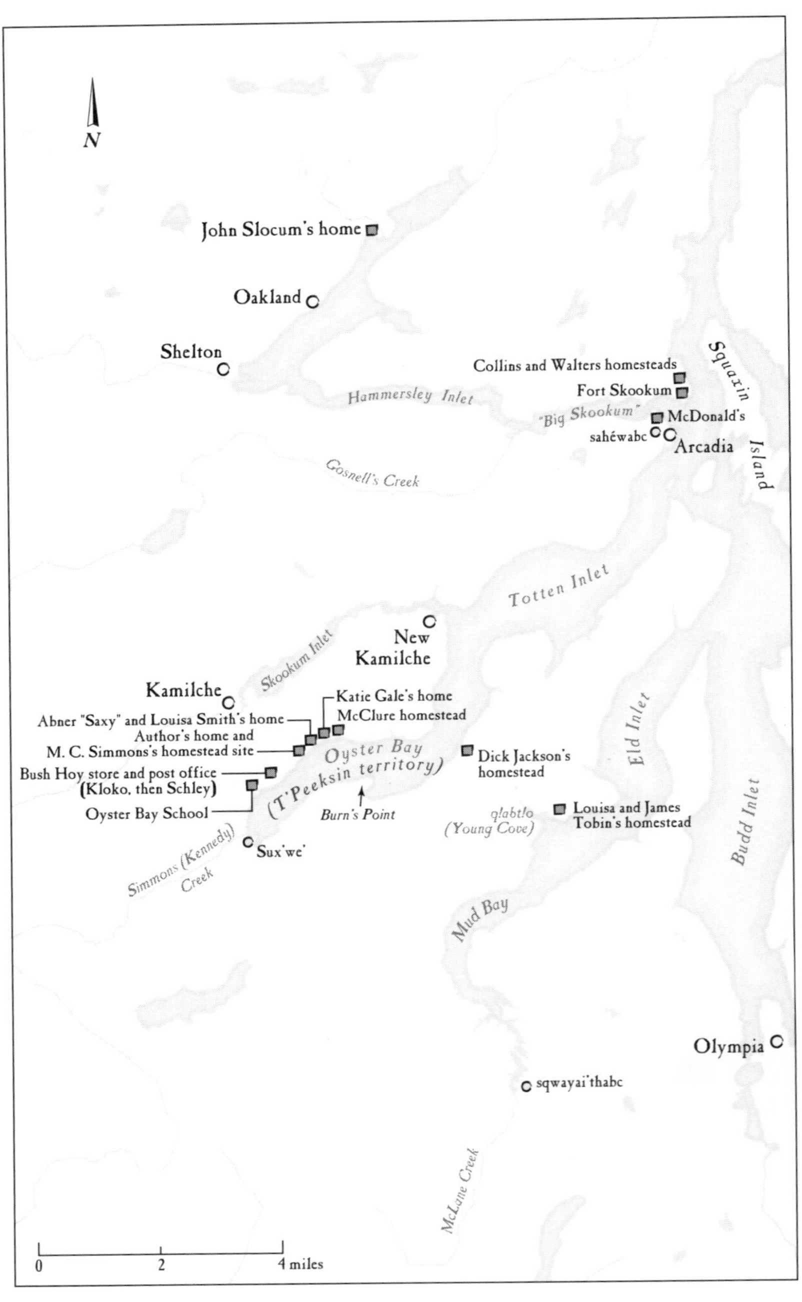

Map 1. Southern Puget Sound inlets and locales of importance to the narrative.

1 *My Lodestone*

KATIE KETTLE GALE was born into violence in an era of violence. As a child, she was surrounded by people who had lost everything and to whom promises from the government seemed not to mean much. She was close to Chief Kettle, a man whom her kin, James Tobin, said was wary of Indian women marrying white men. His words and warnings must have been repeated to her often as life with her husband, Joseph Gale, a white man, became unbearable.

Pete Bloomfield was the catalyst for this story. Pete grew up at Kamilche Point on Puget Sound in Washington State, where his father, Charles James Bloomfield, had acquired an eighty-acre plot. Charles worked for the Olympia Oyster Company in addition to working his own land. Pete, born in 1923, started logging in the area in 1948. He had long remembered a day in the late 1950s when he was felling trees around Oyster Bay, scant miles from Kamilche Point. He had his own logging outfit then. It was called Bloomfield Logging Company. On that day he came across some tombstones deep in the woods. It was common for early homesteaders, ranchers, and farmers to bury their deceased near their home and on their own property, so there was nothing particularly unusual about his find. Many of these little plots have been long since forgotten and overgrown as land has changed hands and descendants have abandoned the rural life for other prospects. Most of these graves are never visited and many have been desecrated; many tombstones have been broken or stolen and some graves have been dug up and robbed of their contents.

Pete's mind must have wandered back to that little plot on and off through the years. That memory just wouldn't go away. It was one of those things he always meant to do something about. So one day he got into his car and drove into downtown Shelton, the administrative seat of Mason County, Washington. He pulled up in front of the little repurposed Carnegie library building that contains the artifacts and documents cared for by the Mason County Historical Society Museum staff. Billie Howard, the director, was probably sitting, as always, behind a desk that allows her to see anyone who comes in through the door. Shirley Erhart was there if it was a Tuesday. Shirley is a bloodhound on the trail when it comes to finding great source material. She can spot in an instant something she knows I'll be interested in as she peruses newspaper files and dusty ledgers. Her memory for what she's seen and where she's seen it is enviable. I often receive the bounty of her serendipitous finds: a bundle of copied clippings in my mailbox along with a cheery note.

Stan Graham, a part-time employee of the museum and a retired assistant fire management officer, was there. He fought fires for the Olympic National Forest for twenty-nine seasons and then turned his attention to his longtime love, local history. He is a big, bright, inquisitive, and garrulous fellow. Stan listened to Pete carefully. He knew the spot Pete was talking about was near my house, so he gave me a call. Stan was aware that I'd worked for Puget Sound tribes for years and knew of my growing absorption with documenting the cultural and economic history of Oyster Bay. We had some common interests and I had mentored him through his effort to catalogue the prairies of the Olympic Peninsula. He helped me learn to read and use mid-nineteenth-century survey maps while I was working for the Puyallup Tribe of Indians.

On a summer day in 2004 Stan and Jan Parker, who also worked at the museum, picked me up at my place. My house is on the way to the site, just a half mile from the driveway that leads to the Olympia Oyster Company, near where Pete had said he remembered seeing the markers. As we bounced along gravel roads in Stan's oversized pickup, I examined a small-scale map on which Pete had marked a huge black *X* with a felt pen. We had clippers, loppers, pruners, leather gloves, and a couple of cameras with us.

After a few inconclusive inquiries at company houses located on the incline above Oyster Bay, we hacked our way up a bushy hill we thought might be the right one. It had been enthusiastically overgrown with alders and blackberries since Pete's decades-old clearing.

Through vines and branches we saw, all at the same time, what we were looking for. We shouted to each other, "Look, we've found it." It seemed so unlikely. We were astonished at our own capacity for sleuthing. We had been given so few clues and the territory where the plot might have been was immense.

Now silent, aware that this was a sacred space, we walked toward the stones amid the ivy and brush. There were several visible. We knelt near the biggest block. This inscribed slab leaned against a gray, stout, moss-covered base. It took a few minutes to make out the letters through the lichen and discoloration on the monument. "The children of Mr. and Mrs. Johnson," it read, "Hattie and Henry." Henry died in 1895 at age seventeen. Hattie died in 1897 at age eighteen, according to the inscription.[1]

We stood a few moments thinking about these children. We wondered out loud about the causes of their deaths and imagined the grief of losing, so close together in time, two nearly full-grown children. Then we saw another pillar. It was a column of cool, pink granite engraved in low relief with twin doves. It was lying, unbroken and still smooth as silk, on the ground beside its base. Stan lifted it. The face read, "Katie, wife of J. A. Gale, died Aug. 6, 1899, aged 43 yrs. Gone but not forgotten."

Katie Gale. It eventually made sense. Henry and Hattie were Katie's children from before she married Joseph Gale, the "J. A." noted on the stone. Katie was, I knew, the "Kitty" Gale talked about in late nineteenth-century accounts of life on Oyster Bay. She was an Indian woman who had her own oyster business and who stood up for her rights, the stories said.[2] She was known by other names, including "George" and "Kettle" and "Kittle," I came to know later. But I'm getting ahead of myself.

At the moment I was simply thrilled. I had wondered for years about the woman I'd barely caught a glimpse of in an old memoir by Cora Chase and in the yellowed ledgers that recorded nineteenth-century tidal transactions in the Washington State Archives. I'd always believed there was a story to be told about Katie Gale. Now here was her grave, less than a mile down the road from my own Oyster Bay home. I went a bit crazy, I suppose, because Stan finally let me know I was hooting and pounding on his shoulders and back and maybe I'd like to stop now.

It was hard to stave off the excitement because, though I knew little about Katie, I was absolutely and instantly convinced that this was the opening of a new chapter for Katie and for me.

2 *First Salmon*

AUGUST 11, 2010. A large, cedar, salt-water-worthy canoe, the sun dappling its bright-red gunwales, plows through Puget Sound waters near Arcadia Point, Totten Inlet, toward a waiting throng. Many standing on the beach are members of the Squaxin Island Tribe, the people who have for years conducted this First Salmon Ceremony and have invited others of us to witness with them. Some of these are descendants of the people with whom Katie Gale lived and worked on Oyster Bay in the late nineteenth century, including her kin.

The canoe's prow makes an elegant, energetic gesture skyward as it breaks the water and crosses the narrow passage that marks the head of Big Skookum, now called Hammersley Inlet. The canoe's paddlers, adorned with cedar headbands, execute strokes that are nearly perfectly synchronized. Their path across the water is sure and steady. The canoe bears the first salmon of the season, in obeisance to time-honored dicta.

On shore, cedar boughs line a rough path over a cobble and shell beach, marking the way for the officiates to receive and carry the slippery, honored fish, so recently pulled from these inland seas. This is the great body of water now called the Salish Sea, which the predecessors of the Squaxin Island Tribe navigated for centuries. Youth in "Squaxin Island Summer Recreation" T-shirts stand along the cedar path and form a protective corridor for the onshore journey the salmon will make after the canoe beaches. Drumming and singing begin. The drums join the pulse of the paddles.

The canoe makes land. The salmon is carried respectfully on a beautifully wrought cedar plank, held on four corners by carved "legs," to a platform above the waterline. Farther up, above the beach and along roadsides, are tangled masses of vegetation and bloom: wild sweet peas or lupine, drying ironwood plumes (*Holodiscus discolor*, known locally as oceanspray), and invasive Himalayan blackberry, the fruit not yet ripe. Next month the ditches will be ornamented with pearly everlasting, wild carrot (*Daucus carota*, or Queen Anne's lace), selfheal, hawk's beard, goldenrod, and harebell. Many of the plants that do well here are European imports, some having traveled in the stomachs and intestinal tracts of animals brought to Hudson's Bay Company farms in the region in the early 1800s. By autumn they'll be nearly smothered by salal and fern. Shaggy manes and amber-colored chanterelles and rare, ghostly Indian pipe (known also as the "corpse plant") will push through the soggy, mulched forest floors.

When this land was inhabited by Squaxin Island Tribe predecessors and when the first European Americans built their humble structures on these shores, deer, cougar, bear, otter, beaver, and skunk were plentiful. "Grouse and squirrel rustled in the huckleberry and salal. In the deep shades of the forest white and pink trillium sought sustenance in the fallen leaves. . . . On the water mudhens, sea pigeons and hell divers ducked to get food," one settler wrote. Along Little Skookum Inlet, just up bay from Big Skookum, "One could stand on a point on the incoming tide and catch big salt water trout and salmon until one was tired of fishing. . . . In springtime came the smelt run as large fish or salmon pursued the smelt schools." The smelt some years would run in thousands. They'd slap around in and about the shallow water and onto the beaches, "where residents would fill tubs and barrels" with them. On occasion a school of whales came as far down Totten Inlet as Arcadia. One did in February 1893. A reporter for a local paper on

Kamilche wisecracked, "They came up probably to see if the Senatorial fight at Olympia was over yet, and to give the winner a whale-back ride through the Seattle canal."

But today, August 2010, in a natural world diminished by industry and population, not yet the end of summer, we celebrate not the deer and helldivers, what some call the cunning, abundant grebes, or even the rascally politicians, but the return of the salmon.

The Squaxin Island Tribe members and their many guests, Indian and non-Indian alike, watch the approach of the canoe with the symbolic first salmon expectantly, even reverently. Other salmon have been, earlier this morning, split and skewered on cedar stakes. Now, their bodies flayed and the stakes they are on pounded into the ground all around the fire pit, they are cooking. Their back skins form a circlet of shiny shields. They stand, sentinel-like, roasting around the flames. Nearby, under a makeshift shelter, platters of macaroni salad, baked beans, clams, and fry bread with honey are arranged on long tables, ready for the feast that will follow the ceremony. There will be much more than enough. Later, Squaxin youth and young adults bearing platters will pass through the rows of visitors. Their guests or elders, some happily arranged on massive beached logs, will have loaded plates balanced on knees. The youth will offer cold drinks and more helpings of clams and perfectly cooked, tender salmon. This is but one of many abundant gestures of hospitality we guests have grown to expect and appreciate on these splendid days.

The canoe that came ashore is a veteran of the Canoe Journey, a Northwest tribal event for twenty-five years now. Davey "George" Krise was, I'm told, absent from the honoring of his leadership of the Squaxin canoe during Canoe Journey celebrations at the home of the Makah Nation, the People of the Cape. The journey had ended earlier in 2010 at the Makah home, located at the farthest western tip of the United States. Now Krise is to be extolled and receive his due. He is draped with a red-and-black blanket that is inscribed with words celebrating the 2010 journey. An elegant speech is delivered in which he is honored before we eat. A sturdy block of a man, he wears a woven cedar hat and accepts the recognition of his work with grace.

It is impossible to understand Katie Gale and the world she lived in without understanding a little about the people she grew up with and the culture and politics that informed her life and times. I'll start with the people on the beach paying homage to the first salmon because many of the Indian people who were part of Katie's life were affiliated in some way with the people now known as the Squaxin.

The predecessors of the Squaxin Tribe were signees to the Treaty of Medicine Creek in December 1854. In this treaty they and many other bands of indigenous people living throughout Puget Sound or the Salish Sea ceded four thousand square miles of land, or over 250,000 acres, to the U.S. government. Many prime locations had already been claimed and settled by Americans of European descent by the time the treaty was ratified in April 1855.

Anthropologists have subsumed Squaxin predecessor bands under technical terms that include Lushootseed Coast Salish, Lushootseed culture, South Puget Salish, and variations on these.[1] These are, of course, analytical terms, not designations the indigenous people themselves would have used in pre-treaty times. The term "Lushootseed" itself signifies the Salish-language variant spoken by people in the South Puget Sound. There was apparently no single name used by the original inhabitants of the area that referenced all the people of Puget Sound.

Names of individual villages or bands, often used to refer to whole river or stream drainages, were used to denote one's home or the place to which one was traveling. People gathered and lived together in unity around place and water. Jay Miller, in *Lushootseed Culture and the Shamanic Odyssey*, suggests that the cedar plank houses located along "the shore near spots rich in local resources, such as a salmon stream, berry patch, and hunting territory," were "major nodes" in a system that recognized and valued those who shared hearth and kinship.[2]

Points along the shores where important resources were to be found or where some significant event occurred were labeled — these points, which could be seen from the water when traveling and therefore were handy for navigation, were more important than the names of whole land masses.[3] However, linguists and others have come to understand the home territory of the people of the sound as roughly contiguous with the boundaries of the Puget Salish, or Lushootseed, language. Some in the area, of course, were bilingual or spoke several languages.

Generalizations are often misleading. As a Squaxin Island Tribe report suggests, "Each family had a particular way of doing things. . . . No one can say that, 'All Squaxins or Skokomish did something this way or that.'" Each inlet, each river, each drainage system had villages associated with it, and the resources available there and the history of those who settled the area led to significant differences in cultural practices. At the same time, abundant sharing of resources and intermarriage led to blending and appreciation of ways of doing things. As Miller notes, "Important families had far-flung networks of friends and kin, forged by marriage, adoption, trade, and social obligations."[4]

One practice that seems to have been fairly universal in the region was and still is the honoring of first salmon, the ceremony hosted by the Squaxin Island Tribe in August 2010 on the shores of South Puget Sound. The enduring practice around the First Salmon Ceremony in some ways exemplifies the strength of the people's ties to and respect for resource and source as well as their own history and spirituality. Just as it is impossible to understand Katie Gale without understanding something of the Lushootseed Salish culture and the treaty and post-treaty period in Washington State, it is impossible to understand Lushootseed culture without understanding the people's relationship to the water, to the salmon, and to the other resources in the region that sustained them and informed their culture.

This honoring of first salmon is an ancient practice. That practice, renewed and made more public since *U.S. v. Washington* (1974; also called the "Boldt Decision") and the passage of the American Indian

Religious Freedom Act in 1978, has become one of the cultural underpinnings of contemporary tribal fisheries management practice. The First Salmon Ceremonies were always directed toward "insuring the continuance" of the salmon run. Henry Allen, the Skokomish elder who in the late 1930s and early 1940s generously taught a young anthropologist, William Elmendorf, about his culture and history, said the river had to be kept clean before the run began. "From this time no rubbish, food scraps or the like, might be thrown in the river, canoes were not bailed out in the river and no women swam in the river during menstrual seclusion. The object of these precautions was to insure that the salmon would want to come." These values and this ideology serve an environmentally fragile Puget Sound region well. It is this love and respect of the waters and the gift of healthy streams that may save the sound for everyone.

First Salmon Ceremonies, of course, varied from band to band and village to village and in accord with which species of salmon was running and the time of that run. The rivers and streams on which the people established their communities, built their weirs and traps, and wielded spears and gaffs hosted the Tyee (or Chinook or king) salmon, the Coho (or silver), the chum (or dog), the pink (or humpies, humpback), and the steelhead. Sockeye were also taken from rivers that included the freshwater lakes that are visited as part of their life cycle. Puget Sound salmon, of the genus *Oncorhynchus*, are mostly anadromous, meaning they spawn in freshwater streams or rivers, go out to saltwater for a period of years, then return to their home territory, or "natal waters," to begin the cycle again. The spawned-out fish die. Only the steelhead are able to survive, sometimes, and return again to the ocean. Each species has its run, its river, its special habitual time of return, and its special nutritional benefits for human predators. Some species have a higher fat content than others. Some are more suitable for drying than others. It is the regularity of the fish, the returning, dependable food supply, that allowed people to settle and thrive along the banks and shores of Puget Sound and its drainages once the last glacial period ended. The ice withdrew from the area about eleven thousand years ago. By, arguably, five thousand years ago, the waters of the rivers were less turbid and had settled to a level and temperature that could support the salmon's needs. Of course, the earliest inhabitants of the region took other finfish. There were bullheads, cod, flounder, and perch, for example. Canoes were specialized for particular jobs: those for use in the river, those for long trips and carrying many people and freight, and those for fishing in saltwater.

Other food was abundant, in its season. There were roots and berries: tiger lily bulbs, wild carrots, licorice roots, fern roots, and the camas that blooms still on undisturbed or restored prairies and along old fence lines. They bear a waving, delicate blue flower and are a welcome sign of spring in the region.

Sprouts were taken, as were the acorns that grew on the Garry oaks that dotted glacial till prairies. These were steamed or roasted. The prairies were tended and maintained by fire to encourage the growth of camas and other root foods and to halt the incursion of firs and other plants that would interfere with the abundant native crops. Chokecherries and wild plum, native blackberries and cranberries and elderberries, gooseberries, huckleberries, and thimbleberries — these are just some of the sweet or tart treats that came in the spring and summer. They might be gathered near one's home or necessitate long trips to the mountains or the foothills, along blazed paths with friends and kin, all carrying baskets ready to be filled. The berries could be eaten fresh or dried and made into cakes.

Deer were hunted and ducks caught in great, high nets that could capture whole flocks for a feast. Elk were plentiful, though they had their own seasonal routes. They might stand in herds in low meadows during part of the year, then circle up into and along mountain ridges. A hunter who understood the animals knew where to wait at which time of year. And a hunter would not take an elk for a "trophy." The biggest and strongest were left to produce the next generation.

There were also the abundant shellfish, including clams, geoducks, and the delicious and bountiful Olympia oysters that grew inches thick on Oyster Bay.

Finfish, shellfish, and other foods such as roots and berries were the bounty that gave the people what they needed and more, barring, of course, catastrophic floods, earthquakes, volcanic action, or other natural events that blocked rivers and kept the salmon from their spawning gravels.

All these foods were scattered throughout the area, ripening and showing themselves at their own pace, each ready for harvest at its own moment.

The habitat and what it had to offer necessitated a fairly flexible people who had the technology that allowed them to engage successfully with a range of resources. They had weirs, dip nets, seines, nets, and other fishing devices for many and varied fish and circumstances. They had well-developed weaving and cordage industries and woodworking skills for crafting structures as well as carrying and storage boxes and baskets. These same skills were needed for felling, burning, and scouring out large trees for the manufacture of canoes appropriate for the different and often challenging waters through which one must travel.

The people also had a loosely structured kinship and social system that allowed for peaceful movement and relations throughout the territory. This system permitted many individual choices and a variety of options about where to live, whom to marry, and where and with whom to make use of resources. People in pre-treaty times would have framed their identity to include a vast web of kin who were members of interconnected villages. They would likely have been, many of them, multilingual and able to relate to landscapes, territories, and people far beyond the place of their own birth.

They could and did reckon family relations through both their mother's and father's lines and could choose whether to live in either the mother's or father's village after marriage. People who live in this kind of kinship system are part of extensive webs of relations who can count aunts, uncles, cousins, and other kin far and wide.[5] And these kin were able, as custom allowed, to give permission to use local resources to a grandniece or second cousin who might come visiting in the spring or summer. They could give permission to use a local fish trap so that distant relatives might take advantage of a particular salmon run that preceded the run in their home river. As Jay Miller notes, "sharing was all pervasive, both in and out of the community." There are and were no words in the Salishan language that mean "exclude." Federal court cases involving fishing rights, he continues, have "relied on notions of approval — expressed through invitation, permission, or kinship."[6]

Anthropologist Marian Smith wrote about villages in the region in her 1940 book *The Puyallup-Nisqually*. She reports, based on her interviews with elders (whose memories went back to the mid-nineteenth century) as well as notes from other elders collected by anthropologist Arthur Ballard, that these settlements were mainly composed of persons related to one another by blood or marriage. But "village participation was not restricted to related persons either in theory or practice." "Wanderers," she continues, "however far afield and for whatever purpose, sought out groups in which they could claim relationship and the trail or direction they took was usually dictated by that possibility."[7]

Homage paid to high status or wealthy persons, Jay Miller writes, "came down as hospitality and generosity. It was perfectly in keeping with this ethic, therefore, that the predominant institution of Northwest societies was the potlatch or give-away feast, drawing together diverse members of a community. Social position and prestige derived not from membership within a local community but from links — forged by visiting, visibility, hospitality, and generosity among a network of such communities. People who did not share were low class, and perhaps only marginally human. Generosity had the effect of creating in the social fabric a knot that contributed to increasing attention and regard over time."[8]

Jerry Meeker, a well-known Puyallup Indian whose stories about his late nineteenth- and early twentieth-century life were recorded in several notebooks, remembered and recounted the longhouse that his extended family and friends occupied in Carr Inlet, southern Puget Sound, during the treaty and early post-treaty era of the 1850s.[9] The composition of that house, as he described it, affirms what Smith's other informants told her about the form villages and marriages typically took. Indeed, marriages between and among persons around Puget Sound, on the coast, on Hood Canal, into the foothills, and across the Cascades were common and continued to be relatively widespread throughout the treaty period and the assimilation era. Incarceration on Fox and Squaxin Islands during the conflict sometimes known as the Puget Sound War or Indian War in 1855–56 and experiences in boarding schools after the late 1870s in some ways increased the range of people one might meet and among whom one might find a life partner. Certainly the treaties and the reservation system dramatically changed the relationship the people could sustain with their home village, customary hunting and fishing grounds, and gathering places. These imposed changes forced new and, importantly, different choices about where to make a home and with whom. Significant differences in post-treaty living arrangements included those caused by the loss of longhouses or multiple-family dwellings and the loss of multigenerational households. After the 1860s very few Oyster Bay families, Indian or European American, had more than two generations present in a household. In the later part of the nineteenth century many Oyster Bay families were refugees, torn from their old homes and lives, fending for themselves the best they could while forging new economic and social structures. Yet their resilience was evident in all that they did.

This is the world into which Katie Gale was born. It was in this world of change, of loss, of shifting U.S. policies, and of ever-expanding populations of European and American settlers and entrepreneurs that she was compelled to make her life.

3 *Where You Come From*

HERE, TODAY, August 2010, near Arcadia Point public boat ramp, down the Lynch Road, looking across the water to Squaxin Island, someone is wearing a T-shirt that exhorts, "Think about the Salish Sea — What it is. Where you come from." The Salish Sea is the new "official" name for Puget Sound. Multitribal conferences are held these days to discuss the future of the Salish Sea. A new social and cultural identity and sense of mission and purpose are emerging. What is evident, wherever one travels in the region and speaks with Indian people, is a new determination to save this threatened, ailing, and all-important body of water that has been home to the people gathered here on this beach today for eons.

Although Arcadia Point is a bit down Totten Inlet from Oyster Bay proper, it is a fitting place to begin this story. Arcadia attracted early donation claim seekers who apparently saw in the lush woods, favorable, mild waters, and forgiving climate a similarity to the Greek poetic domain of the same name. These early European Americans spelled the name of the area "Arkada." It was changed to Arcadia before long. The fabled Arcadia was an almost but not quite idyllic spot where inhabitants could live out a golden life in uncorrupted wilderness. This Arcadia, located at the mouth of Big Skookum, was called QE'lbld, or "rainy place," by the indigenous people. The "large village site" called sahéwabc was there, presumably, when the first whites arrived. "It practically commanded the outlets of Budd Inlet, Mud Bay and Oyster Bay, as well as Shelton Inlet," Marian Smith says in *The Puyallup-Nisqually*. "Its name was sometimes extended to include that entire drainage and the peoples upon it."[1] Of course, the dream of the golden life was rarely to be attained. Furthermore, what idylls the newcomers managed were at the expense of the original inhabitants.

The damage was enormous and multidimensional. Those original inhabitants, the indigenous people of southern Puget Sound, had years of hardship and challenges as they sought to regain the rights they were promised and resources they retained in the 1850s treaties. Landmark legal decisions in the ensuing years were the result of herculean work by activists, some of whom trace their ancestry to people in Katie Gale's story.

For example, a precursor to the salmon-welcoming ceremony and the renewed community and sovereignty it represents was a 1964 "fish-in" at Frank's Landing on the Nisqually River, just a few miles from the Squaxin Island tribal community and Oyster Bay. Maiselle Bridges and many of her extended family members, including Billy Frank Jr., helped lead that extended fish-in, a public protest that drew attention to the injustices visited on Indian people in the sound and one that provided the impetus for lawsuits in the 1960s and 1970s. The most famous of these cases, *United States v. Washington*, resulted in the Boldt Decision of 1974.[2] The ruling, named for the presiding judge in the federal case, George Hugo Boldt of the U.S. District Court for the Western District of Washington, restored to the federally recognized tribes the legal right to fish as they had in pre-treaty times.

Arguably of more direct significance to the history of Oyster Bay, however, was the next big case to come down the line. The tribes originally filed what became known as the "shellfish case" in 1989 as a subproceeding in *United States v. Washington*, which is the continuing umbrella case that supervises all tribal fishing claims. In December 1994 U.S. District Court judge Edward Rafeedie ruled that Puget Sound and Olympic Peninsula Indian tribes have treaty rights to take, with some limits, shellfish on certain private tidelands, and they have rights to half of all deepwater shellfish.

The court's ruling was appealed to the Ninth U.S. Circuit Court of Appeals by the state, tribes, and several private shellfish growers and property owners. In September 1998 the Ninth Circuit issued a final order that affirmed Judge Rafeedie's ruling. The U.S. Supreme Court refused to hear the appeal from the state of Washington, the Puget Sound Shellfish Growers, and private landowners.

This day, therefore, this happy time together here on this beach, is full of history: the history of a people, the history of our waters, the history of encounters between and among people, and the history of determination and resilience.

The people here on this beach, many of them, are connected deeply and personally to that history and to the story of Katie Gale.

4 *Indian Policy during Katie Gale's Time*

LONG BEFORE the landmark fish and shellfish cases and even long before Indian religious freedoms were restored in 1978, Indian people in the Puget Sound area and beyond had been standing, or trying to stand, on the ever-shifting sands of U.S. Indian policy. Understanding the political context in which the colonized people of Indian Country were embedded allows for a much more sophisticated understanding of the history of the Oyster Bay people and the choices they made in their lives in the mid-to-late 1800s.

The story of Katie Gale and her friends and neighbors who labored on native oyster beds in South Puget Sound is set largely in the time of President Ulysses S. Grant's "Peace Policy." This period in the federal government's dealings with indigenous people has been called the "assimilation era." It falls roughly between 1866 and 1900, as does the bulk of the narrative that follows. The term "assimilation era" broadly refers to policies for the governing of the many western bands and tribes of indigenous people displaced by European and European American settlers, miners, and railroad construction. During this time Indians were pressured to move to reserves set aside for them. The reserves weren't safe from encroachment if there was good agricultural land or mineral resources within their boundaries. Various acts of the U.S. Congress, enacted just before and during this period, only made sweeter and more undeniable the hold the promise of the West had on developers, entrepreneurs, and land-hungry farmers from the East. The Donation Land Claim Act of 1850, the Homestead Act of 1862, the Pacific Railroad Act of 1862, and the Dawes Act of 1887 all served to make the West more attainable and the idea of settlement more attractive to landless European immigrants and European Americans. Each of these acts served to further diminish the lands available to Indians. At risk were even those lands specifically set aside for indigenous people and rights to resource use on ceded lands, as written in treaties made between tribes and the U.S. government.

Stories of mistreatment, neglect, and outright genocidal acts against Indians in the West are legion. Though genocide in its broadest definition was not official U.S. policy, this nicety was a detail with no significance to the hundreds of innocent, peaceful Indian men, women, and children slaughtered. Well-documented episodes of unjust acts and massacre after massacre, often retaliatory or vengeful, are innumerable.

There were good people on both sides and among those good people of European American descent were some who witnessed firsthand the horror wrought upon Indian people by implacable and avaricious settlers and by U.S. policies and those whose duty it was to carry out promises written into treaties. Among these good people was John Beeson, who courageously stood up in a meeting in Jacksonville, Oregon Territory, in October 1855 to speak his contrary convictions to the people present who were determined to exterminate the Indians in the Rogue River Valley. Another was Episcopalian bishop Henry Benjamin Whipple, who witnessed firsthand tragedies of misguided policy, injustice, and neglect from his frontier post in Minnesota, where he lived amid Sioux and Chippewas.[1]

It is written in accounts of the period that "Christian principles" moved these men to action.[2] However, both Beeson and Whipple and many other European American men and women seem to have been inhabited by the more universal quality called compassion. And their compassion was what in Buddhism is called the "Great Compassion," one that made them feel committed to bring about the well-being of others, so much so that they were willing to do whatever it took to make it happen. The beliefs, commitments, and words of Beeson and Whipple, among others, mark the beginning of a well-organized and persistent lobby for change in U.S. Indian policy and the governance of reservations. These changes, long in coming, resulted in what has been called Grant's Peace Policy. Taken as a whole, these policies were meant to improve the wretched conditions that the reservation system and its politically appointed administrators had imposed on Indians. By 1866 Whipple and an Episcopalian named William Welsch managed to petition Congress for a board of inspection. This board was to be made up of people nominated by various religious denominations. Eventually, the Society of Friends joined the Episcopalians in their efforts. The Friends lobbied President Grant. Grant did not turn away. In his second inaugural address, March 4, 1873, Grant promised to rethink the treatment of Native Americans, referring to them as "the original occupants of this land." He pledged

> to bring the aborigines of the country under the benign influences of education and civilization. It is either this or war of extermination: Wars of extermination, engaged in by people pursuing commerce and all industrial pursuits, are expensive even against the weakest people, and are demoralizing and wicked. Our superiority of strength and advantages of civilization should make us lenient toward the Indian. The wrong inflicted upon him should be taken into account and the balance placed to his credit. The moral view of the question should be considered and the question asked, Can not the Indian be made a useful and productive member of society by proper teaching and treatment? If the effort is made in good faith, we will stand better before the civilized nations of the earth and in our own consciences for having made it.

The board of inspection that Whipple and Welsch had petitioned for was authorized in April 1869 and became known as the Board of Indian Commissioners. It was to be composed of ten persons selected by the president. (Protestant men filled these positions until 1902.) This board was to work directly with the secretary of the interior to advise on budgetary matters and Indian policy. Furthermore, the board was charged to investigate and make recommendations regarding the administration and conduct of those administering the reservation system. In addition, army officers were no longer allowed to serve as Indian agents, a major change in a policy that had been driven by the need to find work for Civil War officers during peacetime.

The Peace Policy was, in hindsight, flawed in many ways. It put more pressure on Indians to move to reservations, and once there they were subjected to agents, teachers, and other staff who were representative of churches and were determined to turn the Indians into white men and women. Religious groups had been sending missionaries to the West and opening schools from the beginning of the expansion of U.S. settlement. Now they could obtain federal dollars for their efforts. In Puget Sound and other places, church and state worked hand in hand to control, convert, and educate. The Eells brothers, sons of Cushing Eells, a teacher and minister at an eastern Washington mission, were well known to the people of southern Puget Sound. Edwin Eells was an Indian agent from 1871 to 1895. He was first appointed to the Skokomish Reservation in Mason County, not far from the setting of this story, and later became agent for the whole Puyallup Consolidated Agency. Myron Eells, his brother, was a missionary on the Skokomish Reservation and a preacher who served European American settlers' needs from 1874 until his death in 1907.

Conversion to Christianity and acceptance of its system of values and morals was a major goal of the new regime. Christianity would also, the reformers hoped, provide a counter to Indian spiritual movements that the United States feared would provoke resistance and rebellion in the hearts of their adherents. For Puget Sound agents and others in the Indian service, the Indian Shaker Church, first organized after John Slocum's visions in 1882, was one of these movements.

In general, traditional religious leaders and healers were undermined and discouraged from openly practicing their beliefs. At the same time, ceremonies were banned. "Civilizing" projects were especially aimed at children. Schools were established. Usually these were boarding schools, institutions designed to keep children away from "roving" parents and the influence of indigenous language and culture. Traditional dress was not allowed at these schools. Photographs from the period regularly portray before and after pictures of children plucked from their home village and made "civilized" by haircuts, high collars, and pretty, fashionable city dresses.

Pathways to citizenship and voting required disavowing tribal membership. A challenge to the survival of customs, languages, and social structure was, for example, the extended Homestead Act of 1875, which enabled Indians to claim homesteads off the reservation in exchange for abandoning ties to the tribes and embracing European American "civilized" ways.

Later, the Dawes Act, or General Allotment Act, of 1887 undercut the collective reservation land base and allotted parcels (generally 160 acres) to individual Indians. It was designed to encourage farming and the adoption of European American values and lifestyles. That included eradicating communal living where it was the norm. Some reservations — for example, the Squaxin Island Tribe's assigned home — were not big enough or did not include enough suitable land to provide allotments for all. On bigger reservations, the Dawes Act made available to white settlers the "excess" of what had been reserved Indian land.

Many liberal European Americans believed the Dawes Act was a helpful and proper next step in aiding the assimilation agenda and improving the lives of Indians. Alice Fletcher, an anthropologist and the first woman Indian agent, was one who fought for its passage.[3] The act seemed benign enough, even a good move. However, it served to eradicate tribal nations and their tenure over reservation land. When all was said and done, the Dawes Act had provided an additional ninety million acres to white ranchers and farmers and had deprived Indians of the use of that land for their own future development.

National policies and agendas had an enormous impact on the Indian people of Puget Sound before and during the assimilation era. They had been moved from their home territories, incarcerated on poorly managed island reserves during an 1856 "Indian war," and consigned to inadequate reservations after the war. In some cases, reservation land was too poor to support crops, though Indians were expected to give up gathering and hunting for customary foods and to become farmers. Indians were encouraged or forced to surrender their children to the boarding schools, an action meant to extinguish the culture, language, and religious beliefs that would be taught by their parents and grandparents if the children were allowed to stay in their community of birth.

Residents of the maritime community of Oyster Bay, populated in the 1870s through 1900 by Indians, European Americans, Europeans, and mixed families of white men and Indian women and their children, were living their lives in this era of enforced assimilation. They were also living in a time when rewards of land, position, status, and privilege were available largely only to men and to whites or those bestowed with some legal standing through white paternity or a marriage recognized under territorial or state law. Some Indians threaded their way into the weft and warp of the ever-growing European American population. Some mixed-blood children, including some in this book, were urged to do so by their white father. Some saw the advantages of leaving the reservation and reservation life and attaining land in former territories through other means.[4] Some sought to be free of the demands and oversight of agencies and found ways to do so by acquiring a homestead and disavowing tribal connections. Changing policies and laws laid down by the territorial and state legislatures, and even differing interpretations of laws by judges and justices, made the slippery issue of "identity" even more challenging.

At the same time that assimilation was made a goal of U.S. Indian policy, the country was, as a whole, "racialized" in both ideology and practice.

A racialized society is one in which race and inequality based on race are both backdrop and frame of the economic and political system. Race mattered in daily interactions, in who slept with whom, in who owned what, and in who was eligible for the rights and responsibilities granted by the state and the opportunities afforded by the economic system.[5] Even so, in some pockets mixed-race and liberal-minded persons of goodwill created communities where, for a time, identities could be multiple and overlapping and boundaries between and among people highly permeable.

Statehood seemed a certain thing in this period. Those already settled on the land counted on it. The shift from territorial to statehood status was achieved for Washington, finally, in 1889. The territory had experienced enormous growth in the European American population, particularly after the Civil War. The European American population in 1860 stood at approximately twelve thousand. By 1870 those numbers had doubled, and by 1880 the count stood at approximately seventy-five thousand.

With a growing economy and the influx of people into the territory, the region became decidedly subject to the ups and downs of national and world events. In this new capitalist world of trade and commerce, tidelands and shellfish became commodities, rather than subsistence resources for people. The impact of two major economic panics (1873 and 1893) touched the people of Oyster Bay, as did the arrival of the Great Northern transcontinental railroad (1893) to its Seattle terminus and the great Klondike Gold Rush of 1897. The gold rush transformed Seattle almost overnight and attracted even more settlers and investment money to the region.

A Nez Perce band led by Chief Joseph made a final, exhaustive attempt to escape the confinement of U.S. Indian policy in 1877. This was the same year that Crazy Horse was captured, then shot dead while in captivity. The prophetic Ghost Dance religion began spreading its message around 1887. In 1886 Geronimo's band surrendered in Skeleton Canyon. The band members were incarcerated in Florida for many years.

Sixty-two children from the band were sent to Carlisle Indian School, many against their will and against the wishes of their parents.[6] The school, in Carlisle, Pennsylvania, was one of the institutions formed to assist in the assimilation of Indian children.

It was the age of the long reign of Queen Victoria and a period when people on much of the African continent and in Asia and the Americas, some of whom had been colonized for three hundred years by this time, were ruled, treated as inferior, and marched lockstep into a European universe by bureaucracies, schools, and churches established to civilize the world.

It was the age of presidents who embraced a "Westward ho!" attitude toward the continent. Perhaps most important to the history of Western Washington was President Franklin Pierce. It was he who sent the soldier, treaty maker, first territorial governor, first superintendent of Indian affairs in the region, and railroad surveyor Isaac Stevens to Washington Territory in 1853.

During this period women's suffrage was frequently debated, both nationally and in territorial and state legislative bodies. Women, including those in the area near Oyster Bay, organized and campaigned for it ceaselessly.

This was the complex and busy time, then, when Katie Gale and all her friends and kin lived on Oyster Bay. How did Katie Gale, Indian men and women, mixed couples, and European American men and women who lived and worked on and around this Puget Sound maritime community cope with and navigate their positions in that not-so-long-ago world?

5 *Sometimes I See a Canoe*

SOMETIMES I see a canoe, or I think it is a canoe, edging up the sullen, foggy bay. It is for a moment only a sliver of dark, floating silently, just a whisper of a line, barely discernible through the mists. There are no trees to be seen or sky or water, just that dark line of intention in the hazy, overcast landscape. Maybe it is only a needle from a fir tree, waiting for a young girl to take a big drink from the water below, swallow it whole, and then give birth to coyote. But, no, I think it is a canoe and it belongs to one of the old people who lived here long ago. If I get closer to it, I think, I'll see the adze marks, the cuts made by the man or men who hewed this craft from a giant cedar.

The old whites and mixed homestead families used to watch the Indians (Squaxin Island Tribe predecessors and their kin and friends from other parts of Puget Sound) coming up bay in canoes. They were coming to the bay to visit relatives still living here, to celebrate and take the fish in season, to pick berries from the shore, or to trade for cherries or apples. When did the last flotilla paddle past Little Skookum, toward the mouth of Kennedy Creek? When did it stop, that life? Did it ever really stop?

I got a fish from one of the descendants of those people, below my house on the shore just a few years ago. One of my newer neighbors was indignant. She came, her irritation written clearly on her face, partway down the stairs to the beach from her three-thousand-square-foot house.

"They are not supposed to fish this far in," she called out to me from a landing, loudly enough so the fisherman could hear her too. That may be. But I thought it was a miracle to meet this man and his cargo of big chums, or dog salmon, spent from their long journey at sea on their way to their spawning ground on Kennedy Creek. Thousands of them return every November to churn the stream gravel and lay their eggs. This is not my beach, I thought as I looked from the fisherman to the neighbor. And it certainly isn't hers. And he has the right to return as surely as do those fish, I thought.

He wouldn't let me pay for the fish. The neighbor watched as I hauled a heavy salmon back up the hill to the brine and smoker, peeved with me as much as with him. She could not imagine how it had been here in the 1870s, when neighbors got along and a European American would be happy to trade some orchard fruit for a big salmon.

This is the bay where Katie Gale lived. She was an Indian woman from up the White River area, arguably from a village where some predecessors of the present-day Puyallup Tribe of Indians had lived. She moved to Oyster Bay or Mud Bay when she was still a child, sometime in the 1860s. She was likely taken in by relatives, for she was orphaned at a young age. She married a white man, ran a business, and raised children until her death in 1899 from tuberculosis.

The Treaty of Medicine Creek was signed on December 26, 1854, and ratified in March 1855. This was a treaty made between the United States and the bands and villages of Indians known today as the Nisqually, Puyallup, and Squaxin Island Tribes. The first people of the region retained many rights, including the right to fish and hunt in usual and accustomed places, but ceded nearly two and a quarter million acres to the United States.

Some early comers to the area had appropriated land before the treaties were signed, that is, before Indian land was legally transferred to the United States. They surveyed and claimed prime forest and prairie in Indian territory under the authority of the Donation Land Claim Act of 1850. Michael T. Simmons and Wesley Gosnell, associates of Isaac

Stevens, the first governor of Washington Territory and architect of the Washington Territory treaties, had already set up on land claims in Township 20 North, Range 3 West, on Big Skookum Inlet, for example. The pair built a sawmill on the southern shore of Big Skookum, known now as Hammersley Inlet. A salmon stream was blocked and a large settlement of indigenous people lost a prime fishing site. Not far from that stream, called Gosnell or Mill Creek, is Skookum Point bend. A thousand-yard-long shell midden was surveyed there in 1949.[1] It marks the site of that long-occupied village.

The taking of that land and the damming of that stream were among the countless examples of white prerogative overriding Indian interests and legitimacy and of settlers manipulating laws and lawmakers to their own advantage.

The Donation Land Claim Act made 320 acres (a half section) of Oregon Territory land available to unmarried white men and 640 (a full section) available to married couples. The married woman could hold half of that land in her name. The Donation Claim Act also made land available to "half-breed Indians" who made a declaration of intention to become a citizen.[2] Those who filed claims had four years to improve their claim, that is, to build on the land and cultivate it. Exceptions were made for those who could not occupy their property during the 1855–56 "Indian War."

I've made a map of all the claims and homesteads that sliced the uplands around Oyster Bay to bits and pieces after the United States acquired the property and surveyed it. My own 5-plus-acre piece of the map is part of M. C. Simmons's land, purchased by him in 1869, well after the treaty was ratified. His parcel encompassed 183.5 acres. Most other farms around Oyster Bay from this era were acquired under the authority of the 1862 Homestead Act, the Donation Land Claim Act having expired. Under the Homestead Act an individual could attain up to 160 acres (a quarter section) and obtain a deed after submitting proof that the land was occupied and improved.

Michael T. Simmons had a 40-acre homestead grant, in addition to his 639.7-acre donation claim, a little south of my place. To the north were properties acquired by the Northern Pacific Railroad that later were part of Katie and Joseph Gale's holding and now are the site of the Olympia Oyster Company.

My map, embellished with lots of Post-it-type markers with my own codes and symbols, shows that Katie and Joseph Gale's holdings and home were in Township 21 North, Range 3 West, Section 21, the same township and section that my own home is in. Theirs, however, was not homestead or donation claim land but rather purchased from earlier owners. It was on that property that Katie's little house stood. It is within view of my own if I go stand by the bank, past the location of my garden and compost bins, and peer between and beyond the big Douglas firs that mark the edge of my property. Katie Gale lived there throughout the 1880s and 1890s with children from her first marriage, Henry and Hattie, until their deaths, and her son and daughter by Joseph Gale, Maud and Ray.

Katie felt the same mud under her feet as I when she walked along the shore. She saw the antecedents of my chum salmon as they raced through the bay and up Kennedy Creek in the crisp, hazy yellow fall afternoons. She saw the bufflehead, the scaups or bluebills, and the terns. She saw the sapsuckers and grosbeaks, the kingfishers and black-capped chickadees. She saw the same lonely grebes, forever hunting for small fish on the water, as I see. Dandified synchronized swimmers, the surf scoters, grabbed her attention when they came close in to her own oyster beds. She may have shooed them away when they dove for shellfish tidbits. She was screamed at by the ancestors of my crows. They were perhaps trying to steal some food from her or give advice or maybe just trying to protect their fledglings, as crows do. She was heckled by my same scheming, lively blue jays, the same fat birds who dominate my bird feeders most of the year. Her nut trees were assaulted by ancestral matriarchs and patriarchs of the little red native Douglas squirrels that snatch all my walnuts each October.

But it was different then, in Katie Gale's not-so-long-ago days. There were still giants and dwarfs in the woods in those days, and tall stick Indians who whistled in the distance and played tricks on the people at night. My giants are more apparent and scarier and travel the world with their backpacks full of terror and misery. And the noise I hear in the distance at night is the rumble of traffic on Highway 101. Still, Katie is very close to me, though she died in 1899.

The knowledge that Katie Gale lived so close by gives me a special sense of responsibility to her and her life. Somehow it seems to me that simply setting down the bare bones of Katie's life that I can glean from old documents and archived news pages will not tell the truth about it or about the history of the place in which she lived. It will not tell about the hurts, the loneliness, or the suffering. So I will elaborate, imagine, and share my musings as well as the "facts" I've learned about her life.

As I watch the canoe, I see the water shimmer around it. As the fog rises I can see a sky above it and the piercing light of the sun, so that the mist on the bay becomes a wooly white blanket floating a few feet over the water and the canoe is no longer visible. I can see long distances now, all the way down the bay toward Little Skookum Inlet, a two-plus-mile-long finger of water, the lip of which marks the entry to Oyster Bay and the point where the main body of Totten Inlet, the bay's path to the sound and, ultimately, the Pacific Ocean, begins.

6 *Oyster Bay*

A DAPPER oyster barge cuts a jaunty path through the dark, choppy waters just a few waves' width from my neighbor's home, formerly the Oyster Bay branch of the J. J. Brenner Oyster Company. My neighbor and longtime friend bought the structure and the property it sits on and uses it as a unique home and art studio.

I watch the barge from my window, looking over what the locals call the "high rise," the second-floor structure of a working oyster plant, where a ramp and pulley system is used to offload oysters from boats. It's a late November day. It'll be a 16.2 tide in another hour and a half. It'll be low again at almost 8:00, down to a 1.9. This is a usual late fall day on Puget Sound — blustery, gray, and drizzle to full-out rain through the daily diminishing hours of light. Sun will set at about 4:30, so even the little almost day we cherish this time of year will be gone. The water is moving fast around the barge as the long, aqua, crab-like arm of a gantry crane dips over port side of the craft, pinching and prodding the muddy beds for the dumping tubs that contain oysters picked and stashed by men and women who fill them during low tides. Above the engineer's cabin, a glassed-in housing at the back end of the craft, a long pole stands, spotted here and there with twinkling lights. The barge makes grand, productive circles, then heads back down bay to its home berth.

All this water, this many-fingered salt sea, was called Whulge or Wulch by the Indian people in pre-treaty times. Saltwater. Most of my life here it has been called Puget Sound. It got that name from Peter Puget, the twenty-seven-year-old adventuring third lieutenant on the HMS *Discovery*. He accompanied George Vancouver to the area in 1792 and was sent with two smaller boats and a group of men out into the far reaches of the fjord-like expanses to the south of Admiralty Inlet and the Tacoma Narrows. He was charged to search the southern reaches of the sound. As he traveled he recorded impressions of people and places he passed along the way. He also commented on the delicious small oysters that were in abundance. At what might have been near the head of Mud Bay, one bay east of Oyster Bay, a place with whose people the Oyster Bay people sustained a long and close cultural affiliation, he enjoyed meeting a band of Indians: "These people I should suppose were about Sixty in Numbers of all Ages and Descriptions. They lived under a kind of Shed open at the Front and Sides. The women appeared employed in the Domestic Duties such as curing Clams & Fish, making baskets of various reeds, so neatly woven that they were perfectly water tight. The occupations of the men I believe consist chiefly in Fishing, constructing Canoes and performing all the laborious work of the Village."[1]

In this, among the earliest of recorded encounters with people of the region, European men decide to test and comment on the moral character of Indian women:

> They appear much attached to the Women and hold Chastity as one of the Cardinal Virtues, and not like our friends at the Sandwich Islands make Prostitution a Trade. Immense Presents would not tempt these Girls, though coaxed with Rage to violate the Marriage Bed and much to their Credit be it Spokan they remained Stedfast in this Refusal.
>
> Credit is apparently due for this steady attachment and affectionate Conduct to their Husbands in such trying Situations, as the

Articles offered were of inestimable Value in their opinions, and such as would have flattered their Vanity; not that their Beauty or Appearance created any violent Desire for the possession of their Persons. Such Questions were put merely to try, how far they conceived Good Conduct was binding in the Matrimonial State, and I may say from these Circumstances that a Contract of that high Importance to Civil Society is among these poor and uncivilized Indians preserved in its greatest Purity.[2]

Vancouver named waters and inlets of the area in honor of Puget's exploration. Many of the names still hold. Meanwhile, reports of the mild climate, attractive landscape, and potential for development were sent home. The land was viewed as up for grabs.

As of 2009, Puget Sound was renamed the Salish Sea by the U.S. Board of Geographic Names. The old sound, less inclusive geographically than Salish Sea (the Georgia Basin plus Puget Sound make up the Salish Sea), is bounded to the west by the Olympic Mountains and to the east by the Cascade Mountains. It is a huge, multiarmed trough scoured out by the Wisconsin Glaciation that covered most of Washington State between about thirty thousand and ten thousand years ago. It is fed by the Pacific Ocean and contains approximately two million acres of sea water.

Human occupation of Puget Sound began perhaps as early as twelve thousand years ago. "Little in depth investigation of sites in the inlets of southern Puget Sound has taken place, so the actual time period of earliest habitation is somewhat speculative." From the "late Holocene," or 2,500 years ago, Indian people developed village sites along shorelines and especially at river mouths and the confluence of streams or side streams. These settlements, selected for access to rich resources, included "permanent or semi-permanent winter villages with seasonal upland and lowland camps where gathering, harvesting and processing of particular resources such as salmon, shellfish, camas, berries and cedar bark took place."[3]

The T'Peeksin were among those who settled Puget Sound. They are ancestral to and a predecessor band of the present-day Squaxin Island Tribe. Their home was Oyster Bay. That bay, less than a mile across at my place, lies at the extreme southern end of Totten Inlet, one of the extensions of the sound. It is located in southwest Washington and split down the middle now by the invisible political boundary between Thurston and Mason Counties. It was arguably the most productive site in Puget Sound for the tiny Olympia oyster. Nearby Mud Bay was also known for the quality of its tidelands and the richness of the resource.

Some commercial harvests by whites began in the 1850s, though Indians had been harvesting and trading oysters for centuries. After the 1850s things got fired up for real. Yields reached 100,000 kilograms annually in the 1890s and 358,000 kilograms by 1905. It was during these decades, especially the years immediately following the signing of the Treaty of Medicine Creek in 1854 and again just after statehood in 1889, that the cultural and ethnic flavor of the bay altered dramatically.

The T'Peeksin people were among the signees to the Treaty of Medicine Creek. This treaty (like other treaties in the region, all of which used the same template) had a number of provisions that were arguably not made clear to the people who were present for "negotiations" on "She-na-ham or Medicine Creek" near the head of the Nisqually River. "Chiefs," "head-men," as well as "delegates of the Nisqually, Puyallup, Steilacoom, Squawskin, S'Homamish, Stehchass, T'Peeksin, Squi-aitl, and Sa-heh-wamish tribes and bands of Indians, occupying the lands lying round the head of Puget's Sound and the adjacent inlets," represented the Indians of the region, "who, for the purpose of this treaty, are to be regarded as one nation."

This treaty was one of several negotiated by Isaac Stevens between 1854 and 1855. It was followed by nine more in quick succession after Medicine Creek. The Americans and Stevens, as an agent of the Franklin Pierce administration, were in a hurry to have the land legally ceded to provide for the thousands who had come west on the Oregon Trail and were still arriving, wagonload after wagonload, hauling household goods, animals, and hopes for a better life. The British had given over claims to the Oregon Country in 1846, thus opening the way for the United States and its plucky people, including missionaries, to go west, "multiply, and subdue the earth."[4]

Isaac I. Stevens, governor and superintendent of Indian affairs of Washington Territory as well as the leader of the railroad survey to determine a route to Puget Sound from the east, acted on behalf of the United States. As Kent Richards notes, "His task appeared straightforward — he would extinguish aboriginal title to the land, establish the best lines for roads and railroads, and inaugurate a government that would provide the political stability necessary for the population to grow and the economy to flourish in the Northwest sector of the nation."[5]

A reservation, one of three described in the Treaty of Medicine Creek, was established on "the small island called Klah-che-min, situated opposite the mouths of Hammersley's and Totten's Inlets, and separated from Hartstene Island by Peale's Passage, containing about two sections of land by estimation." This was the reservation, a short paddle down Oyster Bay and Totten Inlet, on which the people of Oyster Bay, the T'Peeksin, were meant to settle.

The land opened up for American settlement, with its promise of fertile homesteads, fueled enthusiasm among eastern farmers and entrepreneurs. The land and waterways were lauded in brochures published all over the United States. These depicted a virtual paradise with abundant opportunity.

Oregon Territory and its government were created by the U.S. Congress in 1848, two years after boundary disputes with Britain were settled with the Oregon Treaty, and included areas now known as Oregon, Idaho, and Washington and part of Montana and Wyoming. By 1843 a wagon trail ran from Missouri to The Dalles, in the Oregon Country.

The trail was nearly two thousand weary and difficult miles long but passable and soon to be improved. The trail was heavily used, with the promise of free land (through the Donation Land Claim Act of 1850) and homesteads (the Homestead Act of 1862). The population of the Oregon Country grew by over fifty thousand between 1843 and 1859. The completion of the transcontinental railroad in 1869 linked Omaha and Sacramento, making the journey to the West easier and dreams more likely to come true.[6]

European and American loggers and farmers as well as professionals, business people, artists, writers, and adventurers arrived to make their fortune or just to try their luck at something new. Some, like Joseph Gale, the man Katie Gale married, were restless from their overland journey from the eastern United States. They settled only for a few years, if that, in the southern part of Oregon Territory, that is, south of the Columbia River, often in the Willamette Valley area. Then they came north into what is now called Western Washington. Their eyes were on bigger prizes. Surely there was wealth to be had in this up-and-coming area.

As the laws allowed and land was surveyed, European American men and women purchased not only uplands and homesteads but also tidal land, land that had been harvested for shellfish by Indian people for generations. They positioned themselves to build lucrative oyster businesses.[7] They established new methods for growing oysters, increasing production, and introduced technologies that changed the surface features of Oyster Bay and other rich shellfish bays. Beds were filled and raised and the muddy flats eventually were crisscrossed with dikes to hold water and better nurture and fatten crops of oysters.

An enterprise that had provided subsistence for Indian people was now linked to fluctuations in the national financial picture, and those who labored in it were subjected to the oscillations of economic processes over which they had little control. Steam-driven boats instead of Indian canoes pumped their way through the waters at high tide, carrying passengers and freight to Olympia. The freight included oysters from the small float houses and culling houses that dotted the bay. Indian oyster farmers and paid laborers, as well as non-Indian owners and laborers, lived and worked on the barges and float houses. Later, by the 1890s, Chinese and, after 1900, Japanese people worked as cooks, ran floating laundries, and labored on the mudflats for the oyster growers.

Some Indian people, too, claimed tidelands on the bay. The 1887 Dawes (General Allotment) Act and the Indian Homestead Act of 1875 required that an Indian adopt "the habits of civilized life" in order to secure land.[8] If an individual took an Indian homestead or received an allotment and agreed to disaffiliate from a tribe, that person was eligible for citizenship and attendant rights. Those individuals were also eligible to apply for tidelands.

Thus, on Oyster Bay Americans and Europeans, Indians, Chinese, and by the early twentieth century, Japanese met and worked together, sometimes side by side, for a wild, energetic, and significant era. They were touched, even driven, by a world of commerce, politics, and territorial and state laws that informed their lives and ability to work for a living in subtle and not-so-subtle ways. Events and legislation that were arguably most significant for the prospects of workers and their presence on Oyster Bay included the Chinese Exclusion Act of 1882 and anti-Chinese riots in Tacoma and Seattle, the Dawes (General Allotment) Act of 1887, the economic panic of 1893, and the 1895 Bush and Callow Acts, which allowed the sale of tidelands to private citizens.

Broken fire rock, remains of fish traps in the estuarial area of Oyster Bay, and shell middens (lenses in the bank composed of crushed mollusk shells and organic matter) indicate an early and long occupation of this lush marine shoreline by Indian inhabitants. A large midden on the east side of the bay was still visible in the 1940s.[9] It ribboned along the exposed earth between layers of sand, mud, and silt for 150 yards. Sites on Oyster Bay found and recorded over the years corroborate the detailed testimony of informants to anthropologists who worked around the sound with aged Indian people in the first half of the twentieth century. That is, the middens are located in areas men and women remembered as villages or campsites.

Near the mouth of Kennedy Creek, the creek that enters the bay from the south, stood a village. During a 1927 Indian Court of Claims case Johnny Scalopine remembered "three houses on the head of that Oyster Bay where they were drying salmon at that creek."[10] Don't be misled by the term "house." Houses were made of split cedar planks and provided comfortably for several families, usually related in some way. The houses were built near shores of salmon streams, sometimes several of them in close proximity with one another. The floors were earthen and walls and living spaces were adorned with shelves, blankets, storage baskets and boxes, and cedar-bark mats. Roofs were typically of a shed type or composite gable with a lean-to on one side.

Though many of Katie Gale's friends were born elsewhere in the region and made Oyster Bay or Mud Bay home after the treaties and war, they knew the history and the place-names of the land and shores they occupied. They learned quickly from those who remained in their home territory and with whom they now shared a destiny.

Indeed, when Katie and the others looked up and down Oyster Bay they saw places that they called what they'd always been called: the landscape was a text and a history book. There were literally hundreds of sites the people had knowledge of and by which they navigated and arranged meetings. There at the mouth of Simmons Creek, now Kennedy Creek, was TEpi'lkwtsid, or "caving down mouth."[11] Anthropologist Marian Smith wrote the name "tapiqsdabc" and understood it to be a village site. Louisa Tobin, one of Katie Gale's relatives and a contemporary, however, seems to have used this name for the creek or mouth of the creek from which the village took its name. Nearby was Sux'we', perhaps the site where the three seventy-two-foot-long houses John Scalopine remembered in his Court of Claims testimony for the Squaxin Island Tribe in 1927 had stood.

Sux'we' was named for a singing fish that resembles and is often called a "bullhead." The species found in Puget Sound is *Porichthys notatus*, also known as the plainfin midshipman. It is a bottom-dwelling fish with a gas bladder that it uses to make a range of "humming, grunting, and growling noises." These noises reportedly attract the female to the nest the male has dug under rocks.[12] Old-timers said that one could hear these fish humming under rocks at low tide. T. T. Waterman, an anthropologist who studied Puget Sound indigenous geography in the early twentieth century, called Sux'we' "an important village site," based upon what elders told him.

There were fish traps all around the area where Oyster Bay met the creek. Even now reminders of those days can be seen close to where the longhouses must have been. Skeletal remains of the old traps, rotting, barely visible at low tide, poke forlornly out of muddy sloughs and channels.

People from all around the bay, and, after the reservation was established, from out on Squaxin Island, came there to get the fish when they ran in the fall. The anadromous chum salmon that returned were plentiful and still are. The fish swim to the head of the bay and enter Kennedy Creek. Kennedy Creek, formerly Simmons Creek, is an abundant chum stream that originates high in the Black Hills at Summit Lake, then winds its way down and through the bay. The stream courses through the mudflats on the bay; the deep, meandering streambed is visible at the lowest tides. The chum run is from late October through November. Up the creek, the females make depressions in the gravel and lay their eggs. Then the males fertilize them. The spent fish die along the banks and are eaten by bear or eagles and other animals that feast along the creek. Even the small fish, after they hatch, feed on what is left of the carcasses. Eventually, in March and April, the fry leave their home territory and swim to the saltwater estuary of Oyster Bay. After they've adapted to saltwater they swim out to the ocean and feed there for three to four years before returning to Kennedy Creek to begin a new cycle.

It was no doubt the history of this site and its location at the mouth of the salmon stream that attracted and sustained the cluster of float houses occupied by Indian oyster workers after the war and the establishment of reservations in the 1860s. The extended network of kin and friends, living in close proximity in their anchored homes, must have allowed in some ways for the cooperation, camaraderie, and interaction people would have enjoyed in their now-appropriated longhouse sites.

Long before Waterman collected information and Scalopine testified in the Court of Claims, that vibrant, productive life at the head of Oyster Bay was gone, village sites had been usurped, and longhouses all around Puget Sound had been demolished or burned by white settlers.

Each year, still, legions of human sport fishers line the banks of the stream in the estuary and haul in large fish. These past few years the spawning grounds of those fish have become a weekend tourist destination. Red-cheeked, well-trained guides, some my friends and neighbors, stand on wooden bridges or soggy banks, ready to explain the salmon life cycle, salmon mating behavior, the requirements of habitat, and details of the chums' journey to the sea and back. Dead fish litter the banks. The nearly dead bull their way up the side streams, over rocks and fallen trees, bent on reproducing themselves.

Right across from Katie's house, what is now called Burn's Point, was T'EbE'x^{u}, or "gooseberries." A bit farther out toward Totten Inlet and on that same shore was Tsaba'L. A little creek there marked the spot where people who were "sucking doctors" lived. These were healers who used a variety of methods to treat the sick, including "sucking" illness through tubes or through direct contact of lips with the body of the patient.

Between the gooseberry place and the mouth of Simmons Creek was the big rock Ts!ikewls, an elk changed to stone by the Transformer.

Katie knew the names and the places well. In fact, it was Katie's friend and relative Louisa Kettle Tobin who later told these names to T. T. Waterman's research associate Ruth Greiner in 1927, so that they would not be forgotten. It was Louisa's husband, James Tobin, who drew a map of the area and labeled it with names he'd learned from elders.

The banks and shores of Oyster Bay hold evidence of later times: the coming of the European and American settlers and the development of the early shellfish industry. The story is in the dumpsites that spill out medicine bottles after winter storms claw at the clay banks. An empty glass bottle labeled Angier's Emulsion, prescribed for colds, coughs, and bronchitis and as a tonic for the nervous system surfaced once as I strolled along the shore. It is a reminder of the scourges that visited the people on the bay. It promises to "give prompt and effective relief." An early 1900s ad for Angier's claims it has "no equal as a lung healer" and that it is "the most palatable of all emulsions." It was made of petroleum and hypophosphites.

The Oyster Bay people probably used it for treatment of pulmonary tuberculosis. Hypophosphites were touted as an effective remedy in the late nineteenth century. Of the 173 deaths in the Oyster Bay area between 1891 and 1906 recorded in newspaper accounts and funeral home records, 30 were from consumption (also called tuberculosis or phithsis for the wasting-away properties of the disease) and 18 were from pneumonia or other pulmonary problems. (Other causes of death were railroad accidents, drownings, men crushed between logs or "killed by tree," and even a murder-suicide: two loggers in a lethal, drunken dispute that ended in the death of both of them.)

Another day when I was walking the beach an unbroken vial of Perry Davis Vegetable Painkiller — a small, aqua-tinted bottle — fell from a section of muddy, root-infested bank. Perry Davis branded his medicine in the 1840s. A label claims it is useful for "slight ailments" that occasionally afflict us all. "For cholera, morbus, cramps and all bowel troubles," the print on the box continues, "it has no equal." It purportedly contained opiates and alcohol.

Near that vessel was a lovely little Colgate and Company perfume bottle, perhaps a gift to a sweetheart or the possession of a woman who longed for a more delicate life. Colgate was making over three thousand different soaps and perfumes and other products during this era, and even the oyster workers and steamboat crew must have trekked to stores in Olympia or Arcadia or Shelton to buy and indulge in a taste of a more refined world.

Shards of crockery also wash out of from under tangles of madrona roots and from behind ancient tree trunks that line the shore. There are sometimes chunks of ironstone from China, KT and K granitewear, and crackle-glaze porcelain. A pile of empty soy tins lies in a jumble in the woods just above the beach from the ruins of cabins where some of the many Japanese laborers in the shellfish industry lived. Canceled money orders to families back home in Japan and even dank, moldy notes from citizenship classes have floated out of derelict shacks no longer occupied by the workers. The falling-down structures yield flotsam and jetsam dating through the 1950s.

The technologies of the early oyster entrepreneurs are here too: rusted iron mesh mud shoes protruded from the banks near the old Brenner Oyster Company buildings after a high tide sloughed off a layer of mud and silt one day. There are plenty of posts and pilings associated with the industry that I can explore from my kayak; skeletal remains of old docks, like spars of sunken ships, still stand like dark sentinels here and there. Many of these were mooring posts for floating cull houses. Others are remains of wharfs where the wood-burning and, later, gasoline-driven launches came to carry bags of oysters from the bay to Olympia and markets beyond. Some low-lying beach fronts are still scattered with the shells of Olympia oysters, denoting places where small growers had their culling operations. Some places along the shore, visible when the tide is out, mark winter resting places for float houses.

7 *The Duties of a Woman*

KATIE GALE is standing beside her house up the hill from the bay washing clothes in a seventeen-gallon wooden tub. Katie wears her everyday work clothes, a plain, checked calico cotton dress that has no shape at all. Someone offered her a bolt of this fabric at a giveaway last Fourth of July on Mud Bay, where many South Sound Indians gathered each year during the late nineteenth century to celebrate, feast, game, and visit with one another. The estuarial, C-shaped Mud Bay is at the head of Eld Inlet. Rich tidelands, good for oyster cultivation, are exposed at low tide in that bay. It is an easy walk or horseback ride or paddle from Oyster Bay to Mud Bay.

An archaeological project has found evidence of long habitation of Mud Bay by Indian people. There are also ethnographic and geographic notes as well as oral histories that confirm the bay's long-term occupancy. McLane Creek was, according to T. T. Waterman's informants, called Sqwaya':iL. It flows into the bay at the southern extension of its estuary. Marian Smith, in *The Puyallup-Nisqually*, says there was a village there called sqwayai'thabc. This was probably another of the villages John Scalopine remembered in his Court of Claims testimony. He said there "were two big houses on the head of Mud Bay on the creek there where they used to dry salmon, and three of them below the Mud Bay head on the east side of the bay." He said that each one was about seventy-two feet in length.

People stayed or returned to that village site after the signing of the Treaty of Medicine Creek and the 1856 war. People were living there throughout Katie Gale's time. Photographs taken in 1892 of the site, the people, and the dwellings there attest to its continued use and the vibrancy of a culture. Judge James Wickersham took the photographs with a No. 1 Kodak camera, first offered on the market in 1888, around the time of the 1892 Fourth of July celebrations and potlatch and during the time he, as a young attorney, had come to the bay to help draw up articles of incorporation for the Indian Shaker Church. I'll come to that story later.

The big Fourth of July congregations were an opportunity to visit with people from near and far, including relatives from Yakama. A Yakama bag, collected by T. T. Waterman for the Heye Museum in 1920 from an Oyster Bay woman, was probably a gift given or traded for during one of those July celebrations. The Fourth of July meetings were also opportunities to spend money on others, give away accumulated wealth, and mark major life passages, including the deaths of loved ones.

Calico was among the popular fabrics purchased and given at these gatherings and was used regularly by women on Oyster and Mud Bays. One of Wickersham's photos shows a woman sitting by bolts of what was probably calico. Other popular fabrics were gingham, muslin, and even cashmere. All of these were available at local dry goods stores, including the little stores in Kamilche and on Oyster Bay and Totten Inlet.[1]

Katie Gale, standing there on her hill, is wearing that dress made from calico she got at the last Fourth of July celebration. She used it to make a garment for herself and one each for her daughters, Hattie and Maud.[2] The sleeves of her outfit are loose but they button at her wrists. The collar is simple, untrimmed, and closed with matching buttons around her throat. Over the dress is a large, white, utilitarian apron with pockets made of a canvas-weight cotton twill.

Her black hair is pulled back into a tight, smooth knot at the nape of her neck. Sometimes she lets it hang loose; it falls like an ebony river and ripples down the whole length of her back. After she washes it, as she did last evening, she stands near the stove. It makes a dark storm around her head as she waves it in great arcs until it dries.

She smiles at a thought that passes through her mind. Perhaps it is an image of little Maud preparing, in her serious, intentional way, to recite a poem for school, or the pleasure she knows dear Ray will have when he brings his pal, Adolph, home for creamed salmon dinner tonight. Her face is broad; her mouth seems too big for her jaw and her smile seems too broad for her mouth, so when she is happy that smile overwhelms one. Her eyes are a starburst of deep amber folded all around with soft flesh of lids and dark lashes. Over those are the heaviest of arched brows. Above one brow is a deep scar.

Her house is made of rough-sawn planks from a friend's home mill. The sides and roof are covered with thick, unevenly cut, lapped, hand-split cedar shingles. They've been nailed to strips of lath. The lath has been nailed to sturdy posts. The house or cabin is what architects call "vernacular." There was no particular plan or design used in building it. Local materials were used and nothing beyond the merely functional was a consideration in its construction. It is similar to all the other houses on the bay in this period. And it is similar, too, to the float houses and cabins in Mud Bay and Oyster Bay, dwellings occupied by Katie Gale's friends. Attention to fashionable details came to Oyster Bay architecture later and for the few with accumulation of wealth and affluence.

The house has three windows and two doors, one facing the bay and the other leading back to the outhouse and the woodpile. There is a small, low passage cut into the back wall so that split logs can be slipped into the house to feed the fire. This opening has a little hinged door so that the cold can be shut out after the logs are passed through. The two rooms are fitted with wooden tongue-and-groove fir floors and interior walls. The old-growth fir has a fine grain. Originally quite light, it's grown dark with years of smoke from the stoves and lamps.

The doors would have cost around five dollars and the window frames not more than ten. Enough shingles to cover the structure would have cost about twenty-five dollars, unless Katie Gale and her family split the shakes themselves from cedars on the property. A box of nails cost about ten dollars. Labor to build this small dwelling would run about sixty-three dollars unless, of course, family members did the work in exchange for a few great home-cooked meals.[3]

In one room stand three beds of various sizes. On the bed frames are straw or feather-packed mattresses and wool and flannel blankets. The flannel was bought in bolts and cut and sewn to size by Katie.

A wood-burning cookstove sits in one corner of the other, larger room. Smoke rises up the tin smokestack that pokes at an angle through the far side of the gabled roof. Katie is baking bread and biscuits today. She and other women in the area bake what they called "light bread," a wheat bread made with yeast. She moves in and out of the house, keeping one eye on the laundry and laundry fire, another on the stove.

She's baking and washing but also preparing for next steps she'll take with the clean, fresh clothing. Four flatirons, solid metal, each a different weight and size appropriate for the job, sit on the stove, heating. The heaviest is eight pounds. Katie hopes the clothes on the line will dry by late afternoon so she can press and smooth them with the heavy irons before the day is done. This is Puget Sound, so good, long, sunny days for drying clothes are numbered. She is counting on a bright, clear sky today and has her clothesline well away from any shade.

When the clothes are as dry as can be expected, they will be taken inside and folded before pressing. Katie Gale has a heavy cloth that she covers the kitchen table with when ironing clothing. Then, after they are pressed and meet Katie's standards, they'll be placed on shelves and in cupboards. If mending is needed it is done in the evenings in the quiet, warm light of her kerosene lanterns.

Along the walls in the main room, not far from the stove, hang bundles of herbs, dried or drying, bundles of basket materials, and some string bags and loosely woven cedar baskets as well as tightly woven cedar, bear grass, spruce root, and sweetgrass baskets with imbricated mountain designs. She's had to repair some of them where they've been worn or nibbled on by rats. Near them hangs a slightly worn and tattered cedar mat that she cuts fish on.

Some baskets are full of gathered foods, including camas and licorice root and sun-dried berries from her summer trips to the foothills of the Cascades with relatives or out Cloquallum with the Krises. Her cow-horn berry rake is on a shelf near the baskets.[4]

The largest open-work cedar baskets on Katie's wall are used when she is digging clams, the clams allowed to clean themselves in the cool rush of freshwater streamlets that run out of the bank into the bay from one side of her property. There is a barrel of salted fish, and there are dried clams on strings hanging from an iron hook next to the bags of roots.[5]

Open shelves are built along the rough walls of the cabin, and on them Katie keeps plates she's purchased in Olympia and Tacoma, an assortment of those with designs that suited her fancy.

Near the stove, on the kitchen table, are three glass-chimney kerosene lamps with tin reflectors. The lamps are used most often in the winter, when the days are short and Katie needs more illumined evening time for sewing and baking and the children need it for their homework.

Kerosene lamps were ubiquitous, still, in rural western settlements in Katie Gale's day. According to newspaper accounts from the period, these lamps or their misuse were responsible for many home fires. People often stored kerosene in unstable containers and "filled their lamps at night or over the stove," unwittingly asking for an accident. Women apparently "blew down into the chimney," a habit compared by contemporaries to "blowing down the muzzle of a gun to see if it is loaded." The breath was said to release toxic gases into the home. Women were advised not to carry a lamp from one part of the house to another while it was lighted. It was easy to slip and fall and start an unquenchable blaze. Katie Gale is careful because she has heard stories of disasters.

A box of candles is ready to serve as backup, and several oil lanterns hang near the door to be used for outdoor work in the dark. These are essential equipment when Katie works on the mudflats in low winter tides. Boots and gloves and heavy coats and hats are ever ready on wooden pegs near the door. There are more hooks close to the stove, designated for drying wet work clothes.

The dancing flames of lamps and candles make lively shadows on the uneven walls of the little cabin, especially on long, dark nights. Playful winged things come flap and flash against the fatally attractive bright glass globes in the evening.

Today the lamp globes have been cleaned, handled carefully by the light of the morning that streams through the windows. Wicks have been trimmed.

Stoves require lots of wood to keep them going and the house heated during the long, damp winters. Katie can get by with, maybe, six cords during the coldest months on the bay, when the wind comes strong across the water and bare branches freeze. Preparing for these winters means felling trees up on the back property, then sawing them into stove-sized logs. They have to be hauled down to the cabin and then split into quarters with axe and wedge. Kin or friends would have helped with this chore, but Katie and other women could do this work on their own. It had to be done early enough in the summer or spring so that the wood could dry, thus one didn't wait around for others to do it. Green wood would be a problem to start.

Some people on the bay could be hired to help with chores like chopping and hauling wood in exchange for goods or a little cash, a bushel of apples, or the like.

Heating and cooking with wood isn't easy. Aside from the wood to be chopped and kindling split, there are maintenance chores. The heavy, cast-iron cookstove takes time: to clean and check flues, remove ashes, add wood, and adjust dampers so the stove will burn just right and last through the night. Katie's stove would have had a firebox with an ash and cinder box beneath it, on one side. A second stove for heat would have been in another part of the room or house if the cookstove didn't warm the whole cabin sufficiently. The iron cookstove would have had four "burners" with removal plates, plus a large oven, or even two, below. Both the heat stove and the cookstove leaked soot and smoke into the house no matter how carefully adjusted. Sometimes ashes backed up or spilled when emptying the ash box. Keeping up with the dirt was a chore. Breathing in the close, dirty air during long winters was another problem.

Sometimes, during the summer, Katie and the children picked up large chunks of bark that floated up and down the bay with tides. The bark, once dried, added to the winter wood supply. The bark was scarred from logged trees that came slamming down the dogfish-oiled skid roads and V-shaped water flumes into the saltwater. The logs started their journey up in the hills in one of the many lumber operations down bay on Little Skookum, Big Skookum, or further out on Totten Inlet. The logs from these operations were rafted up and towed behind steamers to mills. The bark, once dried, burned better and longer than some other fuels available, people said.

It is too warm on this particular Oyster Bay day for the stove to be needed for heat, but she'll keep it stoked for the week's worth of baked goods she'll produce for herself and her kin who live in float houses on the bay near the bank. The family are always within eye- and earshot of one another.

The float houses, occupied by both Indians and European Americans in the mid-to-late nineteenth century, were a constant presence on Oyster Bay down through the 1930s, with a few around after World War II and into the 1950s. After the early 1900s most of the occupants were Japanese and Japanese Americans working for the oyster companies. Big oyster companies owned and leased them to workers. In Katie's time, however, individuals and small oyster operations built and owned them. They were useful. They were highly mobile and didn't require that one own real estate. They could be brought to shore, stabilized and leveled on a bank, and used as year-round dwellings. Oyster Bay wasn't the only area where Indian people chose them over life on a reservation. They were also used on Mud Bay and on many inlets and coves around Puget Sound.

In the 1880s and 1890s worker float houses abounded on Oyster Bay. They could be attached to pilings right over or near oyster beds so that, as the houses settled on the muddy bottom of the bay at low tide, one could go to work on the beds. Long board walkways allowed for beach access when the float house was closer to shore, as many float houses in this period were. A house still went up and down with the tides but was anchored to the bank adjoining the oyster grounds of the owner. Small skiffs or canoes were tied to the side of the float house and the surrounding deck was used for storage or gardens or as fenced-in play areas for children.

The cull house was a separate structure. It might be anchored with a sink float over or near the beds being worked.

During the late 1800s float houses were built "without a partition. . . . There was a big square place built somewhat the fashion of the logging camp fire place right in the middle of the one room and there was a big chimney that goes up through the roof comes down so your head won't strike it like." A cookstove was installed off to one end. People "lived and ate and slept right there in that float house."[6]

Without the "conveniences" of the modern household, everything is done by hand. Katie Gale is busy with chores most every day. Katie is the kind of woman who is consumed by her tasks and always pragmatic. Sleep is the time for dreaming, not when you are stoking a fire. Her work is intentional and conscious. She moves slowly, patiently, without haste, to accomplish her work. There is nothing to run from or run to. Imagine: this is a world, a time, without the demands and distractions of the twenty-first century. What sidetracks or flusters in Katie's world is different from what perturbs most of us today.

Yet worries there are. Crop failure means hunger or additional expense to buy food. Wet summers will ruin potatoes. Late frost or snow will ruin fruit crops. Oysters sometimes suffer from freezes that hold them solid in the ice and float them away. Diseases are rampant. People drown, trees crush them, and babies die before taking a first breath. An innocent buggy ride might end in tragedy; the poor roads built along precipitous bank areas often contribute to disastrous tips and spills that could injure or kill occupants. Though she is not bombarded with daily news of global economic meltdown, bailouts, and riots over lost pensions and higher tuition costs, the realities of worldwide financial debacles do reach Oyster Bay and do have an impact on Katie and her life.

During this period in the West, life was difficult by today's standards. This was true not just for Katie Gale but also for all women, including Indians. It's why Lydia Pinkham made money with her homemade medicinals, turned commercial in 1875. Lydia knew what women suffered from and how to induce guilt when a woman seemed to herself to fall short of expectations. Wives, her ad copy said, were to be helpmates to husbands and tireless keepers of the hearth. If you didn't have the gumption for it, you had to do something about it. A woman, the Pinkham line continued, was to "love and admire" her husband, to "inspire him to make the most of himself." If she found her energies flagging, should she "get easily tired, dark shadows appear under her eyes, she has backache, headaches, bearing down pains, nervousness, irregularities or the blues, she should start at once to build up her system by a tonic with specific powers." That would be Lydia E. Pinkham's Vegetable Compound, trumpeted her ads.

Of course, there were many reasons to have the blues, most causes not easily assuaged by the bottle or tablet. Not only was the daily life of the farm or "pioneering" woman difficult, but she could look forward to the great possibility of losing babies or her own life in childbirth. Sometimes a woman lost one newborn after another; sometimes she lost all of her newborns. If the youngster survived babyhood, a mother could still not be certain that he or she would live to adulthood. Local period papers are laced with accounts of tragedies involving youth. For example, a sore throat could mean a death in two weeks. A tree could fall over and crush a child, and did. The little ones died of unspecified causes like "spinal complaints," and death often followed short, brief illnesses with few signs of their gravity. Notices from the periodicals abound of bizarre and sudden endings for children: a twelve-year-old named Alfred Thompson "shot his brains out with a 22 cal. rifle while hunting" in 1892, and a five-year-old ate some poison laced with "rough on rats."

A frequent cause of death for children in the 1880s and 1890s was cholera infantum, though scarlet fever, typhoid, and consumption were also present and devouring. Cholera infantum brought on a high fever, diarrhea, and pain. Severe vomiting and emaciation followed. Children often died within a mere twenty-four hours of onset. The term "cholera infantum" is an "archaic" one and seems to have covered a range of gastroenteritis-type complaints that seemed to have no explanation.

Other diseases came to Oyster Bay, did their evil deed, and then left behind bereft families and a saddened community. Whooping cough, or pertussis, made its rounds in 1888. One of Harriet and Adam Korter's children died of it that year. They were Katie Gale's near neighbors.

Katie Gale's demeanor is often solemn, though she is capable of great humor, especially when around her close friends and kin. She is passionate about things that concern the rights of her friends and kin. She is a broad-shouldered, thick-waisted woman. Yet she is a woman whose feet, though large for her body, make no sound when she moves across the floor or in her garden. Although she is most often quiet, especially when at her daily work, she does have a voice. It is a big, hearty voice that is audible at long distances. She has a big laugh to go with that voice.

Cora Chase, a child on Oyster Bay in the late 1890s, wrote a memoir of that time.[7] It is the manuscript in which I first read about Katie Gale. Cora's father was one of Katie's employees in the oyster business she owned and ran in the 1890s. Cora wrote that even out on the float house where Cora and her family lived, Katie's voice could be heard when she called to her children. Water carries sound, it is true. Still, a small voice will not do to summon your children when they are out on the bay in a canoe or in the woods or to get the attention of relatives and friends working out on the mudflats or in their float houses.

Now Katie bends over a flour barrel, caulked and sealed and made into a washtub. She is scrubbing a shirt on her ridged tin washboard. The washtub is a few feet from a fire where water is heating in a large kettle. The water for washing has been carried from a nearby ground spring, bucket loads at a time. The children sometimes help carry, but usually Katie has collected enough rainwater in a big barrel under a downspout from the roof to save on trips.

She scrubs the clothes, some between her two hands and some on the washboard, using a special soap she's made for her whites and calicos and flannels. Those whites and calicos she separates from other clothing to spare them the harsher treatment she gives clothes used to work in the staining mud of the tide flats. After she has rubbed the soiled clothing carefully, it is ready for boiling and rinsing. The especially filthy pieces, usually the ones worn while working the oyster beds, may soak overnight. When the clothing has been thoroughly rinsed, she "wrings" it, taking care with the more delicate pieces, and then attaches the soggy garments to a long hemp cord with whittled pegs.

Some clothing already hangs on the line, underclothing concealed by larger garments. The rope is stretched taut from a porch post to a high limb of one of the fifteen or so apple trees planted on the hill. The neighboring homesteaders up and down and even across the bay can see those clothes. The people out in their float houses can see them too.

Katie is aware that her neighbors and the kin in the float houses can see her activity and the results of it. She thinks of her neat, colorful clothes flying in the breeze that rises from the bay as her flags, the *banderas* of duty. She knows by signs such as these that she announces herself as an industriousness woman and a woman of value and virtue. Katie knows, long before her husband challenges her worth in courtrooms, that love and merit can be expressed in, as the saying goes, "even . . . the whiteness of a washed pocket handkerchief."[8]

Today she hangs many pieces of the children's clothing on the line: a pair of handmade pants, an apron of simple gingham, and two rough shirts for play and work. She's made most of the things the girls need, as well as household bedding and linens. She buys bolts of cloth from Hoy's store or McDonald's at Arcadia Point or in Kamilche from Kullrich's to supplement what she's been given as gifts. She can get gingham, calico, cashmere, muslin, needles and thread, really anything she needs, from these nearby stores. She can even trade shellfish for dry goods when the steamer *Otter* comes into the bay to collect bags of oysters for resale in Olympia and Tacoma.

A cow grazes under one of the apple trees, a tree set back up the hill a bit, away from the others. She gets a good crop of apples from these trees and dries a fair number for winter eating and cooking using a wood-burning fruit dryer she found at Frost's hardware in Olympia. Frost is well known to Oyster Bay people and friendly with a number of them. He carries many tools and other products they need for their rough life as homesteaders. And he is a fair man.

It is still early in the day but the cow looks as if she will produce a good amount of milk this evening. Katie Gale can count on her for over a gallon a day. She has three others, all decent producers. Thus she always has lots of good milk for butter and buttermilk as well as cream and cheese. She churns every few days. Then the butter is put in molds.

A few layers peck around the yard. Katie purchases good hatching eggs in town when she needs to enhance her flock. She raises poultry for meat and eggs. Her chickens provide enough to share with the folks on the float houses. Katie also has three horses, four yearling cattle, and four calves. Any extra food her animals produce, beyond what the kin require, will be taken to Kullrich's store in Kamilche for sale to those who don't raise their own cows or chickens. Though it is not an entirely barter economy, there are regular exchanges of produce and fish and shellfish (as well as labor) among white and Indian neighbors. For example, Catherine Walter's diary on Skookum Inlet notes many instances of Indian people coming for apples and cherries, sometimes bearing fish for sale or trade. These were sometimes cash transactions, but not always.[9]

The cows come in at night, unbidden, to a small barn with a hayloft. In the simple structure are stalls for three dark, alert horses, room for a little buggy, and of course, an area designated for the cows. An unlit henhouse contains several staggered boxes filled with sweet, dry straw. There are a few high roosts, cut from small branches, and a snug door to be closed at night against foxes and weasels and any other roaming greedy ones, including possums, raccoons, and coyotes. Of course, sometimes a hawk will swoop down and pick off a chicken in the middle of the day. These quick, feathered predators are not impressed by Katie Gale's vigorous curses and shouts.

The hen's coop is protected against drafts. Extreme weather, especially the cold, can kill off a flock. Also, food is difficult for the hens to find if the ground is frozen or snowy. So Katie must make sure they are fed. Water pans need to be watched so they don't freeze over and deprive the chickens of a drink. Laying drops off in the winter with the few hours of light available in the Pacific Northwest, so Katie Gale and other women preserve enough eggs to have a few available even when the hens are molting or not producing.

Under the porch of the house is a trim pile of split kindling, and nearby is an open shed stacked with two or three orderly cords of seasoned firewood. A root cellar just south of the house is lined with sturdy, rough-cut cedar shelves on which jars of canned blackberries, huckleberries, beans, and corn stand in neat rows.

Katie's garden is lush, hand-tilled, hand-weeded, and cropped with cabbages and potatoes and sweet onions. She can buy garden seeds at

Kullrich's and puts in a variety of vegetables. She sometimes experiments with new selections recommended by her neighbors. By 1888 she could purchase "West Test" seeds from Lewiston, Idaho, in local stores. These were seeds that promised to "give better results than Eastern seeds as they are grown in a cold climate, without irrigation and tested to heat and cold."

Whatever the crop, she is up at dawn to check for signs of varmints that might have been burrowing in the garden. She picks at nearly invisible and elusive leaf-chomping insects that might still be out in the misty half light. Later in the day she carefully hoes around the developing plants.

The cleared land on the hillside is fenced. The fence's uprights are made of rough, split posts. She's built this fence to guard against the rapacious deer and to keep the livestock from roaming too far.

The omnipresent deer are a constant worry, though Katie's prowess with her rifle has scared off many and provided her table with an abundance of good meat. Better the meat than to have an entire year's supply of cabbages and potatoes nibbled away in the middle of the night.

And as for straying animals, up and down bay cows have often been found mired in deep mud. They must be rescued with elaborate slings and the strength of a platoon of neighbors. They may die of stress and exposure to the elements, help too long in coming.

Thus fences are critical, to keep critters both in and out.

Even so, sometimes Oyster Bay people like Dick Jackson, whose homestead is across the bay from Katie's place, allow their cattle or sheep to range on the many acres around Oyster Bay owned by Puget Mill or granted by the federal government to the Northern Pacific Railroad.

No matter how vigilant or hardworking Katie Gale was, not everything could be grown on or otherwise eked from the land. She could make her own yeast from potatoes and sugar, but she had to buy the sugar and, of course, the flour.[10] Katie Gale also bought lard, salt, coffee, tea, rice, and kerosene for lamps. She dealt mostly with Joseph Kullrich, a Russian-born storekeeper in nearby Kamilche.[11]

Spelled "Kamilchie" in those days in newspapers, letters, and journals and even on later maps, the name derives from the Puget Salish word for valley, *Qabl'Lteu*, according to T. T. Waterman.[12] It may be translated as "valley" or "peaceful valley." And a lovely valley it is, though cut down the middle now by Highway 101, along which cars and trucks and buses speed between Olympia and Shelton, Washington. The road from Kamilche toward a small plywood mill town, McCleary, follows a long, broad, verdant basin that attracted farming families in the late 1800s. Even today the "Kamilche herd," a large assembly of fat elk, can be seen grazing in the lush fields that span that valley.

The little settlement of Kamilche proper is located at the head of Little Skookum Inlet. On one side of the highway there is a train crossing, a few houses, a gas station, a small coffee kiosk, some Squaxin Island tribal offices, and a fire station. On the far side of the overpass the Squaxin Island Tribe owns and operates a booming casino, a beautiful hotel and performance arena, a grocery store, a gas station, and a resort-quality PGA golf club. Across the road from the casino entrance is the Kamilche cemetery, the resting place of some of the people Katie Gale would have known.

Kamilche was, in the late nineteenth century, a logging center and site of a logging railroad, hotels and boardinghouses, and other amenities. The few memoirs and notes that I've found suggest that in the 1880s and 1890s Kamilche was a fine little place to grow up in. It was the closest settlement by land to Katie Gale's house.

New Kamilche, at the mouth of Little Skookum, was closer to the Gale property if traveling by water, and in its prime it had a store and dance hall and a landing for steamers. Arcadia also had a store. It was operated by Margaret McDonald. She had taken over the place, previously a hotel and bar with limited stock, after her husband died and with the financial help of William Renton and the Port Blakely

Mills. Later, in the 1890s, R. B. "Bush" Hoy had a small store right on Oyster Bay. It was located on the waterfront at the point farthest up bay a steamer would dare travel, lest it get stuck on mudflats as the tide went out. A small post office called Kloko (from the Salish for oyster, *Tlóxtlox*) was established in association with the store in the late 1890s. Its name was changed to Schley in honor of Winfield Scott Schley, a controversial commodore known for his role in the Battle of Santiago de Cuba in 1898. The post office was short lived.

Seams of shell middens on either side of the store site suggest that the site was a gathering spot where local inhabitants held feasts for many years in the 1890s, perhaps later, while waiting for supplies or mail to arrive. From there a steep lane led to the hardscrabble road. It wound its way to Old Kamilche and thence to Shelton.

At these small general stores in the 1880s and 1890s, a can of lard cost $1.35 and a twelve-pound bag of sugar cost $1.00. A hundred-pound sack of flour cost $1.50 (the equivalent of about $30 today). Katie Gale would need more than five hundred pounds a year to make three four-pound loaves a week, enough for her children and to share with kin. The empty, washed and bleached flour sacks were used to make underwear or aprons.[13] Thirty pounds of bacon went for $6.00. Work shirts could be purchased for $1.00. A pair of shoes cost around $3.50. Other items people bought at the local stores, especially the loggers from the camps, included tobacco, a popular brand being Climax chewing plugs, the favorite of baseball players of the day.

People also spent money on overalls, crackers, apples, potatoes (when their own crop was insufficient), candles, rope, raisins, and socks. Stores carried yard goods, including gingham, muslin, and flannel for bedsheets, shirts, and sleepwear; calico; and cashmere for crafting the soft, warm shawls that were popular at the time.[14] One could also buy ready-made shawls as well as blankets and axe handles and shovels and work gloves.

Staples like potatoes were within Katie Gale's budget. If her potato crop failed, she could buy them for two cents a pound. She bought Mason jars for putting up her own fruit. Wild berries, like blackberries, were free for the picking but she needed something in which to store the ones she didn't dry. A half-gallon container was $1.15 and was used year after year. Cooking molasses cost 35 cents a gallon. She stayed away from the extravagances available, like canned pineapple, condensed sour cream, Knox gelatin, and Fig Newton's, all on Kullrich's shelves along with Coca-Cola and even Jell-O.

Katie procured other items, such as needles for hand sewing or even leatherwork, in the Kamilche store. For necessities, such as embroidery thread for handwork and needles for the sewing machine on which she tailored most of the family clothing, she went to Mrs. Schlesener's ten- and fifteen-cent counters in Shelton. She budgeted for some store-bought clothing for the children, such as gloves and mittens, and for ribbons for blouses and decorations for hats. Sun hats for the children could be had for thirty cents and dressier ones for fifty cents. The children were always attractively dressed and well cared for. It was the little details that she added to their frocks and suits that made a big difference.

Katie's care for her children included providing tasty, ample meals made with the freshest ingredients she could muster. She was a good cook and even had a reputation to go with those skills. Adolph Johnson (one of her son's schoolmates and his friend) remembered with relish her creamed salmon and biscuits even years after Katie's death, when he was an old man. She knew a dozen ways to cook the fish and stew the oysters and cream the corn. Everybody on the bay looked forward Katie's contributions to the summer community picnics in Kamilche and the Oyster Bay School socials, when local families whose children attended the school came together for covered-dish fundraisers and socializing.

Katie Gale maintained her household easily with the income she earned from her work on the oyster beds.

Kullrich, for one, liked Katie's business and admired her business acumen, as did other old friends on the bay. He wrote in an 1898 affidavit filed on her behalf that she'd bought "a great many groceries and a number of pairs of shoes for the children" during the previous couple of years. She always paid her bills, he added.

A little dog is often by Katie Gale's side as she moves about, doing her chores. He is a black-and-terrier. Her uncle, Chief Kettle, gave her the pup from his dog's recent litter. The dog and Katie can look out from her hillside and see the Kettle and Tobin float house on the bay. It is held firmly by thick hemp rope to a stout spar along the shore. It stays there, hugging the beach and bank, when the family is not occupied working the oyster beds and when storms hit the bay and it fills with runoff from water-swollen hillsides and streams in the winter. Also on the shore below her house, at the foot of the hill, is Katie's oyster-culling shack. It is the cull house where the Frank Gingrich family, Cora Chase's family, labored for Katie.

Kettle or other relatives, especially the women, holler for Katie sometimes from out there on the water or the mud. They urge a visit or hint broadly for one of her special treats. It's usually a basket of biscuits or loaves fresh from the oven or a jar of fresh jam they crave. If the tide is right, Katie takes Maud and Hattie, jumps in a small, hand-carved dugout canoe or a skiff, and paddles or rows out to spend an afternoon visiting or working the oyster beds with them. In the winter work on the beds takes place in the middle of the night and the family works by the light of lanterns and torches. It is then that a hot stew or loaf is especially welcome. The family is close and related to most of the others on and around the bay, on Little Skookum Inlet, on Mud Bay, and out on Squaxin Island Reservation. Though some on Oyster Bay have come from up north around Snohomish or British Columbia or Duwamish, or Quinault or even Yakima, and certainly from other inlets in the South Sound, they can trace relationships back a few generations and laterally through marriages. This is as it has always been.

The oyster beds are the source of Katie's wealth and she shares it with kin. This is also as it has always been.

8 *"Picking Grounds" and the Making of Community*

OLYMPIA OYSTERS (*Ostrea lurida*) are thumb-sized delicacies native to the Pacific Northwest. They were an important food source for Indian people long before they became a commercial crop after the 1850s. They grow, uncultivated, on rocks and shells near estuaries. It's been said that they were layered up to a foot deep on the flats of Oyster Bay. People came from all around Puget Sound to harvest them. It was these Olympia oysters that were the source of Katie Gale's livelihood and it was these oysters that informed, in many ways, the story of her life.

Before European Americans came to the bay and began oystering with technology and methods brought with them from the East Coast of America or imported from other countries, Indian people like Katie and her family used open-weave baskets for collecting oysters and other shellfish that they raked and dug from the mud with wooden tools. They traveled to picking sites in canoes and built raft-like devices (later topped with iron) that provided a stable surface on top of the mud flats and on which one could build a fire for illumination and warmth while working on the beds during dark, winter low tides.[1] At the end of a night's work, the moon perhaps low in the sky, the phosphorus in the water sparkled magically when gatherers leaned over in the dark to wash the mud from their hands.[2] It was difficult work that required hours of stooping. While working, women characteristically bent at the waist and lowered their upper body and arms so that their elbows almost touched the surface of the mudflats.[3] Sacks of harvested oysters were loaded into canoes, transported to Olympia, and sold directly to customers from the early days of white settlement until the late 1870s, by which time middlemen had taken over the oyster business almost wholly.

Before the commercialization of the industry, an independent-minded woman like Katie who wanted to make her own money could take a little canoe, when there was enough water in the shallow bay, and have a run to oyster beds that she worked on her own, maybe for years. She would work while the tide was out and wait for it to come in before paddling home. Sallie Hall Weatherall, a neighbor and kinswoman of Katie's, was doing this to earn her livelihood before she married Harry Weatherall. Sallie and others took sacks of oysters from natural "picking grounds" to sell in Olympia or to homesteaders around the bay. That was before people like Joseph Gale began to organize labor and create a more systematic, lucrative way of working the beds.

By the early 1870s oyster workers, at the behest of the new bosses and owners who wanted to increase production and sales, were using top floats and sink floats and living and working out of cull houses and float houses. There was still lots of hard winter work in the dark with torches or lanterns and it was still mostly Indians working for the whites, who were gathering oysters in the earliest days of commercial growing, that is, from the 1870s until about 1900. Also, most of the early gathering was still being done on natural beds. The earliest cultivation was simple and only mildly environmentally intrusive.

As time went by a system and hierarchy developed; that is, a clear relationship was established between those who owned the rights to the tidelands and oyster grounds and the workers. Good tidelands were "staked and claimed" by entrepreneurs. An oyster farmer wanted a good location, James Tobin said, in "a slightly sloping flat" bit of tideland with a "fresh water stream running through it." The farmers had to keep an eye out for starfish and snails that would eat the small fry. Spat, or spawn, from mature oysters would be "caught" in "depressions on the flats," and when the tide receded the spat was exposed long enough in shallow basins of water to be "warmed into life by the rays of the sun." It was said that the Olympia oysters were "so indigenous to the soil" that the oyster grower need only "scatter them out so they will propagate." The Duwamish Irish James Tobin and his family owned beds and hired people to help. He was in the business at the same time Katie Gale was. In early twentieth-century court testimony he described the regular tasks of the oyster farmer when it came time to harvest the four-year-old mature crop: "The first thing we do, take up the oysters. If there is only one [person] he has to rake first, then take his sluice fork and fork them on to the [top] float."[4] The harvester might rake them into a "wind row," then put them on the float to take them to the culling house.[5] "It is the usual way of oystering and has been for years and years," Tobin said, describing the way he and others worked on the mud flats in 1870s. "If there is two, one rakes and the other one forks, and in the morning he takes that float (top float) in to his sink, what we call a sink float, forks it into that, then washes it then gets it ready for the cullers on to the floating house, then set around — but if he has two or three cullers or if he has one, they set around and cull it." The sink float goes up and down with the tide but is built with a depression so that the oysters are kept wet. Culling involves selecting and sorting oysters in an effort to produce the best product for the marketplace. The oysters are tiny and hard to separate. They sometimes grew in large clusters.

It takes three years for an Olympia oyster to grow to about the size of a quarter or a fifty-cent piece, or about thirty-five to forty-five millimeters, its maximum size. That's when it is ready for market. In the 1870s smaller oysters were put back on the beds and scattered about so they could continue to mature. Laborers had to be sure the oysters weren't piled up on the bed but were separated from one another "so they don't get too thick on the bed . . . so they don't get too thick piled up." Spreading them like this was done by hand, "sort of raking around by hand and making sure the oysters are scattered."

After the oysters were culled, they were kept on the sink float to keep them wet until shipping day came. Then they were sacked, tagged, and put on the steamer that came up bay to collect them. If two people were working, one held the big burlap bag open and the other forked in the market-ready oysters. Of course, they must be kept wet at all times. Some accounts say that A. J. Burr was the first to ship sacks of oysters from Oyster Bay, thence to Portland and Olympia by steamer.

Bills had to be made out and accounts kept, including who was purchasing and where the oysters were going. Keeping those accounts and overseeing the whole operation later in the 1880s and 1890s often fell to overseers. Both Joe Gale's and Harry and Sallie Weatherall's managers were Chinese men.

Oysters were being harvested in Oyster Bay to the tune of about 130,000 bushels a year by the 1890s. The industry was based on these wild, native oysters until after the turn of the century.[6]

Katie Gale, the Tobins, and even the Weatheralls were successful enough to hire friends and relatives and even Chinese workers to help with the hard hand work on the mudflats and oyster beds. However, "there were times," Tobin said, "when oysters wasn't worth very much and a person couldn't afford to have the work done if he could do it himself." The prices the oyster farmers could demand from brokers in Olympia fluctuated. Bush Hoy, who had a small oyster operation in the 1870s and 1880s, reported, "Sometimes they sold from a dollar and a half to a dollar and a quarter a sack. Other times two or three dollars a sack." Hoy added, "They were oftener lower than they were high. They commenced to increase in value about 1897 and '98 somewhere along there."

After 1893, when Katie ran her own operation and was hiring, she had a house on land, a float house for workers, a sink float, and a cull house. The sink float and cull house were at the foot of her upland property.

Although Katie was living outside of the village world of her parents and grandparents and was a participant in a new economic, political, and social world in the making, she was not isolated from sources of deep cultural knowledge, for there were many Indian women on Oyster Bay and Mud Bay. Though picking and culling oysters and managing her household took most of her time, Katie Gale must have valued her friendship and kinship with other women in her little maritime community. She must have visited them regularly and found ways to lighten her own work by sharing some tasks. They must have helped each other with illnesses and births and expressed their grief with one another when spouses and children died. Indeed, all the women in the maritime community that included Oyster Bay and Big and Little Skookum regularly saw one another. "With all their work the women found time for visiting and a visit was a matter of several days. The mother of a family would take the youngest child and leave the others in the home to carry on, and go to visit a friend or neighbor."[7] Katie, for example, visited neighbors and kin on the bay but also made trips to the Puyallup Reservation to see kin and made other trips with friends to gather herbs or seasonal crops.

At least once a year, Katie Gale, with or without one or more of her children, took the steamer from Olympia up to Tacoma and joined relatives on the Puyallup Reservation to journey above the White River along the blazed trail into the family's old berry grounds. Sometimes the women paused along the familiar path to make berry baskets from bark. Other times, when the season was right, Katie went with Jennie and William Krise to the Cloquallum Creek area northeast of the town of McCleary. There they could find an abundance of native blackberries, the *Rubus ursinus*. This blackberry grows on a long, trailing vine and produces sweet, small berries, unlike the invasive Himalayan variety. The Krises loaded up a wagon and headed up into this prime habitat every summer. Upon return the pickers laid the berries out to dry, then stored them in baskets. Back on the bay, women also helped each other cut and smoke or salt fish from the fall chum run when the fish returned to Kennedy Creek to spawn. All the food gathered and fished and hunted during the summer and early fall had to be smoked and dried or salted, and it was good to have company for this work. The Krises even traveled out to Grays Harbor (and possibly Willapa Bay) to collect sweetgrass for weaving or cranberries, and Katie and some of the other women may have gone along occasionally.[8]

Though commercial tonics, especially for congestion and coughs, were popular and used by people on the bay, they were expensive and of questionable benefit. The women on the bay had known mothers and aunties and grandmothers who made their own medicine from local herbs and roots. They all had learned the recipes and used them regularly. Gathering medicinal flora required other trips together into well-known wooded and mountain areas. Katie, who used home remedies she learned from other Indian women, traveled with them and learned how to use each plant. She consulted these women when she was at a loss for how to treat a child's stomachache or head cold. She used blackberry roots and alder buds and bark for tonic. Louisa Tobin, her cousin who was close to the same age and who, with her husband, was also in the oyster business, was known for her skills with herbs and medicines and was called upon throughout her life when children were ill or women were pregnant or low. People all over Oyster Bay sent for Louisa by boat, though she was a comparatively young woman. She was even more popular and called upon later by the people on Mud Bay and Eld Inlet. That was the bay where she and her husband ultimately settled on a homestead and made a prosperous ranch for themselves and their several children.

9 *The People in Her World*

JENNIE KRISE, one of the many local women Katie Gale knew, was another Indian woman from the Kamilche area married to a white man. Jennie was also a midwife and was known as a healer when Katie was raising her children. Jennie's spouse, William, had a small house and oyster business for a while just in front of the Gale place. During that time Jennie and Katie may have seen each other every day. William Krise was a European American adventurer born in Warren County, Ohio, on July 2, 1822. He traveled from Dayton, Ohio, to Western Washington with the "John Lane Immigrant Train" in the 1850s. Along the trail he shot game for the immigrants' stew pots. The Lane group became the first of the wagon trains to cross into Western Washington at Naches Pass, 4,928 feet high in the Cascade Mountain range. The pass was heavily used by Indians, who traversed the mountains for trade or hunting, to gather shellfish, to visit kin, and to establish new ties through marriage. The route was certainly known for hundreds if not thousands of years. Indeed, many well-established trails led back and forth between Puget Sound and eastern Washington.

Charles Wilkes, the allegedly contentious and clearly scientifically minded leader of the U.S. Exploring Expedition, sent a party to explore the Naches crossing in 1841. Therefore, its features and aspects were not unknown to those European Americans who came later. At some point in the early 1850s, during his own crossing, William Krise apparently met up with and joined a party of surveyors working around the pass for Isaac Stevens and the Pacific Railroad Survey project. They were under the leadership of Capt. George B. McClellan.

Krise arrived in Washington Territory in August 1853, ahead of the wagon train with which he'd started the journey west. Those wagons struggled up the steep, rocky grades of the Cascades over a rough road that was barely, if at all, carved from dense forests and stone. It was a fine pathway for foot and horse travel, but it was a challenge for the heavy wagons and hard on the hoofs of the poor oxen required to pull those wagons. Still, as they passed over the Cascades, what glorious views they would have had of the river valleys and canyons below and of the loveliest of volcanic peaks, the stately Mount Rainier.

After celebrating the heroics of reaching the summit, the travelers had to brace themselves for the downward, still farther westward journey. Theodore Winthrop described the eastern descent down a trail that those already settled in Puget Sound had wrought as "an elaborate inclined plane of very knobby corduroy down the steepest slope."[1] After much struggle (they were forced to cross the meandering White River seven times, for example) they reached Connell's Prairie and the Puyallup River, where the salmon were running in abundance. Perhaps the promises of the bounty of the Northwest they'd heard at home were true! In October they reached Clover Creek, south of Tacoma.

By 1855 William filed for a donation claim of 160 acres in what was then Sawamish County, named for the village and people at the mouth of Big Skookum, now called Hammersley Inlet. In 1864 the territorial legislature renamed the county Mason after the late Charles Mason, who was Washington Territory's secretary of state and acting governor during the war of 1855–56. This act of naming was among the many that tended to wipe out evidence of the territory's roots.[2] Charles Wilkes, for example, named local waters and land masses largely after his own officers. We have him to thank for the appellations Budd Inlet, Fox Island, McNeil Island, and Eld Inlet, for example. It was George

Vancouver who bestowed the name Puget's Sound, after Lt. Peter Puget, who journeyed to the inland sea's southern reaches.

William Krise served in what has become known as the "Indian War" of 1855–56. He was a volunteer militiaman and served in F Company in Fort Skookum, located just across from Arcadia Point on the A. M. Collins donation land claim. One can see the site of the fort easily from where the present-day Squaxin Tribe holds First Salmon Ceremonies. The distance from Arcadia Point to the site of the Collins claim, the entrance to Hammersley Inlet, is a little more than a mile. It was on the sandy buttress in front of the Collins claim that a lantern on a pole signaled that entrance for steamers many years ago. The protection that the buttress afforded, its proximity to Squaxin Island, and its location at the entrance to Big Skookum were among the reasons for the choice of this location for Fort Skookum.

William was there to serve and ready for action from February to July 1856, along with literally all the other European American men who had taken donation claims in the immediate area. Most of the people with donation claims had moved, lock, stock, and barrel, onto the land they'd staked out before a treaty was signed. So the land had not been legally acquired from Indians when the new settlers came. The treaties followed quickly after settlers arrived, and the one of that included the land on Big and Little Skookum was the Treaty of Medicine Creek. It required indigenous people to cede nearly all the land that they lived on, the same land on which they hunted, gathered, and fished. Though they retained the right to continue to use the land for the sustenance activities they had practiced for centuries, over two and a quarter million acres were transferred to the U.S. government. These lands were now "legitimately" available to settlement by the newcomers. The return to the bands and villages whose land it had been was $32,500 in goods and services.[3] Now there was a rebellion: the Indians, many of them, were outraged to find their reserved land inadequate, the promises made to them shallow, and the treaty process unfair.

William and Jennie were legally married in 1874. Jennie, born in

1852, was twenty-two years old. However, records show that the pair began their lives together earlier, perhaps when she was as young as fourteen. A 1910 census suggests that Jennie was born in British Columbia and that her parents were Skokomish. It may be, as one story recounts, that her parents had been captives of the Skokomish in pre-treaty times. Cesalle, her father, was born around 1831, so he might have been brought to Skokomish territory as a boy. Another account calls Cesalle, Tulalip. The Treaty of Point Elliot, for successor bands, established the Tulalip Reservation after Cesalle was born. Thus Cesalle was probably from a Tulalip predecessor band of Snohomish or Snoqualmie ancestry or from Penn's Cove and the Whidbey Island area if "Tulalip." There were others on Oyster Bay with a Snohomish/ Tulalip connection. These included Snohomish Mary, a frequent visitor to float house people.

The Krise family were part of Katie's life in many ways. Not only did William have an oyster bed near Katie's own, but also Cesalle and his family worked with the Kettles, Katie Gale's kin, on the oyster beds. Katie would have known the Krise children and would have called on Jennie's wisdom as a healer.

Ultimately, many Krise children survived and their descendants have made their mark on local history. Jennie and William seem to have had a long and happy marriage.

Another woman in Katie Gale's circle was Mrs. George Gibbs. Mrs. Gibbs lived nearby and was also a midwife, wise in the old ways. She herself was famous locally for giving birth to a twelve-pound daughter in 1892.

Midwives were critical to the health of mothers, and doctors across the West were often eschewed in favor of the groups of women who carried experience in their bodies and hands, the wisdom passed to them through stories and the gathered intelligence of generations. Their tool kits were full of herbs and rubs. They knew what to say and how to reassure new mothers with their confident, matter-of-fact approach to birthing. With birth rates low and infant mortality rates high, it was better, women thought, to trust the experience of other women rather than the unknown methods of unfamiliar male doctors.[4]

In any case, there were few doctors and they were not close by. Women on Oyster Bay and Little and Big Skookum, on the other hand, were always "ready to emergency calls . . . to attend at child birth. Often long trips were made at night on horseback or in rowboats."[5]

Katie also had a friend in Louisa Smith, the Indian spouse of Abner Smith and the daughter of Indian homesteader Henry Isaac. There was also Mary Slocum down the bay and Harriet Korter down the bay a bit farther. All these women were members of her immediate circle, along with the family of Chief Kettle. She knew Big Frank's family, too, still on the bay for a period even after they sold oyster beds that eventually became Gale property. Big Frank had been a Skokomish signer on the Point No Point Treaty and was a highly respected leader.

These people were influential in the development and establishment of a new way of living on the land and water that so recently had been the home territory of the T'Peeksin. Some of them, no doubt, could trace their ancestry to those T'Peeksin. However, some came from more distant places and were now establishing a life together in an unaccustomed, emerging economy. They were the people who formed a community within a community, and they were the people who stood by each other in times of need, who helped with births, and who mourned with each other at times of death. They were people who helped to raise each other's children and who shared small victories and grave disappointments.

In addition to her Indian peers on Oyster Bay, there were many others from farther afield, away from Oyster Bay, who were mentors for Katie. These were the people, kin and friends, whom Katie visited in Puyallup and Tacoma or, closer, on Mud Bay. She saw and talked with people from all around Puget Sound, from the Chehalis or Cowlitz drainages, from the coast, and even from over the Cascades during giveaways and Fourth of July celebrations or before and after Shaker Church meetings.

Though there were gratifying periods, life in the communities of Mud Bay and Oyster Bay was not idyllic. There were burdensome times and peculiar incidents that marred and marked lives forever. The story of Dick Jackson's father was one of those that circulated for a long time.

Dick Jackson, who was of Skokomish descent (now called the Skokomish Tribal Nation) and born of two Skokomish parents, was a good neighbor to Katie Gale. He lived across the bay, farther out toward Totten Inlet, on his own homestead. He was a sturdy, capable man whose father, Tyee Jackson, had been an important, though apparently feared, doctor on Mud Bay. Katie was arguably one of those who witnessed his murder.

In 1874 a man named Henry (Harry) Fisk, who believed Jackson senior had used supernatural powers to bedevil and sicken Fisk's wife, Susie, shot him with "1 leaden bullet." Fisk was a mixed-race man, a fact that weighed heavily in the outcome of his trial.

Witnesses called in the trial included Sam, Lewis, and Jim.[6] These were, presumably, the men who became known as Mud Bay Sam, Mud Bay Louie, and either Doctor Jim or Olympia Jim. They all were prominent members of the larger community of Indians and oystermen and were friends of the Kettles.

A "Kitty," a name Katie Gale sometimes was called, was also brought to witness. Katie Gale would have been about eighteen years old at the time. If the Jim who witnessed was Doctor Jim, he may have been called to the scene before the murder to counter the deadly illness Susie Fisk suffered. A "Sally" was also present and witnessed the slaying. This may have been Tyee Doctor Jackson's wife, Sally Numpton, or even Sallie Hall, both also part of the Mud Bay and Oyster Bay communities.[7] The murder took place at "Sandy's house." That would be Sandy Wohaut. This was possibly a float house, for Sandy Wohaut lived on one at times during his life and certainly did so while he was on Oyster Bay. He occasionally moved it about. Fisk had "arrested" Doctor Jackson without authority and with some manufactured pretense and had taken him from Olympia by canoe to Sandy's house in the Mud Bay Indian settlement.

It was late, four o'clock in the afternoon, on December 14, 1873, when the murder took place. The sun went down around a quarter after four; thus it would have been nearly dark when the handcuffed man was delivered to the house where Mrs. Fisk lay dying and weakly accused Jackson of causing her torments. She called on her husband to shoot him then and there.

James Tobin, who was living and working in Oyster Bay and with whom Katie and all the others had close ties, was the translator for the judicial proceedings that followed the slayings. He was often called on by the court to help with language.

The judge who listened to the case was Roger Sherman Greene. Greene was a Civil War veteran who had been the commander of Company C, Fifty-First U.S. Colored Infantry. After some years of practicing law he was appointed associate justice of the Supreme Court of Washington Territory. He was a Prohibitionist who ran for the governorship on that platform (he was defeated) and a champion of women's rights. He had a well-developed, educated, and thoughtful view of differences among and between people, of justice, and of the role and responsibility of law.

Greene declared in his instructions to the jury, "I must ask you to consider the nature of defendant's [Fisk's] act. The defendant appears before you . . . as of a barbarous race, and having in him uneradicated, perhaps ineradicable, what we might term a dark and wild belief, the belief in *mustachee tomanowas*. This belief, the testimony goes to show, is shared by all his race, and has descended upon him through countless generations of ancestors. . . . In our language it would be denominated witchcraft, of the species sorcery." Greene suggested to the jury that given all the beliefs and facts Fisk had at hand, there was little Fisk could have done to save his wife other than kill Jackson.[8]

Judge Greene's comments in the case had far-reaching implications for the status of Indian people and ancient practices and beliefs in the eyes of the law.

In this case, Fisk was found not guilty based on Greene's reasoning.

This case raises complicated questions as we read it today. On the one hand, Greene certainly had experiences that led him to appreciate and understand the power of beliefs and values and the crucial role they play in determining human affairs. His instructions suggest a fairly sophisticated approach to the case at hand and even posit a defense for Fisk. One would like to have seen what books were on the shelves of Judge Greene's library, for his language seems to suggest that he had read social evolutionary theory. Many an educated person of the time would have and might thereby be led to believe that Fisk was an unwitting representative of a particular level of social development. Fisk's beliefs and those of others of his "barbarous race" could not be swayed or extinguished, Green suggests.

This was not the last word by far from Greene regarding Indians and their relationships and the status of Indian people in the territory. His words and pronouncements in a later case were talked about and quoted by the people of Oyster Bay, including James Tobin. The Jackson case also is an early example of Indians in the area participating in and observing the ways of the courts, understanding their rights under territorial law, and learning about the construction of legal strategies. This familiarity with Greene among members of the Oyster Bay and Mud Bay Indians is useful to the understanding of some later developments in the story of Katie Gale.

Descendants of the Jackson family purportedly say they were related to the Slocum family and that this incident on Mud Bay "may have led to the founding of the Indian Shaker Church."[9] Dick Jackson himself was involved in the founding of the church and certainly brought to it certain convictions and sensibilities, including, perhaps, those from his father's beliefs and teachings.

10 *Travels*

THOUGH DRESSED for laborious, often harsh work most days on Oyster Bay, Katie Gale has some special clothes that she wears for travel, church, weddings, and school functions. She has one particularly fine outfit: a dark-green velvet dress that fits tight at the waist. It has a high, fitted collar and long sleeves that hug her forearms. Along one side of the skirt is a rakish row of burgundy-red appliquéd roses. The bodice is drawn tight, making a slim, smooth shape of her body. Across the bodice a panel is inset and accentuated with a row of pearl buttons. She bought her dress and hat in Olympia at Bettman's, a "general merchandise store" on the corner of Main and Second, during one of her frequent excursions there. Louis, Sig, and Mose Bettman, three brothers from Bavaria, established the store in 1854. Anyone from Oyster Bay with a little extra money and an excuse for a trip into Olympia made straight for Bettman's. If nothing else, a piece of fancy crockery would be purchased and proudly displayed on a shelf in an otherwise humble cottage.

Katie and Hattie, her elder daughter, and sometimes Maud, her younger daughter by Joseph Gale, boarded a steamer up at New Kamilche on the Little Skookum Inlet. It was an easy, less-than-four-mile paddle down the bay from their home and business.

They rode steamers that were part of the flotilla fondly referred to in Puget Sound as the "Mosquito Fleet." These crafts carried people and goods around the region until well into the twentieth century. They earned the name Mosquito Fleet because they were seen so frequently and buzzed and churned the waters like little insects. There were literally dozens of them coming and going in Puget Sound, up and down rivers and up and down the coast between the Northwest and Alaska and California.

Steamers were not only the principal mode of transportation between towns during the last part of the nineteenth century but also the principal means of getting oysters to Olympia for sale. In fact, they enabled the growth of the commercial industry.

The steamers in the Olympia–Shelton–Oyster Bay area were relatively small craft. Boats like the *Old Settler*, a flat-bottomed sternwheeler steamer built by Andrew J. Burr in 1878 and registered in 1879, were often seen in the bay for a brief period. The *Old Settler* had a secondhand engine and boiler. The boiler and the donkey engine onboard were small, but they were, apparently, powerful enough to keep the paddles moving. The whistle of the *Old Settler* came from a very large ship. The combination of the small engine and the larger whistle posed a problem. Every time the whistle was blown, the vessel lost power.

The *Old Settler* gathered up sacks of oysters around Oyster Bay and took them to Olympia to buyers. It also provided a handy means for passengers like Katie Gale to connect with other small, regional towns. From Burr's Landing at the head of Oyster Bay, where the *Old Settler* stopped, you could hop the Chehalis County Stage for Elma, Montesano, and Grays Harbor and from Arcadia you could go up Big Skookum Inlet and ride to logging camps, thence to Oakland Bay and via stage at Oakland to Union City and the Skokomish Reservation. If there was no stage, people walked or went on horseback or "dragged a narrow sled with oxen" along various trails. Travelers "stayed over at whatever house they were near when night overtook them."[1]

Being flat bottomed, stories say, the *Old Settler* could "paddle along the mud flats like running on water" and "run ashore almost anyplace" so that the engineer could "longshore wood" from "Indian's fire wood, cut and piled along the shore."[2] That is, the *Old Settler* crew would maneuver close enough to the shore to haul in wood paid for in advance. Firewood was used, cords and cords of it, to keep steamer engines fueled. It was sometimes obtained by nefarious means, such as snatching it from unprotected stashes hoarded for the winter by homesteaders.

Andrew Burr, master of the *Old Settler*, was a watchmaker and merchant of sorts. (He lost several hundred dollars' worth of goods with when the *Northerner* steamship, heading up the coast from California in 1860, sank near San Francisco.) He was an Olympia postmaster in the mid-1870s. His occupation was listed as "sailor" by the time the 1879 census was taken. His life seemed to go awry after he undertook the life of a steamboat master. The boat was sold when the "owners became involved in legal difficulties."[3] In 1880 he was foreclosed against. In that same year his wife, Martha, divorced him and sued for custody of their children. He had a row with Oyster Bay oysterman Dennis Hurley and took out a restraining order against him in 1884. He was in the courts for habitual drunkenness in 1889. After a less-than-illustrious career, and apparently a very short one serving the oyster growers of Oyster Bay, the *Old Settler* and Mr. Burr's fortunes "drifted up the wharves of Seattle and sank."[4] The *Old Settler*'s engines were salvaged to power a printing press in Seattle.

Before the *Old Settler* was "repurposed" it undertook some notorious races with its contemporary on the Shelton-Olympia run, the *Capital*, an Olympia-built wooden steam scow. It was called a steam scow because, apparently, both ends of the flat-bottomed boat were blunted, or squared off. It too could "run up onto the beach anywhere, put out a gang plank anywhere and load and unload passengers, freight or cattle."[5] The *Capital* made its first appearance in 1876 and was run, for at least several years, as a "freight boat," coughing and hacking its way around Oyster Bay picking up oysters and delivering goods. George Swan, from Nova Scotia, arrived in the sound in 1874 and later became the *Capital*'s engineer.[6] The *Capital* ran on the power of a threshing-machine engine and donkey boiler and had homemade wooden paddle wheels.[7]

There were steamboats aplenty, in addition to the homemade *Old Settler* and the *Capital*. Some of these made Kamilche-Shelton or Kamilche-Olympia runs during Katie and Joseph Gale's time. In 1881 Catherine Collins Walter kept an ongoing record of her days from her home across from Arcadia on her homestead at the entrance to Hammersley Inlet. The Walters apparently maintained the lantern on their bluff that helped direct steamer traffic; thus they would have been particularly aware of their comings and goings.

Catherine could watch steamers passing while baking "light bread" or canning cherries or churning butter. She mentions seeing the *Zephyr*, the *Capital*, and the *Daisy*. The *Zephyr*, built in 1871, was in the area after it was "secured" by the Merchants' Transportation Company of Olympia, formed in 1872. The *Zephyr* was the company's first steamship. The *Daisy*, built in 1880, was one of a fleet of three with which the Washington Steamboat Company started business in 1882.[8]

The tramp steamer (one without a regular schedule) *Otter*, another sternwheeler, was also running regularly on Oyster Bay. Years later the *Otter*, called locally the "Tacoma Tramp," was nevertheless remembered with affection. The *Otter* was "eighty feet long, [with an] eighteen feet beam and six feet hold." It became part of the Oregon Steam Navigation Company's fleet in 1874.[9] In its early years it towed barges for Renton Coal Company. It later became a trading steamer and conducted business on Oyster Bay. According to one memoirist it carried "mail, groceries, ammunition, clothes, shoes, bolted goods and mail order catalogues."[10] During this period the *Otter* traded straight across with the oyster farmers: goods for sacks of oysters. The *Otter*'s owners sold oysters in Tacoma and undercut Olympia dealers. They also cut into the business of local grocery and dry goods stores. And they made a good profit on the goods they sold or exchanged, though in its later career the *Otter* was reportedly not selling as many goods as formerly. The local paper reported that "the oystermen are tired of paying high prices for poor goods." The *Otter*'s career came to an end after a collision in 1890.

Another steamer of the era was the *Hornet*, just "25 feet long and there was just enough room to walk around the sides and stern and a little more room in the bow." During holiday seasons, when there were more passengers, "a scow was lashed to the side of the Hornet with a plank laid across for seats."[11]

The sternwheeler *Multnomah*, built in 1885 in Portland, was purchased by Samuel Wiley in 1889. It was 143 feet long and 28 feet at the beam. It was originally a Columbia River steamer, but Wiley brought it to Olympia and it made runs to Seattle and to New Kamilche.[12]

In 1893 the steamer *Doctor* was making regular trips from Olympia to Kamilche. It carried mail and made special trips on Mondays and Thursdays "for oysters on the upper [Oyster] bay." In March of that year the *Estella*, built in 1885, was pulled off the Oyster Bay route, but there was still plenty of steamer traffic.

In April 1893 the Kamilche column in the *Washington Standard* newspaper reported, "There is a good prospect of a steamboat war on Oyster Bay. Three boats intend to run on this route, with business enough for just one good boat." Between the steamers and the float houses, Oyster Bay must have been noisy and crowded. What Katie Gale experienced when she looked out was very unlike the seldom-traveled, tranquil waterway I see today.

Though the little freight-hauling steamers were ubiquitous, before 1895 it was the *Willie* that made the main Shelton-Olympia run. The *Willie* made three round trips daily from Shelton to Olympia by way of New Kamilche.[13] The *Willie* had a "ladies cabin" in the bow of the boat. "A continuous seat was built under the windows and a small square table stood against the wall. In the center of the cabin a stairway led to the low level and from it arose odors of cooking . . . and lubricating oil and smoke from the wood furnace."[14] The *Willie* simply sank one night at the dock in Shelton. Someone, it was said, tied the *Willie* to the dock with a too-tight guy line. The tide rose, the *Willie* didn't. Water filled the hull while the crew slept on the upper deck. Everybody was rousted by a night watchman. But that was the end of the *Willie*.

The *Willie*'s successor was the newly built *City of Shelton*, commissioned by the Simpson Logging Company. It was a nearly one-hundred-foot-long sternwheeler. It had a big stack at its fore, an ample promenade deck, and comfortable inside seating for protection from the weather. There was plenty of room for storing goods below. Indeed, it offered a pleasant way to travel around southern Puget Sound if one could avoid the soot and smoke that reigned down from the ample chimney. "Take care where you stand" was the conventional wisdom recommended by newspapers. Wear a duster and cover your hat. A veil on the face was advisable. Indeed, the air of the Puget Sound area in the 1890s was compromised in many ways by the belching of mosquito-fleet vessels, smoke from fall and winter wood and coal fires from homes, slash-and-burn fires along the slopes of logging operations, and smoke from the trains carrying lumber to ships.

Given the lively movements of a burgeoning population and the active trade and commerce required of a growing economy, it is no wonder that recent studies of sediments in Puget Sound show "signs of combustible hydrocarbons" from burning coal and petroleum before 1900. Scientist can see this evidence following the Klondike Gold Rush of 1897 and subsequent population growth in the region. "Particles from chimneys and smokestacks and new industries drifted over Puget Sound, into the water and sunk to the bottom," one writer declared.

Emissions hung in the often dense fall and winter fogs. Sometimes dry hazes settled in valleys and bays. The South Sound escaped, at least, the consequences of the heavy, coal-driven industrial development of the East Coast and the killer smogs that choked workers and citizens in cities like London during this period.

Steamer trips were not without other hazards of more obvious and immediate concern. There were tides, fog, wind, and other seagoing vessels to watch out for. Crews of the various boats were competitive with one another, sometimes recklessly so, and operators, captains, and engineers often arranged wild, unrefereed races and tossed demeaning remarks about the seaworthiness and speed of other crafts. There was a lot of alcohol being consumed by crews.

The settlement of New Kamilche on Little Skookum was a hub of logging activity. The Port Blakely Mill, a William Renton enterprise, had begun operations on Bainbridge Island in 1863 after attempts elsewhere on Puget Sound. By the 1880s Port Blakely Mill was the largest lumber mill in the world, with a capacity of two hundred thousand board feet a day.[15] Indeed, all over the Northwest, entrepreneurs and speculators like Renton took advantage of the natural resources of the area and acquired land that had belonged to Indians for development. There were not only natural resources but also cheap laborers available. Many new immigrants, especially single men, were dependent on wage jobs. Particularly available were off-reservation Indian people who were concerned about feeding themselves and their families as old resources became scarce and access to them was made difficult by state and territorial authorities and white settlers. The new circumstances threatened their very existence.

Wealthy corporations and their masters came to dominate local economies and created a class of workers who could be shuffled in and out of work depending on the national and international markets, those "boom and bust" spikes and dips in economies beyond their control.

Mason County, Katie Gale's home, had great forests and became an important source of timber. Sol Simpson, an entrepreneur born in England and raised in Canada, hauled timber for Port Blakely from his Seattle base. He was lauded for being the first to use horses instead of oxen to haul the log carts to market. In 1890 he formed his own company, based in Mason County, the Simpson Logging Company. By 1898 "it was producing a half million board feet of logs per day from eight logging camps and through 80 miles of tracks."[16] The tracks were known as the Blakely Line and the logs were bound for the docks in New Kamilche, where they would be loaded on a boat and shipped to the Port Blakely Mill. There were several logging camps near the town of New Kamilche with attendant men and horses and oxen. A large dock there was the site of much commerce, generated by the mushrooming logging business, and the little town had its own store and even a dance hall.

The building most used for dancing in New Kamilche's heyday was constructed in the early 1890s. It was a two-story, thirty-two-by-seventy-two-foot structure used as an Odd Fellows Hall. There are some recollections of balls and dances in journals and manuscripts written during this period. These gatherings were popular among the Europeans and European Americans who brought their songs and instruments from their home country or ordered instruments from mail order catalogues.

Montgomery Ward had guitars for sale from about 1880. One source says you could order banjos and mandolins too — everything for under five dollars. People played and danced through the night, according to extant memoirs. These long sessions usually required backup fiddlers to switch off and keep things moving. Often someone played a mouth organ. Other instruments might include accordion, concertina, guitar, mandolin, banjo, jaw harp, clarinet, and horns. Depending on the venue, there might be a piano available. Isaac Van Dorsey Mossman, whose son was an Oyster Bay resident, described the dances in Oregon, which probably were not dissimilar to those held around Kamilche and Oyster Bay: "A dance would start at 4 o'clock in the afternoon and last until 10 o'clock the next day. Plenty of grub and lots of whiskey. Every fellow would try to see how hard he could dance and how high he could swing his partner." Popular tunes included "Nelly Bly," "Rye Straw," "Annie Laurie," and plenty of schottisches, reels, quadrilles, and waltzes for dancing.[17] The New Kamilche dances attracted folks from the Kamilche Valley, Arcadia, and Mud Bay. Callers for dances included Jay Ransom, who was spelled now and then by a man known as "Snag-tooth" Butler.[18] Frank Gingrich, father of Cora Chase, was one of the fiddlers.

Katie Gale and her daughters were part of the passing scene, familiar faces in New Kamilche and among steamer passengers. However, they likely did not go to dances or other primarily, if not solely, European American events. They could hear the music, especially while out on a float house or working in a low tide during a long winter night.

Katie and her children did go to town. And probably often. They stepped onto a New Kamilche steamer and settled themselves among passengers who'd already boarded in Shelton. They took care to avoid or step around loads of cordwood for the engine and the soaking-wet burlap bags full of Olympia oysters, some from their own tidelands. They held their long dresses up past the ankles to avoid dirtying their hemlines even more than they had already just getting to their own canoe and climbing up the beach to the wharf at New Kamilche. The steamer trembled and people on board experienced a small earthquake as the engines started and the boat was about to take off. As they traveled toward Olympia, on clear days they could see the bright Nisqually glacier on the slopes of Mount Rainier from the steamer's deck. Looking west, they could see the long, jagged range of peaks that make up the Olympic Mountains, the most prominent among them the large double crests of The Brothers and the impressive, 7,743-foot basalt summit that is Mount Constance. Of course, Katie knew these notable features of the Western Washington landscape by other names. On the surface of the water as they passed they saw a multitude of ducks and, in the fall, great flotillas of jellyfish. Sometimes orcas could be seen and often there were seals with pups, sometimes big herds of them sunning on an abandoned sink float. On some routes, specifically those going north to Tacoma past the Nisqually Delta, they could glimpse the still-majestic peak of Mount St. Helens far to the south.

When the boat landed in Olympia, Katie, with whichever child traveled with her, conducted business. They could sell the bags of oysters to brokers right off the boat. Then they shopped in the growing town of Olympia, population in the range of five thousand in the 1890s. Washington had become a state in 1889 and Olympia was designated its capital. It seemed destined for big things.

Apart from Bettman's Mercantile, there was a furniture store and myriad other establishments. Telephone lines had been hung and there were telegraph poles and even a horse-powered railway system.[19] If they were hungry they could, as early as 1870s, have a bite at the People's Hotel and Restaurant on the corner of First and Main Streets, right near the steamboat landing. Its advertisements invited people to "place your hungry form in one of the easy chairs which surround the tables of this famous eating house, and fill up your soul's content with the choice viands served by the gentlemanly proprietors of this Restaurant."

Often Katie and her daughter Hattie caught a steamer on to Tacoma. In that case they might board the night before or spend hours on the dock watching freight being loaded for passage to Tacoma or Seattle before departure. From the Commencement Bay dock in Tacoma, Katie and Hattie headed to the Puyallup Indian Reservation, created by the Treaty of Medicine Creek, where they visited relatives. They were among the many off-reservation Indians throughout the region who kept close association with reservation kin and returned often to hunting, fishing, and gathering grounds of their youth and pre-treaty times.

They would always stay a few days. Hattie listened to her kin talk politics while they wove or shelled peas or peeled potatoes or prepared and dyed basket materials: cedar bark smeared with the inner bark of alder for red, immersed in black mud, or boiled with Oregon grape root for yellow. The group was usually composed of a few women kin. They sat outside their houses around a wooden table or on their porches working, dressed in their big cotton aprons and ample calico dresses. They worked together, talking, laughing, and telling stories in their own language. Everyone knew it.

Politics provided fodder for the best conversations. Who is in and who is out. Who's in trouble with whom and why. What the politicians off the reservation are up to. Who is trying to buy whose land. The Puyallup were always, it seemed, righteously agitated about something or other. Hattie got many ideas during those visits. You might say she began to nurture a political consciousness. You might say she was radicalized by these conversations and the bitterness many of the old people expressed about what the whites had done to them and their land and complaints about what they were cheated out of.

Transcripts of testimony presented by Indians in Western Washington before the Court of Claims in 1927 in *Duwamish et al. v. United States of America* are full of these complaints, the same ones often repeated, retold, and rehashed throughout the last half of the 1900s and after. These grievances and the bitterness the Puyallups and many others expressed had been carried forward by elders from the treaty period of the 1850s. During the Court of Claims hearings in the late 1920s, aged tribal members described their memories of pre-treaty life in detail, recounting village names, numbers of houses at each village site, place-names. Insufferable losses were recounted. Incomparable losses. Horrific injustices.

These injustices do not fade from collective memory quickly. Where were the goods promised in the treaty proceedings? The bags of gold promised? Why were their houses burned to the ground? Why were they denied the rights to hunting, fishing, and gathering grounds that they did not "treat" away? As David R. M. Beck writes of tribal people along the Oregon coast during the same era, "The changes in the world around them were made more poignant because the United States government failed to live up to the solemn agreement that tribal members believed they had made."[20]

Still, though the Tacoma visits were important, most of the trips Hattie took with Katie were to Olympia, the bustling little town with its gas streetlights and fancy department store. Before they boarded the *Willie* or, later, the *City of Shelton* in New Kamilche, they tethered their canoe to a piling near the dock. It would be floating there until their return, moving up and down on the post with the tides. Some of the steamer crew were friends and knew them well. The trips were always enjoyable and news from all over the South Sound was exchanged with crew and passengers hailing from Shelton, Kamilche, and points nearby.

At journey's end they walked up the long wooden planks to the Olympia docks, the site of much financial traffic and frenzied business activity. Wooden buildings lined the shore, including buildings hastily thrown together from rusted bits of scrap metal and salvaged, salt-washed boards from wrecks at sea, the flotsam and jetsam brought in on tides or down rivers with spring floods. There were boardinghouses for the dockworkers and fishermen, brewers and working women. These were merely adequate shelter, nothing more, often made tight against rain and wind with mosses, bits of sail fabric, even bits of animal skins stuffed into cracks and holes. The docks themselves were piled with burlap bags of oysters waiting to be loaded and shipped out. Bushel sacks of wheat, hogsheads of leaf tobacco, foodstuffs, and merchandise from the east and foreign ports were being off-loaded from three-masted brigs, the cargo heaved onto shoulders and carried over creaking, springy planks from ship to dock.

The day Katie bought her best dress, she and Hattie bounced their way down those mold-slippery wooden planks past sweaty sailors and piles of cargo and headed into the town proper. They soon stood gazing at the brilliant displays in the Bettman's Mercantile shop windows. There it was, the dress, fresh from the East and calling out to her from behind the large glass panes that undulated and therefore slightly distorted her view of the coveted garment. She had enough money. And she had, she mused, just the right hat to go with it, which she'd bought on the last trip to town. The hat was wrapped carefully, waiting at home.

The hat is large-brimmed, covered all over with large, rambling roses. When she wears that hat and that dress, she is magisterial, the queen of the bay and of her land. And in the hat and new dress she is beyond being hurt by her, by the mid to late 1890s mostly absent, spouse. He has another, younger, white woman. This knowledge does not dishearten or depress her. She knows, when she wears the dress and hat, that she is both powerful and chic and need not be ruffled by the rules or whims of a society or a spouse that would continue trying to control or confine her even as he seeks to replace her. She is a capable woman and has too many allies and too much gumption to allow Joseph to break her.

At home her dresses and the hat are tucked away, carefully bundled in protective, clean cloth and placed in one of her big storage baskets. No dust or soot or loose sparks will find them. All of her personal things — the clothing for the children, the furnishings for her house — have been paid for with her own money, the money she's earned picking and culling. She lives on what she earns for her labors; she has learned to rely on herself, only herself, to keep her children fed and her household secure against the unknown future. She has learned to expect no relief or fostering from her neglectful husband.

11 *Katie Gale's Early Life*

I WONDER if Katie looked out from her home toward the east in the evening and admired the glowing pink cone of Mount Rainier. After a clear day, the bright glaciers that circle its peak reflect the sunset in the west. I wonder if she watched for the color of autumn sunrises as the dawn broke behind that mountain. I wonder if she walked up the hill behind her house, up beyond the rough carriage road, to look toward the west at the last light of December sunsets. Did she stop her work to celebrate the plates of ice that lie, brittle, brilliant slabs, on the mudflats when it is cold enough to freeze the freshwater of the meandering Kennedy Creek and even lift clumps of oysters from their beds? Did she watch the radiant frozen floes as they drifted from the banks with the outgoing tides?

I imagine sometimes that I'm looking out at heron and tern and bufflehead descendants of the birds she saw. Did the return of the dunlin sandpipers, winging their way above her, bunched shoulder to shoulder, twisting and turning in astonishing harmony, sound to her, too, like the breath of God? The dunlins are extravagantly wonderful in flight, wintering on Oyster Bay, far from the Arctic where they breed. Flocks turn instantly, in midair maneuvers that astonish me. The collective flashes, alternatively brown and white, show the tops, then underbellies, of the congregation's individual members. They feed in the mud, in the night, wherever and whenever, on sea worms and small crustaceans, plentiful on the bay. They gorge themselves on the feast provided by the tidelands to fatten up for the journey back north in the spring.

Oyster Bay is home to more than five thousand shorebirds in the winter, "including black-bellied plovers, dunlins, greater yellowlegs and Western sandpipers."[1] Katie saw them all from her home, from the shore below her house, and from the oyster beds where she worked. She knew them and their habits intimately.

She watched the November chum jumping from the bay water against the golden fall skies or blustery storm waves. Some say that females breach before entering Kennedy Creek to loosen their egg sacs. They've returned to their home stream, bent on reproduction, after three to five years at sea. From their beginning in the gravel redds dug by their mothers, they emerged as tiny alevins, and as still-small fry they swam to the estuary at the mouth of the creek around February, thence to the ocean. Now they are back in the fall to begin a new cycle.

On a quiet day the slap of chum hitting the water after a skyward leap can be heard up the hill above the bank as far as my house. I wonder if Katie taught Ray and Maud and Hattie and Henry and poor, short-lived Lizzie, her five children, to slice the guts from the fish, then cut the flesh from the spinal column? Did she teach them to run these plump filleted slabs through with cedar sticks and hang them in the smokehouse? Or did their father, concerned with raising fully assimilated children, prevent any attempt by her to teach her children, especially Ray and Maud, "Indian ways," even of preparing fish?

When Katie began picking oysters she was a girl, working side by side with other family members. They picked the natural, thick and extensive beds of the native Olympia oysters, growing in the largely unpolluted waters of the bay.[2] Katie was picking oysters before the introduction of Pacific oysters and predators that drill and kill the flesh of the Olympia oyster. (The Japanese oyster drill *Ocenebra japonica* and the flatworm *Pseudostylochus ostreophagus* were introduced in shipments of Pacific oyster spat from Japan in the early 1900s, when Pacific oysters were first introduced to Puget Sound.)

Katie and her family were there before the first non-Indian oystermen arrived on Oyster Bay with their values, dreams, and aspirations that rapidly turned a largely subsistence harvest to one based on accumulation of wealth, investment, and growth. Katie and her family were certainly on the bay before human-caused degradations to the bay and its mud and waters began.

Changes began in the 1870s but were coming rapidly by the 1890s, when Katie Gale was in her early thirties. It was by this time that Puget Sound sediment cores show increasing amounts of lead and arsenic, largely from shipbuilding and the Asarco plant on Commencement Bay near Tacoma that was smelting lead from 1890 until about 1905, when it switched to copper smelting.

Shorelines, deltas, wetlands, and swamplands of Puget Sound were already being changed in shape and size by this time as a result of dredging, filling, and diking all around this great inland sea. Beginning in the early 1900s, immigrant Japanese workers were put to work building multilevel cement and wooden dikes filled with shell and gravel in Oyster Bay. These dikes acted as retaining walls for seawater that covered spat and growing Olympia oysters and protected them. However, all the dredging and diking directly affected vegetation, including eelgrass, and therefore also had an effect on native fish and shellfish habitat.

Pulp mills were next to menace the environment and endanger the native oyster beds. One was opened in Shelton in 1927, just a little after the Olympia oyster production had reached its peak. The discharge of sulfite waste liquor from this pulp mill almost destroyed the native mollusks. (The Shelton mill didn't close until 1957.)

Katie Gale and her family were on Oyster Bay before territorial legislation was passed that allowed the acquisition and cultivation of tidelands, those same tidelands that had been worked for generations by Indian people. A territorial act "To Encourage the Cultivation of

Oysters" was passed in January 1863. Parcels of tidelands in Totten Inlet were granted to private owners as early as 1864.[3] This act was amended in 1873 to allow any person who was a citizen of the territory and who had planted oysters to acquire up to twenty acres for that purpose. It was amended again in 1877 to allow citizens to gather from unstaked natural beds. The territorial legislature amended the act again in 1879 to allow citizens exclusive use of natural oyster beds.[4]

These territorial acts were supplanted by the Bush Act and the Callow Act, passed after statehood. Both acts were passed in 1895.[5] The Bush Act allowed for the sale of state-owned tidelands to private parties for the purpose of "oyster planting, to encourage and facilitate said industry." The Callow Act allowed for the "purchase and sale of oyster lands" to private individuals.[6]

Over the years, non-Indians rushed to take advantage of these opportunities to cultivate shellfish and make their fortunes. They filed for oyster tidelands and invested heavily in hopes of future gains. People who never intended to work beds had them surveyed and acquired them for future sale. Oystermen owners hired workers, became middlemen, and organized their enterprise around the cheap and ready labor already on Oyster Bay. Some of the laborers were landless whites like Cora Chase's father and mother in the late 1890s. But early on, and for the most part, they were the previously independent Indians who were already there. Later the white owners hired Chinese and Japanese, who displaced the Indians. The owners shipped oysters. (They shipped to Tacoma, Olympia, Seattle, and hence to San Francisco, among other ports.) The crop was picked, culled, and bagged by people who were paid by the "piece," two dollars for a two-bushel burlap bag when Katie Gale and others were working for Joseph Gale.

The white oystermen had, in a few years, a much greater impact on Oyster Bay's ecology and environment than had a thousand years of Indian occupation. They were growers, not simply pickers. They diked and seeded. They filled and created new beds.

In a 1901 Pan-American Exposition supplement to the *Mason County*

Journal, a staff writer celebrated the expansive oyster business. "The very best white men and shrewdest capitalists are giving this branch of commercial pursuit their attention and making investments and improvements in the oyster industry to such an extent that it is becoming the leading and most important business in this part of the United States," he writes.

It was in this world of expanding capitalism and social and cultural upheaval that Katie had to find her way.

Katie Gale. She was probably born in a sullen and smoky, haphazard dwelling on poison ivy–infested Fox Island; she was likely born a prisoner in a virtual concentration camp during the 1855–56 "Puget Sound War" in Washington Territory. Her mother would have been dispossessed of her land, her culture, and her kin and placed on this island "reservation" with others who had been dispossessed.

The war followed complaints about treaties that had been written, "negotiated," and signed. These treaties had been brought to the regional Indian people by a man of small stature but stately aims. He was a man who vowed to Franklin Pierce to serve the cause of "eminent domain." He was the territory's first governor, Isaac Stevens.

Stevens measured his success by the number of acres he'd mapped out and for which he had "treated." This "treating" was really all to the immense benefit of the United States, not the Indians. It is said that the Indians, in fact, had very little choice but to accept the terms of the United States. The military was the force behind the negotiations, and Indian land had already, in many instances, been claimed and settled by European Americans. Isaac Stevens plodded over mountains and rode high in his saddle as he traced routes for future railroads and sites of future empires. He represented, even embodied, a patriarchal government, so much so that he called himself their "father" when he spoke to Indians at councils. Sometimes he merely said he represented their great father in Washington. Either way, the sense he conveyed to his listeners was that the government was in charge and would care for them as a father would his children. It was a benign message, but one that asked an already-depleted people to give over their land and their way of life and make way for a new world.

The writer Sarah Vowell, in her discussion of earlier American history, provides some insight into the roots of that patronizing way Stevens, and many others of the period, had of speaking to Indian people. Arguably, years before, the Massachusetts Bay Company had begun to pave the path to the Stevens era and to lay the philosophical, political, and linguistic groundwork for Indian-white relations in North America. Vowell writes that a group of "white male religious fanatics" received their authoritarianism from "the same place they derive all their other beliefs — the Bible." John Winthrop, the third governor of the colony, 1630–34, wrote that democracy was a breach of the Fifth Commandment, to honor your father and mother. Vowell cites Martin Luther, who explained how the Fifth Commandment "extends beyond the nuclear family and into public life: 'In this commandment belongs a further statement regarding all kinds of obedience to persons in authority who have to command and govern. For all authority flows and is propagated from the authority of parents. . . . They are all called fathers in the Scriptures, as those who in their government perform the functions of a father, and should have a paternal heart toward their subordinate.'"[7]

Stevens was not unique. He was simply following the examples before him, on the heels of some two and a half centuries of rhetoric.

What did Stevens really tell the Indians who gathered to hear him present the treaties? It is clear from later oral testimony from those who were alive when the Treaty of Medicine Creek — the one that had the most impact on Katie Gale's life — was signed that Stevens's words were not well understood. At least the part about what was promised was garbled. The translation was made from English to Chinook Jargon, a language with a limited vocabulary, and then to the gathered Southern Lushootseed or Puget Sound Salish speakers in their language.

Chinook Jargon was used throughout the Northwest as a so-called trade language. It comprises a Chinookan- and Nootkan-derived vocabulary along with some French and English. Some form of it, minus, of course, the English and French, is said to have been in use in pre-European trade up and down the coast. There was extensive, long-standing trading among and between Indian communities. The jargon was the lingua franca of the time, perhaps for generations. Many European Americans and Indians in Western Washington in the mid-1850s knew some Chinook Jargon. George Gibbs, who assisted Isaac Stevens in the treaty process, collected and wrote a Chinook Jargon word list.

Extensive and difficult concepts are not easily or precisely expressed in Chinook Jargon. It is highly metaphorical and meaning relies heavily on context. Therefore, what was said at Medicine Creek during the treaty "negotiations" was muddled, perhaps in part because the translations to and from Chinook were inexact, misleading, or even erroneous. In any case, people afterward told different versions of what they had heard, and these various impressions, doubts, and translations were passed on to others.

Katie Gale, born a couple of years after the signing, would have known, from the beginning of her life, people who had been at the convocation called to sign the treaty at She-nah-nam Creek, the treaty that became known as the Treaty of Medicine Creek. Those who had been there from southern Puget Sound, including Oyster Bay and Mud Bay, told what they knew; they compared what they had been promised to what they had been given — a reservation on Squaxin Island where nothing grew and where hoary, dissolute men were sent to run the place. These men, maybe, kept money and goods that this absent, presumptuous "father" had meant for the Indians. Whatever Stevens had said, the crucial point was that the Indians were getting nothing or very little in return for the land they'd ceded in good faith.

They hadn't given up everything. This was clear. In return for the ceded land, Stevens had surely promised, people asserted, that the original occupants and owners of the land would be able to fish and hunt forever as they had before, wherever they had before. Nobody would have signed that away. It was the good land and waterways that had always sustained them and provided an adequate, even bountiful, livelihood. That would not have been given to anyone for any reason.

There were problems, obvious problems, shortly after the treaties were signed and ratified. Indian people all over the territory knew of these problems and talked, even ranted, about them.

In 1855–56 a war was waged by the Indian people who were most courageous and vocally and publicly offended by what had happened. They were led by Chief Leschi, a Nisqually-Yakama Indian. Puget Sound Indians, all seen as potential combatants by the European Americans, led by the governor, were told they had to go to Fox Island, a 6.4-square-mile tract of land in Puget Sound near Fort Steilacoom, a U.S. Army post at the time. It was retained and run as a wartime concentration camp for Indians. Meanwhile, the Sa-heh-wamish of South Sound, as some predecessors of the Squaxin Island Tribe were called, and others, including the Squawskin (from whom the present Squaxin Island Tribe derives its name) from Case Inlet, were held on the reservation called Klah-Che-Min, or Squaxin Island, an island with no naturally occurring drinking water and little else in the way of amenities.

It was Fox Island, however, where Katie was likely born.

If one takes the record of supplies sent to Fox Island as representative of what was available for sustenance in the camp, the Indian people, who had for generations feasted on the abundance of returning fish runs, seasonal berries, roots, bulbs, wild green vegetation, and moist, succulent shellfish since anyone could remember, seem to have been expected to live on flour and molasses. There wasn't even much of that.

Some of the Fox Island internees got permission to go to their homes or to old territories of relatives up on Carr Inlet with seed potatoes to plant. These families and individuals no doubt became stronger because they could gather plants and hunt there while they were hoeing and planting. They could do some fishing. The people who never left Fox Island became weak and despairing. People died every day in wretched conditions. They couldn't leave until the government said they could and were trapped in their despondency, watching each other waste away.

In spite of what was surely a harsh beginning, Katie must have been told and later remembered the stories her mother and other kin related during her childhood. Perhaps tales were told to keep up morale or to be sure the culture wasn't completely lost. Perhaps people told of mythic adventures and heroic feats to distract the children from the pain and fear and sorrow so many felt. Some of the narratives were epics that required several nights to bring to a conclusion; thus children as well as adults would look forward to the next episodes and be, perhaps, distracted from their misery.

Katie heard many tales about the mountain many called Tahoma before it was called Rainier. She knew stories about the "changer" who created human beings from other creatures and bestowed on them the rudiments of culture. She surely remembered the narratives that celebrated determination, survival, and transformative possibilities. She would have heard sagas of thunderbird and whale; she would know dramas of blue jay and beaver. Some among those who survived and spoke to Katie would be experts at telling the tales and recounting wonderful deeds in detail.

These stories taught her that the world was not always like this hard one she lived in. Of that she remained certain until she died. The stories taught her that the bitterest times contained possibilities of renewal. They taught her that people are different from one another, each unique, and some not particularly nice or to be trusted. The stories taught her that change was the way of the universe. There were always new ways to learn, new challenges to face, new faces to greet, new masks to don, new rivers to cross, and new stars to explore. When, she would have wondered, did this change — the change she had witnessed already in her life, the one that led to this life she was caught up in — begin?

I'll never know where she was born with any certainty, nor will I know the facts of her early life. I don't know for sure what she heard about the treaty or the war. Katie Gale left no letters or diaries or journals. I can only surmise these things I've written from what I do know about this time and this life in the territory that abutted what we call Puget Sound. Still, there is, regrettably, so much I don't know or even begin to understand.

Of one thing I am certain: Katie Gale was a refugee, a person displaced by war and threats of war from her country of origin.

The White River people with whom Katie Kettle Gale seems to have had some connection were "inland" people (as opposed to "saltwater" people) whose resource area encompassed land between the rivers, streams, and prairies of the area as well as tracts along the western slopes of the Cascades.[8] Trails across mountain passes that led east to Yakama territory, used perhaps for thousands of years, were easily reachable from the White River. Thus there was a centuries-old history of exchange and Sahaptin influence in this territory. Sahaptin is the language of the Klickitats and Yakamas, some of whom settled on the west side of the Cascades or traded regularly with other indigenous people. During the course of contact the locals and some Sahaptin speakers had intermarried, so there were multilingual speakers in the area and a mix of cultures.

The White River was so called for the milky glacial sediment it carried from its source, the Emmons glacier, high on the flank of Mount Rainier. It was not known as a productive salmon stream, but people on the White shared resources with other river people who had elaborate weirs or fish traps on the Green River.

Katie's people had horses. But not many. Those horses may have come originally to the White River people over the mountains from Yakama by way of the trade routes and with kin from that area. Horses were brought to eastern Washington in the early eighteenth century. The horses the White River people had, most probably descendants of Spanish mustangs, may have been similar to the Nez Perce horse, spotted and spicy, an old-line buckskin with appaloosa and paint genes, thus mottled around the middle section. They would not be the kind of horse she and Joseph Gale had later to pull their carriage to barn dances.

Katie's people hunted in the Cascade foothills, dug for roots and bulbs in the prairies, and climbed Huckleberry Mountain with their large burden baskets when the fruits were in season.[9]

The village Katie's family were from would have been one of those caught up in the violence of the war that began in 1855. This was a hard time for Indian people in the region. The Treaty of Medicine Creek had been signed, but Leschi, a Nisqually chief, and others were not happy about its provisions. In fact, Leschi had arguably left the signing grounds in protest.

Katie's kin were no doubt encouraged by longtime and sustained contact with Indians east of the Cascades and in Oregon Territory who were already defying the incursions on their land by whites and already standing together in protest of the unfair treaty provisions. These kin and others who were party to the Treaty of Medicine Creek were increasingly dissatisfied with the terms of their treaty and the consequent size and location of reservations defined by the treaty. Many had already established working farms with cropland, pastureland, and homes outside of the proposed reservation boundaries. Moreover, white settlements were advancing on Indian country at a rapid rate. There was also little evidence, in the way of goods or services, of the compensation the United States had promised to the original owners of the land. It all smelled of a bad deal.

In late October 1855, following skirmishes between territorial volunteers and Western Washington Indians and growing tensions after open, armed, and deadly conflict between Yakamas and the U.S. Army, furious Indians carried out raids and attacked three non-Indian families. Several individuals in the White River Valley were killed. The blood shed here, memorialized with tales of selfless heroism and kindness that crossed cultural boundaries, marked the opening days of the war.

After October 1855 Indians from around Puget Sound were ordered to Fox Island or Squaxin Island, or they would be treated as "hostiles." That meant Indians seen outside of the makeshift prisons could be shot. Katie's family and extended kin were among those forced to leave their villages by threat of edicts issued by the territorial government.

Most Indians, including likely Katie's family, were not yet "settled" on the reservations, while others had resisted the notion of leaving their homelands. Along with those who had "come in" to reservations and were somewhat established on reservation land, they would be ferried to Fox Island as detainees, where they would be confined for the duration of the war.

In April 1856, with many Indians still resisting detainment, Governor Isaac Stevens sent a circular that detailed the dire consequences of refusing to comply. More chose to "come in" rather than risk being killed by now extremely nervous whites. It is unclear when Katie's White River relatives arrived on Fox Island, assuming they did. Such details are lost in the confusion of the period.

By February 1856 the local agent in charge of Fox Island had directed the building of some houses at the campsite and had ordered the purchase of bread and sugar for the Indian prisoners already assembled. Documents from the period show that more Indians came to the island over the next months. We do know some groups of women and children were brought in April 1856 and, in one instance, the record kept by the agent shows that "the most part of them have never been on the reservation." More would have come, his report continues, "had they canoes." On another occasion somewhat later, two Indians with canoes were sent to the Puyallup Reservation to bring in women.

At one time, up to one thousand Puyallups (including people from upriver and Puyallup tributaries as well as from Commencement Bay), Nisquallies, S'Homamish (from Vashon Island area), S'Hotlemamish (from Carr Inlet), and others languished as captives under the supervision of the government's man on the scene. Agent Sidney S. Ford Jr. wrote that when he took charge of Fox Island on May 1, 1856, there were 720 Indians resident. Of these, over 300 were under age sixteen. Eighty of the 720 died in July and August. One recorded cause of death was "bleeding of the lungs," as tuberculosis was called. It is likely that tuberculosis accounted for many more of the deaths.

Financial accounts kept by the agent suggest that rations provided to the Indians were minimal. They included the already mentioned flour and molasses and, less regularly, coffee. The internees could not hunt or fish. Indeed, the army dammed some salmon streams during the war to prevent upriver holdouts from harvesting food. This act would, of course, have consequences in later years, for that cohort of fish would not spawn in those streams and thus a run could not be expected from their offspring in the future.

Residents on Fox Island were expected to grow some food. The previously mentioned seed potatoes arrived at the end of May and crews of detainees were set to clearing and planting in Henderson Bay, up Carr Inlet some distance by water from Fox Island.

Ford, in his reports, called the Indians "destitute of the comforts of life." In spite of the desperate conditions, Governor Stevens wrote in December 1856, when many Indians were still resident on the island, that Ford should keep expenses at "the lowest point compatible with efficiency."

If Katie's mother were resident on Fox Island during her pregnancy, she would have been denied the nourishment essential to sustain health and well-being. She would have been surrounded by sorrow and sickness. Many of her family and friends no doubt died during the incarceration on Fox Island or lived in difficult circumstance, if not in hiding, elsewhere during the war.

In March 1856 the hostilities finally ended where they began, on Connell's Prairie near the town of Buckley in Pierce County, Washington.

William Krise, from Hammersley Inlet described in military records as a five-foot-five-inch man of twenty-nine with fair skin, blue eyes, and light hair, served with distinction in the battle of Connell's Prairie. It was a decisive battle in the short war. Capt. A. B. Rabbeson wrote of his soldiers, "These men [including Krise] deserve the greatest credit for the courage and bravery—each performing his duty." There was not, he continued, "a man or officer engaged in this fight who did not perform his whole duty."[10]

The Washington Volunteers skirmished for two hours or more with Chief Leschi and a group of Indian fighters. It was the last battle of this unfortunate era of the region's history. Afterward Leschi led three dozen or so surviving Indians across the mountains to Yakama Country.

Leschi was later captured and then hanged, in February 1858, for the murder of Washington volunteer Col. A. Benton Moses, killed in October 1855 in the White River area. Leschi's attorney argued that Leschi was a combatant in a war when the alleged incident took place and that he should not be tried in a civilian court for murder. Nevertheless, he was. The first trial ended in a hung jury, but a new trial found him guilty.[11] A carefully surveyed map (made by Lt. Augustus Kautz of the U.S. Army, who befriended Leschi while he was held in captivity at Fort Steilacoom, and by Dr. William Fraser Tolmie, formerly chief factor at the Hudson's Bay Company's Fort Nisqually and a Leschi supporter) demonstrated that Leschi could not have been where he was said to have been by those who accused him and could not, therefore, have committed the "murder" for which he was being tried. This map came forward as part of an appeal for a new trial. The new trial was denied.

Leschi was exonerated in 2004. In that year a specially constituted court, including present and past justices of the Washington Supreme Court, agreed with Leschi's original defense. "Chief Leschi should not, as a matter of law, have been tried for the crime of murder," they declared.

In March 2004, both houses of the Washington State Legislature passed resolutions that affirmed these findings and exonerated Leschi. "BE IT FURTHER RESOLVED," the Senate resolution states, "that the

Senate recognize Chief Leschi as a courageous leader whose sacrifice for his people is worthy of honor and respect and that the residents of the State of Washington solemnly remember Chief Leschi as a great and noble man."

The war was over, but the lives of those exiled from their homes were irredeemable. The treaties had been signed and the old home and village sites and lands ceded to the United States. After the war formally ended at the Fox Island Council in August 1856, Indians were to go to the reservations described in the treaties. The sizes and locations of reservations, the principal cause of complaint and the ensuing hostilities, were changed during that August council. Governor Stevens agreed not only to expand some existing reservations in Western Washington but also to establish another, the Muckleshoot Reservation.

Many of Katie's family and friends who survived the war and captivity must have eventually settled on the Puyallup Reservation, where Katie and her daughter Hattie would often visit "tillicum and kindred." Though the White River was not part of the Puyallup drainage system, some villages on the Puyallup had close ties with White River people. For example, the STUH'kh-ahbsh at the junction of the Stuck and Puyallup had ties with White River people. Also, Puyallup River people were relatively close to a White River village called do'líuq^{u} or doh-LHEE-ook'oo.[12] Anthropologist Marian Smith, in *The Puyallup-Nisqually*, documented these village sites. Her book is based, in part, on extensive interviews conducted during the 1930s. Her aged Puyallup and Nisqually informants remembered early post-treaty times and knew village sites from childhood and stories from their elders. They told her that there had been much visiting and sharing of resources, including shared use of fish traps, among these White River and upper Puyallup people. Given these close relationships, going to the Puyallup Reservation along with people from other Puyallup predecessor bands and villages when forced to leave their homes and freed from Fox Island would have been reasonable for Katie's remaining kin.

12 *The Kettle Connection*

I CAN only speculate that the woman who was in all likelihood Katie's mother died during Katie's childhood, even, perhaps, on Fox Island. Or perhaps she was already domiciled in South Puget Sound and living on Oyster Bay with kin who invited her to join them after the war. The evidence shows that when Katie was still quite young she was in the Mud Bay Indian settlement or on Oyster Bay, either with her mother or sent there during her mother's illness. Katie was possibly sent to be raised by relatives named Kettle or Kethlid, a name she was known by before she married Joseph Gale. The family apparently had Squaxin (Case Inlet), Satsop, and Yakama connections, perhaps through White River/Sahaptin relations.[1] Louisa Kettle Tobin, who in the 1914 U.S. Census lists her tribal affiliation as Yakama, and her Irish Duwamish husband, James Tobin, were both on Oyster Bay when Katie Gale lived there.[2] James and Louisa Tobin later took a homestead on Young's Cove, Eld Inlet, a short walk east across a prairie from Oyster Bay. They had not always been in the area. They were married by Father Eugene Casimir Chirouse, James Tobin asserted in a court case in the early twentieth century. Father Chirouse resided on the Tulalip Reservation from 1857 until 1878.

Chief Kettle, Louisa Kettle Tobin's father, was arguably Squaxin from Case Inlet, according to Louisa. He was probably, at least in later life and before the Treaty of Medicine Creek was signed, from the Sherwood Creek area of Case Inlet. Louisa Tobin knew names for points in that area and Chief Kettle apparently knew the Sherwood brothers who had settled there. Louisa was unequivocal in what she told the anthropologist Ruth Greiner during the 1920s.[3] Her father, she said, was called qwaLbétΔb.[4] He came to be known variously as Kettle, Kethlid, Labatim, Labatum, and Lobatum.

qwaLbétΔb was an acknowledged great leader. Sometimes his name appears as "Sitkum Kettle." This may have been because of his small stature. Both the Chinook Jargon words *sitkum* and *tenas* would convey this meaning when used to refer to a person. The one photograph I've found of him, dated 1892, shows a small but sturdy man wearing a buttoned overcoat. On his head he wears a straw boater or skimmer, popular in the late nineteenth century. He appears to have a cane in his left hand, though it is largely hidden behind his left leg. Perhaps he was still recovering from a wagon accident in which he was involved in July 1891.

At his death it was written that despite his great age "Chief Kettle was sturdy and agile and was not subject to the troubles which generally overtake men of his age. He was always in the best of health and spry and lively as a young buck."[5]

He is an ancestor of both Maiselle Bridges and Billy Frank Jr. Maiselle Bridges, spouse of Al Bridges, worked tirelessly in the 1960s to restore fishery rights guaranteed by the 1850s treaties. She and her family often placed themselves in great personal danger as they went on the river again and again in the face of armed opposition from the State of Washington. Maiselle Bridges envisioned and founded, with the support of the community, the Wa-He-Lut Indian School at Frank's Landing on the Nisqually River in 1974. As a small child she lived for a time with her grandparents, Louisa and James Tobin, on their homestead on Eld Inlet.

Billy Frank Jr., Maiselle's brother, has been the chair of the Northwest Indian Fisheries Commission for over thirty years at the time of this writing. This leadership role does not begin to describe the importance of Frank's work over the years. His presence is dynamic, and his tireless work as a spokesperson for the rights of Indian people, the salmon, and the natural resources of the region and the world has been recognized and celebrated; he has received countless public accolades, including the Albert Schweitzer Prize for Humanitarianism. He is truly a prophet and a visionary.

Both of these dedicated activists inherited, though they would not have known him, the drive and spirit of their great-grandfather, Chief Kettle, or Labatum Kettle.

Chief Kettle, if indeed from Case Inlet, was part of the group from which the name Squaxin is derived. The original Squaxin, or tuxs qwák-sûd (following Ruth Greiner's orthography) or Squawskin (the spelling used in the Treaty of Medicine Creek, ratified in 1855), were from the head of Case Inlet watershed in Puget Sound. It is on the island that was then known as Klah-che-min (now best known as Squaxin Island) and was set aside as a reservation by the Medicine Creek Treaty. It was on Squaxin Island that, according to Louisa Tobin, Chief Kettle "surrendered his guns" to the Sherwood brothers during the 1855–56 Puget Sound War—the war waged in protest of the terms of the treaty.

Before the war the Sherwood brothers had settled on what is now called Sherwood Creek in the present town of Allyn on Case Inlet. They built a sawmill on the creek, no doubt a tuxs qwáksûd fishing area, and in doing so, blocked the salmon run. The principal village site on Case Inlet was at its head. It was what Marian Smith called village number 33, the sqwáksdabc. (Smith's orthography), in the list of village sites she gathered through interviews collected for her 1940 book. The people on Case Inlet had close contact with people from Hood Canal. There was a "well defined path across the land bridge between the mouth of Coulter Creek and Clifton on the Canal."[6] The village was noted by George Gibbs, the attorney who worked closely with Isaac Stevens during the treaty period, and its population was recorded at forty on an 1855 census. Another village was located at Allyn, at the mouth of "Mason Creek," or Sherwood Creek, fed by waters from Mason Lake.[7] Frank Allen, one of the Skokomish men who worked with William Elmendorf, said the Twana name for the village was dusk' ^{w}a'X^{w}sed.[8] The creek was called ^{tux}sqwElts, or "hot," according to T. T. Waterman's Southern Lushootseed orthography. Vi Hilbert's Lushootseed translation for this name is "a place where something is cooked, baked or heated."[9] Both John Winterhouse (1948) and Florence Howard (1949) described shell middens found in this area and around the mouths of creeks and streams.[10] The one at the mouth of Sherwood Creek "extended 102 yards along the bank and varied from five feet to twenty feet in width."[11] Thus the area that Chief Kettle seems to have come from or lived in as an adult was clearly a long-established, well-populated one.

However, there was so much movement of people around this region before the treaty period that it is impossible to say with any certainty where Chief Kettle was born. One family story arguably places him in the Seattle area during a Haida raid. In a letter dated 1910 H. H. Johnson, an agent investigating the legitimacy of claims to allotments on the Quinault Reservation, writes that "Kettle Lobatum," though a resident of Squaxin Island, "was in reality a Satsop Indian." Johnson says that he was related to "Swatser, who was one Chief of the Satsop tribe."[12]

Chief Kettle may have been born on the Satsop around 1818 and then married into a Case Inlet family before 1854. What seems clear is that he was living in or near Sherwood Creek or the village at the head of Case Inlet before the war, was on Squaxin Island during the war, and then lived on Mud Bay and Oyster Bay in the later nineteenth century. Louisa Tobin's Yakama mother may not have been his first or only spouse, which further complicates the matter of tracing family ties.

It was, however, surely from his actions on Squaxin Island during the 1855–56 war that Kettle earned or enhanced his reputation as a peacemaker. His family members were probably detained on Squaxin Island after he surrendered his guns. They would have been required to stay for the duration of that war. They would have lost, forever, their homes and lush fishing, shellfishing, and hunting territories on Case Inlet.

Some of the Case Inlet people, Smith says, moved to the Skokomish Reservation after the war.[13] This was due to the close relationships that held between the Case Inlet and Skokomish people from time immemorial. Others, including the Kettles, moved to Mud Bay and Oyster Bay with other relatives and friends rather than stay on the unsuitable Squaxin Island Reservation. It was from Mud Bay and his Oyster Bay home that Chief Kettle continued to be a known leader in the region.

"Old Man" Kettle, as his name sometimes appears on census rolls and in newspapers, with three other Indian men, showed up to work on the Olympia-Tenino railroad in 1874. Sitkum or "Chief" Kettle was well known enough in the area to have this contribution noted in the *Washington Standard* newspaper in April of that year. "The head chief of the Squaxon Indians, Kettel, with three of his chosen braves reported early yesterday morning to the foreman on the grade of the railroad." The reporter claimed to have a direct quote from Chief Kettle in Chinook Jargon. The quote, as the newspaper printed it, is "'Nesiki ticki cultus potlatch mamook ict sun copa la-lode" and was translated by the reporter as, "We want to give work one day on the railroad."

The Northern Pacific branch line ran through Tenino with no links to Olympia. Land and money were raised in Olympia to build the connecting line and additional land was acquired. The actual building was a volunteer effort — townspeople and local farmers were asked to donate specified shares of time. Chief Kettle answered the call to donate time, clearly suggesting that he and other Indians on Mud Bay and Oyster Bay felt connected to the Olympia community and perhaps to the future economic benefits of this project. He and his friends were ready and able to participate.

Much of Kettle's life after 1856 seems to have been spent on Mud or Oyster Bay. He and his wife maintained their relationship with Mud

Bay even when working on Oyster Bay and apparently were well known in both communities.[14] Perhaps the family and others took their float houses between Mud Bay and Oyster Bay depending on available work and the season. The fullest account we have of Kettle comes from the recollections of James Tobin, Louisa Tobin, and Mud Bay Sam, among others, from testimony given in a 1911 court case regarding the claims of Sallie Weatherall, an Indian woman, to property left by her late husband, an Englishman, Harry Weatherall.

Sallie Weatherall contested the will that gave Harry's kin the valuable oyster tidelands they had acquired and worked together as husband and wife. The Weatherall kin and their attorneys argued that Harry and Sallie had never been properly married, nor was there evidence that he had ever considered her his wife. Many Oyster Bay people, including Abner Smith, by then living in Wapato, Washington, but willing to vouch from afar for the veracity of Sallie Weatherall's claim; Bush Hoy; and Robert Frost (the hardware store owner), as well as Mud Bay Sam, the Tobins, and others came forward on Sallie's behalf with specific and compelling testimony. Still, the case was found against Sallie, then living in a float house in Eld Inlet near Mud Bay and cared for by the Tobins.

Chief Kettle had performed a marriage for Harry and Sallie in 1879 on Oyster Bay. A Presbyterian minister named John R. Thompson, "a native of Prince Edward Island, and educated in Scotland," came to an already established Presbyterian church in Olympia in 1868. He was not installed until 1875, according to the history of the synod, and continued in his post until 1884. He preached throughout the region and was often called to support other Presbyterian ministries. Apparently he had a ministry in Mud Bay before the Shaker Church was established there. Thompson used to preach to the people and Tobin acted as interpreter for him.

James Tobin testified that Thompson taught Kettle how to marry people, "to take hold of their hands and tell them and talk to them about God and Jesus Christ." Harry Weatherall, eager to settle in with

Sallie, then called Sallie Hall, asked Tobin to translate for Kettle so he could make him understand that he wanted to marry Sallie, Kettle's relative from Case Inlet and a Squaxin, according to her own testimony.

Kettle could not speak English and only some Chinook, according to James Tobin. He only spoke "Indian," Tobin testified. Harry's Chinook wasn't great, so Tobin had to be present to help the men understand each other. "The old gentleman didn't want to marry them at all," Tobin said in 1911, "because Bostons throw their women away and he didn't want Sallie to live with him." Tobin added, "He kicked on white people marrying Indians." Harry insisted he wouldn't run away and that he wanted to be married like the Bostons. Tobin seems then to suggest that he and Kettle and the others knew the Tyees, or "masters," wanted them to all get married now. It was true that other preachers and the local agents were promoting "legal" marriages for Indian people and asking that they eschew "Indian-style" marriages. Many were falling into line during this period. There was a reference made to Judge Roger Greene during the conversation, the judge they knew from the Jackson murder case several years earlier. By this time they'd probably heard his name from other cases as well.

Greene had made an important ruling and pronouncement on marriage in June 1879 after cases were brought to him regarding unions between white men and Indian women. In his "Judicial Review of Marriage Laws," Greene writes that "where the relationship of parties apparently living together as husband and wife, is in question, the presumptions of the law are always that they are married." He says that marriage is a "civil contract, and needs for its validity nothing more than the mutual assent of two persons legally capable of making and fulfilling such a contract." Still, to protect chastity and maintain the honor of both parties, and for the security of parties, it is useful have formal documentation of some kind. He noted that the section of the Territorial Marriage Act, the act that forbade marriages between whites and people of more than half Indian blood, had been stricken on January 18, 1868. The people of Oyster Bay would have known of

Greene's pronouncements and would have heard or read of the lead-up to his decision in *Territory v. Beale*, an "indictment for living in open and notorious fornication," a case that had been brought by Whatcom County against several white men married to Indian women.[15] They could easily have "read" this as a wish from the Tyees in Olympia that marriages be formalized in a way recognizable to the "white" authorities and have fully believed that Thompson had given Chief Kettle the authority to solemnize unions in an acceptable way.

Sallie and Harry Weatherall's marriage took place when the Tobins, the Kettles, and the Weatheralls were living on Oyster Bay in float houses in a community of Indians and whites that included Sandy Wohaut and his wife and Doctor Jim and his wife. This was before the Tobins had their homestead in the Mud Bay vicinity of Eld Inlet.

The testimony in the Weatherall case bolsters other information that posits Chief Kettle as an elder whose leadership was respected among the people of both Mud Bay and Oyster Bay and even beyond. Tobin was asked in the Weatherall case how Kettle was thought of by the people in those days. Tobin answered that "he held sort of a position among his people like a man that is a head man." He "used to talk to his people how to act. He was known in the country as Chief Kettle and was a religious man."

Tobin and Mud Bay Sam agreed in their 1911 testimony that "Kettle was a man that was called all over pretty near all over from one end of the sound you might say to the other if there was anything going on wrong he was called to straighten it and marry people that was his business."

Chief Kettle's wife and Louisa Kettle Tobin's mother was, apparently, Yakama, and Yakama relatives came yearly to stay with the family on Mud Bay and harvest and dry clams and oysters for the return journey. Louisa was born two or three years after Katie Gale and is well known and beloved by still-living kin in the twenty-first century. She worked and lived on Oyster Bay most of the years that Katie lived and worked there. They possibly were cousins and picked and culled oysters together.

They were certainly little girls together, and their lives on the bay must have kept them close until Katie's death.[16]

The Kettles and Tobins and so many others on Mud Bay and Oyster Bay were people, among perhaps hundreds in Puget Sound, who chose not to go to the reservations or left the reservation when it became clear that the conditions there did not allow one to carry on reasonable economic pursuits, ply one's trade, or expect adequate support from often oppressive if not downright corrupt administrators, school masters, or others sent as representatives of the U.S. government. In other words, the choice to leave reservations, or never to go in the first place, was a reasonable choice made by entrepreneurial people in search of economic stability and a free life.

Oyster Bay and Mud Bay were covered with natural oyster beds that yielded a crop as reliable as the salmon. This resource provided a livelihood — the harvest of Olympia oysters was a stable means of earning a living. The Tobins, the Kettles, and Katie Gale, among others, chose to take advantage of this rich off-reservation opportunity.

We can catch glimpses here and there of their laboring lives together and the nature of the relationships that must have held between them. For example, several of the important Indian and white oysterers appear in the record of an 1880 court proceeding. James and Louisa Tobin, "Sys-all" (aka Cesalle), Royal (Sallie?) Hall, Henry Weatherall, "Skookum" George, and Joseph Sherwood, among others, were served warrants to give testimony as witnesses in a case involving a violation of "Acts of Washington Territory 1877" regarding the cultivation of oyster beds.[17] The case was brought by Adam Korter, a German immigrant oyster farmer married to an Indian woman, Harriet, and living down bay on Totten Inlet. Korter claimed to have witnessed Joseph Gale and Abner Smith and "his Indian women" Louisa (Abner Smith's wife) and Sallie Hall (Weatherall) raking and gathering oysters from natural beds and leaving some oysters on the shore to die. The act they were charged with breaching was passed November 9, 1877, to "Encourage the Cultivation of Oysters." Both Gale and Smith denied the charges and claimed to have purchased the oysters in question from Indians.

That this explanation was plausible gives us some insight into the economy of the oyster industry in 1880. Though white men were acquiring and consolidating tidelands for the "cultivation of oysters," Indians were still the primary labor force and many were independently picking on their own beds, then selling to the European American men who were rapidly becoming "brokers," or middlemen, as well as producing and harvesting from their own beds.

The Indian community on Oyster Bay, by all accounts, was large and active in the 1870s through about 1890. This off-reservation community, with some members in the process of acquiring and settling homesteads, was large enough and distinct enough that local newspapers commented on their celebrations, feasts, and ceremonies.

Katie Gale; the Kettles; Dick Jackson and his family; Big Frank and his family; Jack Slocum; Jim and Louisa Kettle Tobin and their first daughter, Catherine; Henry Isaac and his family and John Slocum and his family on Big Skookum; Doctor Jim (Klatab) and his spouse, Susan (Tow a qual chad or Tw-a-hwal-shud), and Sandy Wohaut (Wau ha ta or Wau hata) and his spouse, Mary Sandy (Chitsa Sandy or Tilsa Wohaut, a sister of Doctor Jim's); and others were part of this community. Other Indians (some with a European American spouse) in the Oyster Bay/Kamilche community during the 1870s through the 1890s included Cesalle and his spouse, Jane (Swiss-loo); Louisa Smith, wife of Abner Smith and daughter of Henry Isaac; and Jennie Krise, spouse of William Krise.

There was also Nellie McClure (later Sutton), spouse of a Missouri-born lumberman, A. J. McClure, nearly twice her age, and Harriet Korter, spouse of the German-born Adam Korter, a dozen years her elder. Also, Sallie Hall Weatherall lived on a float house with Harry Weatherall. Mary or Mrs. George Gibbs, spouse of an English-born cook, frequented the Weatheralls' float house and may have been a relative of Sallie Weatherall and the Kettles. She was fifteen years younger than her husband. The Dick Jackson family lived farther down bay on the east side, and Henry Isaac and his family were up Little Skookum. John Slocum's wife, Mary's father was a cousin of Doctor Jim. There were many cross-connections and kin in the community, and there were many connections with the Mud Bay Indian community. News traveled fast between these two tightly knit settlements.

Sandy Wohaut must have been a quite active and visible member of the Oyster Bay group. He is mentioned by Cora Chase in her memoir of the late 1890s. Adolph Johnson also knew him when he still paddled his dugout around Kennedy Creek at the head of Oyster Bay, gaffing salmon, in the 1890s. Sandy Wohaut made an impression on the blond, young Adolph, son of immigrant Danish farmer parents. Adolph thought that Sandy didn't "work," though he knew he fished. Fishing didn't count as work in the boy's world, though he watched as Wohaut loaded his canoe over and over with salmon he gaffed when the chum ran in thousands up Kennedy Creek. The old man taught the boy to fish and how to handle the canoe. Years later, as an old man himself, Adolph had a distorted view of Wohut's labor. He didn't know or mention that Wohaut had filed for tidelands and had oyster beds, for example. He *did* remember that Wohaut did not linger near the trees that still held canoe burials that were "pretty well intact" near the mouth of Kennedy Creek. Sandy "averted his head" when he passed those trees, Adolph remembered many years later. As a boy, Adolph had gathered beads from the site, but his respectful mother "made him put them back."

Though it is hard to credit reports filed by the many local writers who enjoyed poking fun at Indian people in their news columns, it may be that Wohaut did in fact wear a "plug hat," as one article noted. This was likely a bowler or derby. Still, many of the newspaper reports about Indians in local papers were cruel and callous. A writer in March 10, 1893, "jokingly" compared a clam chowder feed Sandy sponsored to the tragic Wounded Knee massacre of December 1890.

Many of the Indian women and their families, even those who were primarily farmers, would have had the monopoly on oyster picking, culling, and trading until the 1878 arrival of Joseph Gale, Dick Helser, and Abner Smith and the territorial and then state laws that supported and encouraged the cultivation of oysters and opened the doors to tideland ownership.

All of the Indians of Katie Gale's acquaintance, even if they did maintain some ties with the Squaxin Reservation (and some do periodically show up on census rolls there), had chosen to take their chances in the off-reservation economy and to find creative ways to forge a life in post-treaty Western Washington. Though she may have lost members of her immediate family, Katie Gale had models and teachers and relatives around her. It was doubtless her hearty and hard-working kin, the Kettles and Tobins, and her relationships with daring, bright, risky friends and some clearly knowledgeable leaders and entrepreneurs that gave Katie the wit, wisdom, and savvy to become the kind of woman she was. But there were historical forces at work as well.

1. Dick Jackson, an early adherent of the Shaker religion and neighbor of Katie Gale. Used with permission of the Mason County Historical Society.

2. Katie Gale's tombstone, in a thicket high above the western shore of Oyster Bay. Photo by LLyn De Danaan.

3. Chief Kettle and Louis Yowaluch, or "Mud Bay Louie," at Mud Bay in July 1892 during a Fourth of July gathering and potlatch. This photograph would have been taken within days of the incorporation of the Shaker Church on Mud Bay. Yowaluch, a Shaker minister, hosted the meeting. Taken with a No. 1 Kodak Camera, first produced in 1889. Alaska State Library, James Wickersham Collection, James Wickersham, PCA 277, Album 18-156.

4. (*above*) Louisa Tobin, healer, artist, oysterwoman, and informant to Ruth Greiner on local place-names. Photograph was taken sometime before 1927. Photo courtesy of Jim Tobin and Steve Lundin.

5. (*right*) A map with Salish designations of significant places around Oyster and Mud Bays. Drawn by James Tobin, circa 1920. Tobin was an oysterman, farmer, leader translator, Shaker minister, and friend to Katie Gale. He died in 1927 at age seventy-one. Washington State Historical Society.

J'wäk'ō'bōd'ūt
(means Skokomish note)
[Olympics]

Dük hoodwhooch
(means little canoe)

Chü gwä'leech

Chü hü lee

Kwä'l hwä'dee

Zō quü'ōks
Hard beating wind

Whē ük whit
[beach at Pt. Defiance Park]

S'jil kum

Klä äh kee
(It was a graveyard)
[Eagle Island]

Schä'talp

Indee Kegeltōd

Sōlāl's

Klä bet chee

S'pi'xwit

⊛ squ'kts

Chō'hält

Stä'shosh

Sgwacht

Sawi'ik

D'kōt

S'tü'chüs

Percivals cr.
K'klä'bit

Chet'wood

Chü pit sp [Moxlie Creek]

S'pootsilf
American Lake
W H Gilstrap, name as given by Kōquiltom an Indian abt 90 yrs old

[K'Klä'bit
Percivals Creek

[D'Kōt
Priest Point

Black Lake

Kä'op
[Black Hills]

Stuck whit
or
Stuck gōō guit
(means dragging a canoe)

Stäkh tubchs
people living away from the salt water

Skwä'kwä'lee

⊛ gē'ig kch is another name I have been given, instead of squ'kts

WILLIE.

6. (*above left*) *A View of Arcadia*, by James Tilton Pickett. This painting was probably based on a sketch made while Pickett lived with Catherine and William Walter. The sketch is dated in one collection as 1885. Galen Biery Papers and Photographs, no. 2809, Center for Pacific Northwest Studies, Western Washington University, Bellingham, Washington, 98225-9123.

7. (*bottom left*) The stern-wheeler *Willie*, a familiar sight in South Puget Sound waters and one Katie Gale and her family would have ridden frequently. Museum of History and Industry/Puget Sound Maritime Historical Society, Seattle, Washington.

8. (*above*) A float house on Puget Sound. Photograph by Kyo Koike, titled *Called a Home*. Dated early twentieth century. University of Washington Libraries, Special Collections, UW 31136, Ph Coll 262, Kyo Koike Photograph Collection.

9. John Leslie, a friend of Katie Gale (*upper level, far right*), on the steamer *S. G. Simpson* of Shelton. He was a crew member and later engineer on Puget Sound steamers. Used with permission of the Mason County Historical Society.

10. Katie Gale's home and oyster operation on Oyster Bay. Note the float house along the shore. Used with permission of the Mason County Historical Society.

11. Oyster Bay School, 1898. *Back row, far left*: Miss Galusha. *Second row from front, second and third from right*: Boys presumed to be Ray Gale and his friend Adolph Johnson. Used with permission of the Mason County Historical Society.

12. Wedding of James and Louisa Tobin's daughter Katie to Edward J. Smith (from Chehalis), 1903. Photograph by Ida B. Smith, Olympia photographer. The wedding was held on the Tobins' Eld Inlet property and was attended by more than three hundred Indians from around the sound and Neah Bay. The Tobins provided all the food. Those in the photograph are (*left to right*) Olympia Jim, Henry Martin, the bride and groom, Annie Tobin, and Mrs. Mary Jackson Jim. University of Washington Libraries, Special Collections, NA 662, General Indian Collection no. 564.

13. The steamship *Willamette* at the Pacific Coast Steamship Company dock, August 9, 1897, ready to leave Seattle for the Klondike. University of Washington Libraries, Special Collections, A. Curtis 26440, Ph Coll 482, Asahel Curtis Photo Company Collection.

13 *No Crops of Any Consequence*

THERE WERE good reasons not to live on the reservations and to choose, instead, to try one's luck elsewhere. From the beginning, the appalling conditions that reigned on these hapless, cramped colonies were no secret. The Indians of Puget Sound had been through a catastrophic, culture-killing period in their history that included disease, loss of land, and war. Now they were confined on reservations and subjected to the folly of ill-advised policies and actions of administrators who were in over their heads. Reports from the various agents on the reservations catalog a litany of missteps and tragedies. Despite these circumstances, the Indians found ways to resist and carry on.

In December 1857 Wesley Gosnell, the special Indian agent at the Puyallup Reservation, writes that "influenza and consumption," among other diseases, had killed fifteen residents during the previous quarter. There had been only four births. He adds that there was a "great scarcity of Salmon." During the previous year the doctor, B. W. Kimball, on the "Squaksin reservation" treated 153 Indians, though it is unclear if he meant this to be understood as 153 separate individuals or 153 cases brought to him. He complains that this number does not represent "the actual amount of sickness," because many people were still consulting their own medical experts. Many people were living off the reservation, he says, and "their habits, morals, and mode of life" he apparently believed to be an obstacle to treatment. Dr. Kimball suggests in his reports that vice, morals, and the influence of depraved whites were the cause of many of the woes on the reservation. The accusation that women's morals were slack was a theme in medical reports from this period. And it is women who were to be blamed, it seems, for the low birthrates. They were, according to these reports, prostituting themselves.[1]

Gray H. Whaley found this characterization of Indian women in records he examined in the course of writing his 2010 book, *Oregon and the Collapse of the Illahee*. In response, he writes that "chastity" was a cultural value trumpeted by European and European American cultures of the period. "It was a standard that 'the better sorts' (wealthy or noble) embodied in their conservative dress, demeanor, and actions. Any violation might damage their reputations and make them unchaste." This ideal "couldn't be reached by many Western women: it was one of several ways of sorting the population into better and lower orders." Speaking of Lower Columbia Indian women, Whaley notes that the language and ideology of purity and morality "made its way into colonial discourse to demean Native women." Prostitution, when it did occur, was, in these desperate times, clearly a means of survival. However, what the whites labeled immoral or prostitution was often simply their Victorian shock at witnessing different standards of dress, behavior, and sensuality.[2]

In putting forward a moralistic explanation for disease and birth and death rates, Kimball, the doctor assigned to the Squaxin Reservation, makes no connection between the demographics of the postwar and early reservation period and the effect of the waves of disease that had visited indigenous populations since the late 1700s, several of which would have deleterious effects on fertility. He also makes no mention of the traumatic changes in people's circumstances, including loss of traditional food supplies and the stresses that would also affect fertility. If only "intelligence and morals . . . may be improved and . . . their sanitary condition be improved," he laments.

A letter to his brother from A. M. Collins, living across Little Skookum from Arcadia Point and what was still the Indian settlement of sahéwabc when he and his wife arrived, provides us with one of the first written glimpses of the health issues that plagued the people of Totten Inlet and Oyster Bay before reservation life. Collins was in a position to witness sick and dying Indians during an 1853 smallpox epidemic. "This part of the country is very healthy for stout, hearty people but it is considered hard on persons afflicted with consumption or rheumatism," he writes. Then Collins describes the local effects of rapidly spreading disease. His letter reports that "the Indians are dying daily with the smallpox. They take no care of themselves when the fever comes and they go in the water and lay on the ground to cool themselves."[3]

This rampant illness, along with prior and subsequent waves of infectious disease, diminished the T'Peeksin, the tuxs qwáksûd, and other Indian populations in the area and arguably affected birthrates and the vitality of the people for years to come. There was simply not enough time between epidemics for populations to recover, and some of the worst of these catastrophic outbreaks, including some forms of tuberculosis that became endemic, wreaked havoc with human reproductive systems.

Smallpox had appeared in Western Washington first in the late 1700s and another wave devastated populations in the 1830s. The disease spread easily by contact or through droplets in the air. A virus, the symptoms included fever, aches, and a rash. Eventually these rashes became festering, swollen lesions. Tragically, the disease killed up to 30 percent of those who suffered it.[4] Stories of these and other decimating afflictions abound in oral accounts passed along by indigenous people of the area and in the journals of observers. Perhaps the earliest written accounts are from the 1792 Vancouver expedition. Peter Puget, sent to explore the South Sound waterways, describes journeys through the Tacoma Narrows and around Pt. Fosdick and Hale Passage, where they met with Indians in an area now known as Wollochet. They went on to the head of Carr Inlet on May 21, 1792.

As they journeyed north they saw, they believed, the "Termination" of Carr Inlet and continued toward the farthest reaches of the inlet. Puget writes,

> When the beach was close to the Boats & in the SW Corner of the Cove was a Small Village among the Trees — beyond the termination the Country had the Appearance of a Level Forest, but close to the Water, it was covered with Small Green Bushes — We pulled in towards the Village but seeing a Canoe paddling from it towards us, induced us to lay on our Oars to wait their Approach, but neither Copper nor any Article in our Possession had sufficient allurement to get them close to the Boats. They lay about Twenty Yards from us & kept continually pointing to the Eastward, expressive of a Wish that our Departure would be more agreeable than our Visit — . . . In their Persons they were apparently more Stout than any Indians we have hitherto seen on the Coast. . . . Two of the three in the Canoe had lost the Right Eye & were much pitted with the Smallpox, which Disorder in all probability is the Cause of that Defect.[5]

Later in the evening, still on Carr Inlet but farther south, probably in Von Geldern Cove, as Puget's party prepared to "seine for salmon" and "dine," several canoes with Indian paddlers approached. They were followed by an Indian canoe bearing the men previously encountered, and shortly thereafter they were joined by even more canoes with Indians. In all, more than twenty-four men approached the Europeans. During this tense meeting Puget noticed that the men wore no sea otter skins. Perhaps this observation was a kind of "note to self" regarding the availability in this area of this highly desirous species. No, these men were clothed in bear, raccoon, rabbit, and deer and might not be worth cultivating as trading partners for the more valuable and sought-after otter skins. Some of the men, Puget notes, "had thick Bushy Beards" and others only a bit on their "Chins and upper Lips."

The accounts of pockmarked adults suggest villagers had been subjected to smallpox, very possibly during the 1775 epidemic. The adult men in the canoes Puget saw would have been children during the epidemic. The men Puget met were the lucky ones. It has been estimated that fully one-third of the indigenous people died in the 1770s epidemic.

Smallpox probably disproportionately affected pregnant women. It may have caused pregnancies to be terminated. The disease has been associated with miscarriages and stillborn births. Smallpox has also been suggested to be a factor in male infertility. However, there seems to be no firm data to support this.

Further evidence of European- and European American–era epidemics in the northwestern United States and Canada is found in published literature and local, period newspaper accounts. Descriptions of other local outbreaks and their consequences can be found in scattered diaries, journals, and government reports.

Robert Boyd's *The Coming of the Spirit of Pestilence* provides a compilation of many of the major diseases known and recorded. Some specifically documented epidemics that may have had an impact on South Puget Sound peoples, population, and reproductive capacity are:

smallpox: 1770s–?
smallpox: first decade of the 1800s
unknown (probably smallpox): 1824–25
fever and ague: 1830s
influenza: 1837–38
smallpox: 1837 (Dr. William Fraser Tolmie of the Hudson's Bay Company vaccinates before it reaches Fort Nisqually)
measles: 1848
smallpox: 1853 (Dr. Tolmie vaccinates at Fort Nisqually)
smallpox: 1863 (Father Eugene Casimir Chirouse vaccinates at Tulalip Reservation, Washington; Joseph Davies vaccinates at Makah)
smallpox: 1907–present among Mud Bay and Oyster Bay Indians[6]

It was the 1863 smallpox epidemic that was perhaps the most tragic of all and truly genocidal given the well-documented neglect of the Indian population exposed to the disease in Victoria, Vancouver Island. Little to nothing was done to avoid the spread of the illness from Victoria to other Northwest Indians. People were not quarantined or vaccinated but instead many sick and dying were sent packing and hauled to home territories in their canoes. Of course, this action merely served to spread the disease to every village along the coast as infected relatives returned.

The 1853 epidemic, as we've seen, was observed by the Collins family on Hammersley Inlet. Catherine Collins was said to be a trained nurse, though whether she put her skills to work during this smallpox epidemic is unclear.[7]

Reports from the Squaxin Island Reservation were sent to external administrators at least yearly. "Diseases of the respiratory organs" are the most common, Dr. Kimball says in one of his missives. Over "one fourth of their sickness is pulmonary." The doctor deplores the fact that he has very little to offer by way of comfort or even palliative care. He was apparently unable to determine or eradicate sources of illness. Deaths during that past year would "exceed fifty," with births a little more than half this number, he reported.

The instructor for the school on the island, established under the provisions of the treaty, was not as moralistic or hopeless as Dr. Kimball. However, in his official accounts of his work, he expresses annoyance that the people had a "roving disposition" and thus his students would go off for "two weeks to three months" with their parents to "procure their favorite food." This, of course, makes it difficult to conduct classes or to see much improvement in students, he says. That they and their families would starve without this "roving" and harvest of food is not considered worth mentioning, apparently.

In 1858–59 Sidney S. Ford, special Indian agent and a man decidedly more sympathetic with the situation of the Indians, wrote of the

"Squaksin" Agency to Michael T. Simmons, Indian agent for Washington Territory, that "my Indians have received but a small amount of goods or money during the past year. Only the old and sick have received presents, and that to a limited extent. Those that are able, work for the farmers around the county, and earn their own living. I strongly recommend this course to them, as it not only provides them the means of present support, but learns them the manners and customs of the whites." Ford reports that the whites and Indians in the neighborhood treat each other justly and humanely. He adds that any disturbances have been have been caused by liquor trafficked by "dishonest and disreputable white men."

Ford, in this account written just a year or so after Kimball's, seems to see the Indians both on and off the reservation through a stunningly different lens. Something in his character and history must account for the difference.[8] Perhaps it was because he had grown up on a claim near Chehalis, Washington, with a family that valued and sustained a close relationship with a band of Chehalis people.

In 1859 Gosnell, the agent for "Squaksin, Nisqually, and Puyallup Indians," wrote of the "Squaksin" Island Reservation that though "great labor and expense" was required to clear it, it "produces good crops." This was an opinion contradicted over and again by future agents. Gosnell says that "three hundred and fifty souls" belonged to this reservation. But, indeed, few "visit the place, being scattered over the country working for the whites; many of them, particularly young men and boys, being regularly retained as servants in the families of the white settlers." About two hundred spent the winter on the island, he says, but in the spring they "scattered off through the country in search of fish, berries and other food, a practice which they follow every year, and one which they could not be easily broken of, even in the midst of abundance at home, such being their roving disposition." Of course, there was no "abundance at home."

In 1860 Dr. Kimball asked a good question of his data, problematic though the figures he had collected might have been. He looked carefully at birth and death records for the Medicine Creek Treaty tribes, then looked at the numbers of men and women past puberty and discovered that there were 524 women and 369 men.[9] Alas, he seems not to have explored this demographic imbalance further, nor does he seem to understand the disparity as a reason why people might wish to continue making plural marriages or why women were regularly finding mates among white men by this time. Nor did he understand that going off for summer gathering expeditions might in fact make it possible to find mates from outside of the rather limited choice of available partners locally. There simply weren't enough Indian men to go around if one were to marry within the Medicine Creek tribal area and adhere to a European American ideal of a one woman–one man marriage. Confining people to reservations and discouraging plural marriages were goals of agents and consistent with their dreams for a morality that fit with their own sensibilities. However, these policies were certain to have even more negative consequences for the declining population.

In an 1862 report to Calvin H. Hale, the superintendent of Indian affairs for Washington Territory, G. A. Paige, Indian agent, writes, "No crops of any consequence have been put in on the Squaxon reservation, the soil being of so poor a quality that the returns will not meet the expenses of planting and harvesting." Gosnell had said pretty much the opposite only three years previously. What Paige doesn't report is that, even if the soil were good, an array of enemies often laid waste to crops before harvest. Potatoes are especially susceptible to scab and various bacterial and viral diseases. Blight, the disease that destroyed potato crops in Ireland in 1845, is a fungal disease that can spoil a crop and controls for it were not available in 1862. Vines wilt and tubers rot underground. One year the summer was so wet that the entire Squaxin Island potato crop, though small to begin with, was ruined. Around this time the Skokomish crops, probably seed crops, succumbed to army worms (probably *Spodoptera praefica*), which apparently infested plants throughout the region.

Why would anyone stay on these god-awful reservations if there were a choice? The laments of the officers in charge continue with seemingly little insight or common sense. Yet somehow it is some shortcoming of the Indians rather than the goals and policies of administrators that usually are blamed for failures. "In consequence of the wandering disposition of the Indians composing the bands belonging to the Squaxon reservation, and who are unable to get a living thereon, the school under the Medicine Creek treaty, located at this point, has been rather unprosperous," Paige continues in his 1862 report. Unprosperous is undoubtedly a major understatement. Maintaining a school would be the last thing on the agenda of a stressed people simply trying to survive.

The school did a little better in 1863. At least "until the novelty wore off, and with it the attendance," Adam Wylie, instructor, writes. In March he had two scholars in attendance. He wanted the children removed from their parents and the "baleful influence of the older ones." He writes, "The separation of parent and child appears despotic, but would not a mild despotism save the young?" Surely one more assertion of authority over a people's culture and social system would not make that much difference, this teacher of the young seemed to suggest.[10]

In 1864 A. R. Elder, agent at the Puyallup agency, was concerned that the Squaxin Reservation was "unfortunately situated for the cultivation of the morals of the Indians." He agrees with Hale that the island's land "is very poor, and not fit for cultivation." He wants it sold. He suggests that the reservation site, selected by Michael Simmons, who himself had happily settled on the good land that once belonged to Indians, is "not fit for cultivation." They had put in a few potato patches, cabbage, and beets. But most food needed to be gleaned from hunting and gathering, he admits. Still, Elder was as concerned with the loose morals of white men in the logging camps, who were habitually cavorting with Indian women and providing the men with whiskey, as with the deplorable state of resources on the reservation.

By 1867 Elder is practically apoplectic in his annual report. He is clearly at a loss about what to do with the Squaxin Reservation and its people:

> I have been trying for the last three years to make something of these Indians but have failed, and have become almost discouraged. They are in too close proximity to the vicious white men who reside upon the border of their island, and who furnish them with whiskey. They have time and again rejected all religious instruction, have ordered priests from the reservation, told them they did not know God, nor did they wish to know him. They say they will not quit gambling, nor will they relinquish their right to a plurality of wives or their arts of necromancy.

One can almost see Elder's red face and bulging veins.

Even so, Elder doesn't see this as an all-out rebellion against the system and religion he represents. He doesn't understand that the people have, in spite of all they've been through, pride, dignity, and a will to live as they wish. He says sell the dang island and move everyone to the Puyallup Reservation, "where there is room for all" (an assertion the Puyallup people would have no doubt taken issue with) — and, presumably, a much better setup for monitoring and controlling these pesky, independent-minded Squaxin.

Elder's report ends with this: "There is an old man and his family who are very generally to be found upon the reservation, while the rest of the tribe, men and women, are roving through the country, or living in towns." Elder, the ever respectful and obedient servant of the superintendent of Indian affairs, T. J. McKenny, pays his respect to the one old fellow who seems to agree to be under his thumb by giving him a "coat and pantaloons, a blanket, flour, . . ."

In 1869, fifteen years after the signing of the Treaty of Medicine Creek, Maj. Samuel Ross writes in the Washington Superintendency's report to the commissioner of Indian affairs that, in spite of promises of training, schools, and resident, skilled supervisory staff made by

Governor Stevens when the Medicine Creek Indians ceded over two million acres of land, "no annuity goods had been distributed to them for several years, and no attention had been paid to their repeated complaints of wrongs and injustice. Agency buildings need repairs; working cattle had been removed and sold; farming implements were lost or destroyed. The large hay crop of the Puyallup reservation was left uncut in the meadows; the school at the same place was such only in name." He notes that the employees are "worthless."

Thus, as Alexandra Harmon writes, "few Indians moved to Puget Sound reservations during the 1850s or 1860s, the government did not even know who or where all the people encompassed by the treaties were. . . . Virtually all but the feeblest of Puget Sound's native people thus continued to provide for themselves. They fished, hunted, and harvested berries and roots as their ancestors had done; but they also sold what they caught or gathered, hired out as domestic servants, ferried passengers and cargo, and labored at mines, mills, and farms."[11]

By 1875, when Mud Bay and Oyster Bay were populated by Indians, mixed couples and children, and whites, working oysters beds and farming, Edward P. Smith, in an annual report to the commissioner of Indian affairs, says that the Squaxin, "numbering 150," are on a reservation, "where *no efforts at civilization* have been put forth." Smith says, "They labor for settlers, hunt, fish, do a little farming, and live in comparative comfort in a *semi-savage* way" (emphasis added).

While Smith lamented, the Indians in the area were busy finding strategies for surviving in the world they'd been handed and finding a niche in the new economy. They were all but eschewing a reservation and a government that had failed them. The lives they had patched together to allow them to endure were disparaged and denigrated because they did not appear to the local agent to be "civilized." They were, in the eyes of yet one more flailing agent, "comparatively comfortable" but nonetheless outside the embrace of the government's assimilationist goals.

14 *Relationships*

FEBRUARY 2, 2011, Oyster Bay. The sun rose behind Mt. Rainier this morning. It was one of those stunning dawns when the eastern sky glows pink and red through wispy clouds and Rainier is a dark silhouette. The outdoor temperature is twenty-six degrees Fahrenheit. It's a killing frost. My chard and collards will survive. If I stand up at my desk I can see the bay and watch the water rise and fall throughout the day. The tide is still in as I look now. It was high, sixteen feet, at close to 6:30 a.m., just an hour or so before the sun came up.

If I were to put on some warm clothing, walk down the steps to the beach, and pluck my kayak out of its storage sling, I could be on the eastern shore in five minutes. I could be at the head of Oyster Bay in fifteen minutes or down bay to the site of New Kamilche and the mouth of Little Skookum within half an hour. I'm not particularly fast or athletic. It is a small bay and all of these points are easily reached by boat. The shore at low tide is also walkable. There are obstacles, sometimes, where trees have fallen from the banks. Sometimes it is necessary to skittle over a wet trunk or pick one's way over twisted, slimy roots of cedar or madrona. It can be done.

At night, after dark, I can see the lights from my neighbor's house, the old Brenner Oyster Company plant, below me or the flicker of lamps on the tide flats in the night when someone is working on the oyster beds.

I live in a house built in the 1950s for Brenner employees. However, I bought my place from Nat Waldrip, a descendant of one of the early oyster growers. The first inhabitants of this little abode, people who migrated to Washington from Oklahoma, have stopped by a few times to visit the old place and talk about the trails they followed between this place and other houses on the bay. Joe Abo has similar stories about his 1950s boyhood, when most of the workers hereabouts were Japanese and Japanese Americans. Those trails were probably used when Katie Gale lived here, if not before. My son and his friends followed them as recently as the 1980s.

When I first moved to Oyster Bay, my next-door neighbor lived in another Brenner house. His name was Shorty and he had a dog named Bandit. Shorty swore that a cougar roamed our woods. I was careful at night when I went out to feed my dog or lock up the chickens or bring in firewood, but I never saw one. It was raccoons that gave me trouble. And Bandit himself, with his prowling and thieving habits. My old apple trees, probably planted by homesteader M. C. Simmons, still bore fruit then but I harvested none, even after I posted my own dog under the branches of the biggest one to fend off the night raiders. Sometimes I could see as many as five pair of eyes shining down on me when I went out to check on the barking and growling of the dog below.

Down bay I can see other simple structures like mine on the hill above the Olympia Oyster Company plant. That was all Gale property in the late 1800s. Farther on, if I paddle all the way to Little Skookum, I'll be followed by seals and pass mussel floats and the Kamilche Sea Farms. As I move silently along the water, I can stop and say hello or holler out to people I know along the way. Maybe I'll see Sally Kaufman or Charlie Stephens. Susan Christian may be out on the deck of her oyster plant home.

Late nineteenth-century Indians and European Americans must have seen and talked with each other every day just the way we do now. They were on the water and tide flats most of the time, except for those who were farmers. They would have hollered out as they passed each other in canoes or skiffs. They would have walked down the beach and scrambled up rough paths to the houses built above the high-tide line to visit or to borrow some sugar or buy some butter. They would have stopped and tied up to a friend's float house to sell a fish. They would have rowed to New Kamilche to pick up letters or packages from the East. They'd see others there doing the same thing or waiting to hop a steamer or buying a few supplies. They'd stop and chat, ask "Where to?," or gossip about politics or the weather or how the crops were coming along.

The Europeans and European Americans came to Oyster Bay knowing only a few people, if any. They were Americans from Kentucky, Illinois, and Massachusetts. Some were veterans of the Oregon Trail, seeking their luck and fortune first in Oregon, then traveling north to Olympia. They took homesteads in thickly wooded land that sloped down to the little bay at the end of Totten Inlet, the bay with the best and most plentiful oysters in the whole of Puget Sound. Some were from Scotland and Ireland and elsewhere in Europe; they were dislocated by the Industrial Revolution or famine or the still-prevalent practice of primogeniture.[1] They were not able to make much of a living on their new farms, yet they were not content to labor in factories located in the dust and slag piles around mines or to live in the growing slums and crowded, unhealthy conditions in cities. Many of them came to farm or log. Many were single men, not so old, cutting timber and removing the stumps to make room for a patch of potatoes or peas or to graze a cow. Some came, surely, because they were simply adventurers looking for a better life. They had to build community to survive.

The Indians came from all over southern Puget Sound and beyond. They had some kinship ties and prior relationship to the bay and the inlet. They had given up on promises and eschewed reservation life. They, too, had to build community. So they did. They all worked together, their children went to school together, they witnessed for each other's homestead proofs and marriages. And the community was built by one of these interactions after another.

The Indians and European Americans asked each other for help with just about everything. There was plenty of work to do to "prove" a homestead, build a home, and make a bit of land productive. Cutting trees, splitting shakes, removing stumps, building, and helping with harvests and planting—all was better done with two or three people working together. Some paid for help. Others traded labor or goods.

Proving a homestead was a condition that had to be fulfilled in order for the homesteader to receive a patent for the land. Once the homestead was filed and it was shown that there were no other applications made on the land, the homesteader was mandated to clear and build and in other ways "work" the claim. The homesteader had to be in continuous residency for five years. After that period, the homesteader signed statements describing the improvements made to the land and swearing that he or she was residing on the land. Two friends or neighbors went along to the land office and swore statements to vouch for the truth of the homesteader's description of the improvements. Once all the forms were filed, with a six-dollar fee, a patent was issued. The patent was signed by whatever president of the United States was in office when the final patent was issued. An option, which some on Oyster Bay elected to take, was to buy a land claim at a fixed price per acre.

Dick Jackson's final proof on his 87.4-acre homestead was witnessed by Harry Weatherall and James Tobin, among others. The men must have traveled to Olympia together to sign and file papers. They each knew Jackson and his farm well enough to vouch for the veracity of his statements.

M. C. Simmons, a white man, came forward on behalf of Nellie Sutton's final proof after the death of her European American husband, Andrew J. McClure. Simmons's homestead was, he said, within two miles of hers, "in sight of my house." When asked if Nellie McClure

Sutton had been absent from her claim during the proof period, Simmons said, "They used to get their butter from us every week as long as he [McClure] lived & I could see their cloths hanging out on the lines from our house."

Henry Isaac, an Indian, filed for and received a forty-acre homestead near the bay. He paid $2.50 an acre for forty acres of land that was mostly suited, his daughter said later, for fruit trees. It was passed on to his daughter, Lucy Simmons, after his death. Lucy was twenty-four years old and eager to maintain the family farm. In her statement accompanying final proof, she says that her father had been dead for four years and that his "family has been in straightened circumstances and have not been able financially to submit final proof and payment . . . within the statutory period of 8 years."[2] The transfer and final proof was witnessed by "Dick Jackson, Dave Helser, John Slocum and Joe Gale" in Olympia on January 18, 1897, in the Olympia Land Office. David Helser described the Isaacs-Simmons place as having a "good house 20 x 14 chicken house, woodshed, 50 fruit trees 3 acres fenced. Six acres slashed and burned." The families were neighbors. Helser's place adjoined the bay and Isaacs's was up the hill behind him.

John Campbell, Margaret McDonald, and Catherine and William Walter all left papers that contain some details of less formal interaction between people in the area. Though their homes were on Little and Big Skookum, many of the people they saw or engaged to work for and with them were from Oyster Bay.

John Campbell, a Scotsman and early settler in the area, kept a nearly daily diary beginning in January 1869. He describes his efforts to establish his farm in Kamilche Valley near Oyster Bay on Skookum Creek at the head of Little Skookum, a site where archaeological evidence shows that Indians had lived before the treaty and perhaps for some time after. A fifty-by-fifty-foot shell midden was surveyed on Skookum Creek in 1949. It was said to have been filled with "one foot of Olympia oyster shell," indisputable evidence of occupation and regular use by Indians.[3] Other sites along Little Skookum include one measured in

1949 at three hundred yards. This midden contained a mix of butter clam, mussel, and Olympia oyster. Another measured 187 yards. The middens aren't the only source of evidence of village sites. A memoir from Campbell's period attributed to a member of the Whitener family describes the head of a good salmon creek near Big Skookum that had a big expanse of pebbled beach and a still-vibrant Indian community:

> A tribal smoke house stood on the south shore with provision for six families or six fires, as designated by the Indians. It had clams and oysters. The smoke house was built of cedar posts set in the ground and small poles for ridge poles and rafters, and these were covered with strips of bark and woven mats. There were no windows. There was a mount that was made of the oyster and clam shells that had been thrown there by the Indians. The beach too in front of the house was white with bleached and broken shells. . . . About 30 Indians would winter in the smokehouse. There would be a line of canoes and nets and equipment hauled to the top of the beach in front of the smoke house.

The householders would "bake bread by the fire on a board" and eat bear and venison, cooked in kettles. Though this memoir is undated, it describes a time well after the treaty had been signed and some other Indians were living on the Squaxin Island Reservation. It is also clear from other comments in this memoir that white farmers and loggers were regularly socializing with households in Indian communities like this one.

However, most of what we know from this era is from accounts of European American lives. John Campbell's diary, for example, contains many details of the struggles and triumphs as well as the more prosaic moments of his life in the area:

> TUESDAY JAN 18TH 1870
> Frost & cold weather Started from W. Walters' in the morning & got home in late evening & found all well

WEDNESDAY JAN 19TH 1870
Rainy weather Employed in repairing my boot & packed up provisions from the bay

THURSDAY JAN 20TH 1870
Cold rainy weather went up the Bottom in search of Cattle got two at Huntleys' place & brought them home shot 9 pheasants

FRIDAY JAN 21ST 1870
Moderate weather went out to hunt Cattle found them all right Saw some Deer Shot at one but did not get it got home & split some slabs for fence on bank of creek

SATURDAY JAN 22ND 1870
Moderate weather Employed making fence on banks of creek & building house for pigs[4]

Thus the life of the homesteader.

Campbell had cows named Becky, Motley, Bell, and Daisy. They were forever running about and found floundering in wet, boggy marshes by streams or near the saltwater. It required extreme measures to haul them out. Their legs had to be bathed in warm water to bring their temperature back up to normal, "lest the chill kill them."

Campbell, perhaps without thought and in a regretful rage, shot his dog for eating apples from a tree. The animal had probably been, more often than not, useful to Campbell's endeavors. For example, the dog had previously treed a wildcat that weighed, Campbell noted, 360 pounds. The poor beast had done his work but paid dearly for what Campbell thought of as an unpardonable transgression. One can only imagine the exasperation on top of exasperation that can lead to such desperate and self-defeating acts. That day the dog ate the apples, Campbell had just had enough. It seemed to him, that day, that he couldn't conquer this new land. Perhaps it was after that same spring when the jaybirds ate his newly sewn oats.

Then there were property-line disputes or heated disagreements with people upon whom a settler might later have to call in emergencies but whom he hardly knew and with whom he may not have shared a language. Campbell fought passionately with his neighbor, Van Horn, whom he seemed to have disliked altogether. Van Horn was lucky not to have been shot like the dog when Campbell found his fence trampled and his potatoes "run over" by what he concluded were Van Horn's animals. Another time a young man was literally banished from the area when he made inappropriate advances on Campbell's daughter.

Campbell lived near William and Jennie Krise and had regular dealings with them. In the first month of Campbell's entries, he mentions hauling hay for "Indian Sam" and "Indian Jackson," probably Dick Jackson. He mentions "Indian Jim" regularly, as well as "Indian Humptulips," whom he assists in getting a marriage license. "Indian Seesall" (Cesalle), Jennie Krise's father, is mentioned in 1874 as "sawing up firewood" for Campbell. "Isaac," probably Henry Isaac, who lived not far from the Campbell place at the time, is mentioned. He assisted Campbell with his hay.

Campbell carefully, perhaps sorrowfully, records the happenings after the death of A. M. Collins. It is a poignant depiction of what must have been a frequent experience in the lives of homesteading families.

Collins had died of "dropsy," Campbell reports. After the death, several men came together around five o'clock on the evening of January 16, presumably to sit with the body, perhaps to make a coffin and dig a hole for the burial, and to comfort the widow. The next day was freezing cold. The little community awoke to a "sharp frost" but a clear, brilliantly sunny morning. Neighbors came together at the Collins home around 11:00 a.m., "& at 12 brought the corpse out into the front room. Self read the 12th chapter of Ecclesiastics" to the small group of friends. "Let us hear the conclusion of the whole matter: Fear God, and keep his commandments: for this is the whole duty of man. For God shall bring every work into judgment, with every secret thing, whether it be good, or whether it be evil. . . . the lid of the coffin was unscrewed & the face of the corpse exposed for the last time for about 5 minutes."

During this time "Mrs. Collins fastened two rosebuds in the breast of the coat which the corpse was wearing & at her request I cut a lock of his hair & placed his razor at his right side in his coffin." This struck me as curious until I read that it was fairly common practice in the nineteenth century to place a knife, a vial of poison, or a razor in the coffin for fear that the corpse was not really dead after all and would awake in the dark casket deep in the ground. The deceased was provided with a means of bringing about final death.

Then "the lid was screwed on the coffin & the remains taken to the grave & buried, after which the people left for their respective homes, wife & self went to the W. Walters house & stayed the night."

Thus ended the life of the man who had written to his brother shortly after he took up his donation claim, "James, I can't give encouragement to anybody to come to this country. It is a long, hard trip any way you take it, attended with a great deal of trouble." Then asked him to send money, "all that you can get."[5]

After the death of A. M. Collins, his wife, Catherine, married friend and neighbor William Walter. Catherine Collins Walter was the foster mother of Jimmy Pickett, son of Gen. George E. Pickett and his deceased Indian wife.

Catherine Collins Walter was engaged in frequent exchange of goods with Indians in the neighborhood. Her diary of 1880 reflects the busy life of a farming family, one eye on the weather, the other on crops or cows or the steamers in Little Skookum. She apparently carefully cultivated abundant and cherry and apple trees. I have a photograph taken in the late 1880s of a cherry pickers' picnic at her place. More than fifty men, women, and children, many with baskets of fruit, are posed in front of a somewhat feeble picket fence. Behind them is a lush orchard. These harvest gatherings must have been grand, glorious, much-anticipated events. They were also, no doubt, much-welcomed days of respite from difficult daily lives.

"Indians," whose names she must have known though she does not usually use them in her journal, regularly came by either to sell fish or to buy or trade for cherries and apples. Sometimes she specifies gender by using the term "Klootchman," a Chinook Jargon word that denotes a woman. In one entry she says "Indian Peter" (and his "Clutchman") came to get some apples.[6] This is probably Peter Clams, who often worked for Margaret McDonald, the owner of a store at Arcadia Point.

Margaret McDonald and her husband, a young farming couple from Canada, lived on Oyster Bay, at Hardscrabble, just a quarter mile up bay from my place, when they first came to the area. The husband died in 1882 after a long illness. Margaret was faced with finding a way to support herself and six small children. The story goes that Captain Renton of Port Blakley Mill Company offered to help set her up in business and did so. She took over an already-established business, including, apparently, a hotel and bar and post office run by her husband, at Arcadia.

Up to the time that I saw the store ledger and the regular correspondence between McDonald and the Port Blakeley Mill Company, this all seemed a bit farfetched. But the meticulous Mrs. McDonald, who recorded each customer's name and the name, price, and date of every item purchased from her, saved what might be the inventory of the first shipment made to her. It is a several-page document with a long list of goods dated November 1883. The Port Blakely logo is at the top of each page.[7]

Catherine McDonald's store was strategically placed just across the entrance of Big Skookum from the Collins/Walter place. Jimmy Pickett, while still living with Catherine Collins Walter, made a drawing and a painting of the site and buildings. It is one of two surviving images I've seen of this important hub of activity.

The store carried most everything a person living on the land and water could need. Margaret McDonald had shovels, rope, gunpowder and shot, towels, syrup, combs, overalls, and even "raisons." She served whites, Indians, loggers, oyster farmers, and tradespeople. She also had a bustling trade with steamboat crews and the Port Blakeley Mill. A store like McDonald's served as a center of activity in rural communities. They often housed post offices and brokered labor deals. Fortunately, some of her ledgers and correspondence have survived.

On Port Blakely Mill Company letterhead:

> MCH 8TH 1886
>
> MRS. MCDONALD
>
> ARCADIA W.T.
>
> Dear Madam
> . . . Was the Barrel of black oil full or was there part leaked out. What Indian did you deliver it to. We charge 25 cents per gallon and call a barrel 50 gallons. let us know if you charge the oil in your account to the Indian and oblige.

On Port Blakely Mill letterhead:

> JUNE 2ND 1887
>
> MRS. D. MCDONALD
>
> ARCADIA, W.T.
>
> Dear Madam
> We wish you to have the Indians get the piles ready we ordered next week, as the vessel is here they are to go on let us know how they are doing and if piles will be ready and oblige.

Port Blakeley Mill letterhead proclaims that the company had "Spars and Piles Constantly on Hand." No doubt these were in demand for the construction of docks and piers all through Puget Sound. Some Indians of the area around Arcadia, Oyster Bay, Skookum Inlets, and Squaxin Island were employed by the Port Blakely Mill and managed by Margaret McDonald to dress logs for this purpose. McDonald was the go-between, and she must have had a crew of ready workers to engage in work the mill passed on to her. She also must have acted as paymaster.

On August 16, 1887, Mrs. McDonald received $120.25 for Peter Clams from Port Blakeley Mill. On August 15, 1888, Port Blakeley Mill credited Mrs. McDonald's account with $231.40, apparently owed to Peter Clams.

On Port Blakely Mill Company letterhead:

> AUGUST 13, 1889
>
> MRS. D.A. MCDONALD
>
> SHELTON
>
> Dear Madam
> We wish you to see Indian Johnny Slocum & have him cut the cedar. . . . we will pay him $5.25 for . . . put in the water & raft (good logs) the same as we pay Welley and McClain.

Welley (Willey) and McClain were European American loggers, and the mill wanted to assure Slocum that his pay for work done would be equitable with what these men were paid. Eli Willey is said to have enjoyed sitting with Indians, including the Slocums, at the beach in front of their house. They shared clam dinners together. Eli is also said to have helped "Old Slocum" fish when he was going blind. Old Slocum had sold meat to the logging camps when he was younger and still able to hunt.[8]

Aside from the commerce with Port Blakely, McDonald's store provided merchandise to many passing through who needed food and dry goods or tools.

From the ledgers saved by family, we know that in 1874 William Krise bought bacon and a sack of flour on March 6 and several pounds of sugar and a knife in April. He had a few drinks and a meal in May. An Indian named Napoleon may have worked for the establishment. He regularly boarded there and took many meals and drinks. His accounts were always covered, perhaps by his labor for McDonald.

Oyster Bay people James Tobin, John Slocum, Henry Isaac, Mrs. Tom Slocum, Sandy Wohaut, and Doctor Jim are patrons whose names appear regularly in McDonald's books, and their purchases give us a sense of what they needed, used, and wanted in their homes. For example, in October 1886 James Tobin bought a can of lard, three yards of flannel, fifty pounds of salt, and a box of crackers. Later in the month James Tobin needed a new axe handle. We know someone in Tobin's household chewed. He bought plug tobacco on occasion. In July 1887 the Tobins needed a new broom. They regularly purchased bacon and boxes of soap. And we know that someone in the household enjoyed coffee. Chief Kettle bought a pair of boots and a pair of socks from Mrs. McDonald on November 4, 1887.

Given Margaret McDonald's apparent fastidiousness, I shouldn't have been surprised to find, tucked into one of the ledgers, her declaration to become a citizen of the United States and relinquish her allegiance to "Victoria, Queen of Gt. Britain," sworn to in March 1883.

After 1887 the Arcadia store closed and Mrs. McDonald partnered with Thomas O'Neill, her son-in-law, to run the McDonald & O'Neil shop in Shelton. Thus an era of brisk commerce between Indians and European Americans on Big Skookum ended and the jobs brokered for Indians by Margaret McDonald were gone.

Both Bush Hoy and Joseph Kullrich had stores nearby and others came along, but their ledgers do not seem to have survived. Still, the little stores were there for a while, and at least Oyster Bay people had places to shop until they too closed. There were no shops near Oyster Bay for years until the Squaxin Island Tribe's Little Creek Casino, with a gas station and convenience store, opened in 1996. These are located on the approximate site of the old Kamilche Valley Grange Hall.

In spite of the many ways that Indians and European Americans interacted and the numerous marriages between them, there were invisible but real boundaries in relationships. Indians were in some ways excluded and in other ways stigmatized by some European Americans. European American men and their Indian wives or partners, whom Campbell calls "squaws" in his diary, came by occasionally and visited Campbell and his wife and children. But though company was often "mixed," the Indian women were clearly not as respected as the white spouses by some of the white men, and they literally didn't "count" in some contexts. Campbell's use of the term "squaw" is just one indicator of this.

Sometimes, apparently, Indian wives weren't taken into white society at all. Women like Sallie Weatherall who, married to Harry Weatherall for decades, was never taken into his sister's house, just up the hill from the couple's float house. Sallie was not, reportedly, taken to parties and picnics by Harry when other whites of the community gathered. The men could, if they chose, make the women invisible and live, symbolically, a double life.

The government sometimes helped with this charade. Though the forty-some children of interracial unions around the bay were recorded on the main census sheets of the 1870 Federal Census, the names of the wives of their fathers — that is, their mothers — were not or were taken on a separate sheet. It was as if they were members of another household.

The term "squaw" was used freely by European Americans. But some, perhaps even Campbell, didn't understand what the word conveyed. There were subtleties in its meaning and use, and those subtleties represented to the world the status and legal standing of Indian women who were partnered with white men. Oyster Bay Indian women and white men were for the most part legally married or at least presumed themselves to be. Records show that people like Henry and Sallie Weatherall, who had been married by Chief Kettle and shared money and property in common, were not exceptional. They presented themselves as husband and wife and were thought of by the broader community as such, even if the wives were relegated to the float house and not recognized outside of the environment of the bay. A married woman such as Sallie Weatherall was not a "squaw."[9] Neither were Katie Gale, Jennie Krise, Harriet Korter, Louisa Smith, and many others.

Sometimes men and women lived together out of convenience or in a mutually acknowledged temporary sexual arrangement. In these instances the women were apparently paid for their work on the oyster beds by their male friend, as was any other worker. They were employees, not partners. The differences between these associations and marriages were clear to people who knew the individuals personally. There are a handful of mentions of such unions on Oyster Bay in the sources I've found. Of course, because they were impermanent and no legal contract between the two was signed, there is not much in the record about them. The Indian women who lived with white men in these relationships were expected to cook for them and, at least sometimes, sleep with them. The relations were casual enough that after a few years one or both of the parties might move on and there was no divorce or formal separation called for. The local whites apparently used the terms "squaw man" and "squaw" to describe this relationship.

The presence of an Indian woman on a white man's float house did not necessarily indicate even a temporary arrangement of this nature. Snohomish Mary, for example, often visited Harry and Sallie Weatherall and stayed over. Someone who didn't understand their relationships might come to an erroneous conclusion.

Robert Frost was an Olympia hardware store owner who frequented Oyster Bay. His store dealt in "wooden ware, willow ware, agricultural implements, crockery, glassware" and had "a full stock of loose and fixed ammunition constantly on hand." He was someone that Oyster Bay people knew well and with whom they did business. Frost was very clear about male and female relationships on the bay and had definite opinions about white men who abused the "system" and women. He said, "Indian fashion, common law or any way and a man is an infernal brute that don't stick to the woman that stays with him."

Frost continued, "Squaw man is a kind of common expression to people that don't understand. A man that lives with an indian woman is called a squaw man. When it comes to a marriage or an indian marriage where they raise a family, — well I wouldn't say as to that. But it is a common expression of those people that don't know and don't understand."[10]

Thus there was honor among many of these men around the institution of marriage, in whatever form. And there were many actions and activities that signaled "marriage" apart from a license from the justice of the peace.

For example, married couples worked oyster beds side by side. They shared a common purse as well as a common bed. If the couple pooled resources and purchased groceries and dry goods in common, that was a marriage. If they jointly hired and paid other workers, that was a marriage. If they were seen or known to negotiate property purchases together, that was a marriage. A man who was in a marriage—and that might take many forms: common law, "Indian" style, made with papers in front of a justice of the peace, or made with a handshake and a prayer with a preacher—was expected not to go off and leave the woman. That was talked about by others in the community and found despicable. This was true whether the husband was Indian or white. Gig Harbor Joe, for example, was disdained for leaving his wife on Mud Bay when she was ill.

A man in a marriage with any woman was not supposed to ask her to continue to labor if they had accumulated wealth. It was shameful if he gave over his own chores to hired hands but expected his female partner to continue daily exertions on the tide flats. That was talked about. It wasn't right. A man who was in a marriage was expected to look out for the future of the children of that marriage. That included providing for them in every way.

White men on Oyster Bay who had Indian wives were criticized by some other white men if they abused their wife in any way, especially if they had labored together on oyster beds and the woman had helped to secure equipment and tidelands with money she had earned.

Though there was much commerce, mixing, and marriage among and between the populations on Oyster Bay, Little Skookum, and Big Skookum and the environs, the solidity of the Indians' previous village life, and the culture and history it represented, was missing for them. (As in some ways the predictability and safety of their former lives was lost to the white settlers who had left families and countries of origin behind.) Indeed, the binding constraints of organized society, the complex, age-old relationships, and the network of support that had sustained the indigenous people of Puget Sound had been shredded by this time. Kin and friendship still held, as for example it did among the Kettles on Oyster Bay and Mud Bay.

However, supportive as this group was, it couldn't replace band and village life. The average family size (among both Indians and non-Indians) was small, between three and five during this period. Few households were multigenerational. Thus the people who held the history and told the stories were missing, dead from the ravages of disease and war or scattered to reservations. People not on reservations were separate from one another, living in independent homesteads or float houses. There were no large village complexes or longhouses to which one might return for winter dances, spiritual regeneration, renewal of cultural and social ties, and reinforcement of mores.

Yet people still traveled to and from Mud Bay together for celebrations and to some traditional resource areas and gathered around the region on many occasions. Some white settlers reported canoe loads of visitors coming in and out of Oyster Bay. Certainly the Kettles' social network was fairly extensive, and there are many indications that they worked and lived together or near each other over time. Later, after 1881 and the founding of the Shaker Church, meetings of Indian people were probably more regular and structured.

Still, the 1870s and 1880s were, for Indian people, a kind of free fall into a different world of property, ownership, and social relations. The government was busy promoting assimilation for Indians through laws and policies. Many traditional leaders were dead. The elders, those who had survived, were treated by whites as quaint anachronisms.

Marriage on Puget Sound had always been a way of establishing new ties with bands and villages in the region. People commonly married out of their immediate territory to establish networks of kin and expand economic and resource bases. One major consequence of the traditional system of "out" marriage was that wealth was constantly circulating. Perhaps the impulse in the late 1800s, still, was to extend the group and keep wealth moving about rather than accumulating in one household. And there were new, compelling reasons to do so. Making alliances with European and European American men may have been seen to be expedient and pragmatic, that is, something advantageous from the point of view of the accustomed and historically effective economic and kinship system and its effect of building alliances and distributing resources.

However, the goal of some of the capitalist European American men whom Indian women married in the late 1870s and 1880s on Oyster Bay was to accrue, conserve, and build wealth. Given these differences alone, the result of alliances between European American men such as Joseph Gale and Indian women such as Katie Gale was, probably inevitably, conflict. Joseph Gale's goal was to become a successful oyster dealer. His actions led to the consolidation of wealth, not to distribution of newly gained prosperity among community and kin.

Furthermore, progressive methods and technologies introduced by the European American entrepreneurs in the oyster trade relegated Indians on Oyster Bay to wage laborers and overwhelmed what small-scale businesses they had established. As wage laborers they were used seasonally, paid by the piece, and had no "benefits." They became less and less useful to the European Americans as the years went by. By 1900 there were few Indians working on Oyster Bay, for even in the capacity of piece workers they had been replaced by Chinese and Japanese. These workers, too, had very little job protection or benefits until, arguably, the mid-1970s.[11]

However, marriage alliances may have in some ways blurred rank and status lines on Oyster Bay, as when Hudson's Bay men took Indian spouses.[12] The legal identity of the offspring of these marriages was tenuous and, in a way, up for grabs over the years, as we shall see in the Gale case. And there were many of these children.[13]

The conventional wisdom, repeated in settlers' memoirs as well as oral histories, is that the white men married Indian women to get access to their oyster lands. However, the authority of ownership was conveyed upon those persons ready and able to take the opportunity offered by various territorial and state laws and acts, such as the Callow and Bush Acts in 1895, and not automatically to those reservation or nonreservation Indians who had gathered shellfish on the tidelands historically. Marrying an Indian woman may have helped to legitimize the legal claims in the eyes of some and, in some cases, may have assured the inheritance of new claims if the woman one married had an Indian oysterman father or mother who had successfully established a legal claim to tidelands. However, clearly there were many more marriages between Indian women and white men than there were marriages with specific economic advantages for the men. It was much more likely the case that white men legally gained ownership of tidelands, including, eventually, natural beds, by appropriating, staking, and filing claims for tidelands that had been used by Indians, not through their wives. The Indian shellfish grounds may have been "usual and accustomed" fishing and shellfishing grounds, but they were not, at this point, recognized by territorial or state law as such unless someone did the work of filing a claim. And certainly some Indians did file. Tyee Bob and Jack Slocum, for example, filed descriptions of their oyster beds with the auditor's office in Mason County in 1880 and 1881, respectively, and continued to grow oysters commercially. Later, after statehood in 1889, other requirements for the ownership of tidelands were introduced and still more Indians filed, including Katie Gale under her own name, as did Sandy Wohaut. It was these surveyed and filed claims that were recognized under territorial law and, later, under Washington State law.

Indeed, the advantage (given the tenor of the time and the extant policies that privileged assimilated Indians, as well as the disreputable condition of the reservation system) may arguably have been to the women in mixed marriages. The Indian women who participated in legalized, state- and territorially sanctioned marriages were, under territorial and state law, guaranteed legitimacy of their children, access to land, full citizenship, and the right to devices such as community property laws that allowed them to keep or acquire property and to pass it on to their own children.

During a two-year period, from 1866 through 1868, territorial law prohibited marriage between whites and Indians. However, the Legitimacy Act of 1866 granted inheritance rights to half-Indian–half-white children, and an election law passed the same year made those children of both genders eligible to vote when they reached the age of twenty-one if they held land, could read and write, and had adopted the habits of whites.

Relationships among and between people on Oyster Bay in the late nineteenth century were complex and layered with meaning and significance. A hearty hello called from skiff to canoe, a salmon traded for a basket of cherries, and a signature or *X* made on a scrap of paper that guaranteed a future land patent or paycheck: each of these friendly, trustful exchanges served to obscure great differences in status and opportunity while at the same time signaling the hopes some must have had for a truly egalitarian community.

15 *Joseph Gale Was an Enterprising Man*

JOSEPH GALE, at his death, was well known throughout the state of Washington. He had forty acres of "most excellent oyster lands," so "especially well located" that they did not "require artificial culture to make them profitable." He had "direct telephone communication with Shelton, Olympia and outside points," and was hailed as one of Mason County's "enterprising citizens." His home was called "one of the most pleasant and delightful" in the county. He had served as deputy state fish commissioner for six years under James Crawford.[1]

Crawford became the first Washington fish commissioner when he was appointed by Governor Elisha Ferry in 1890. In 1896 Crawford announced publicly that he would be glad to have Gale continue in his post, though Gale had said in an Olympia newspaper that his "future work would be to overthrow the party in the state." The party referred to was Crawford's own party. Joseph agreed to stay on and served for two years with A. C. Little, who took the post of fish commissioner in 1899 under the administration of populist governor John Rogers.

Joseph was elected to the post of justice of the peace in Mason County three times and was chair of the board of the Oyster Land Commissioners. He was sworn in to the board in January 1899. In 1899 he also served as the president of the Oystermen's Association of Puget Sound. He was a member of the Fraternal Order of Eagles, among other affiliations with brotherhood organizations. He had put up money to help found a Shelton newspaper. He was also a nephew of a prominent and much-admired Northwest publisher, though their personal regard for one another is not clear. He had been a husband three times over and had two school-age children. Among his other achievements, he had, as a boy, endured an arduous journey to the Northwest with his family on the Oregon Trail.

Joseph A. Gale was an achiever and a man of some influence, and yet he was, above all, a man shaped by the prejudices, opportunities, and challenges of his times. It would be easy to portray him as villainous in the story of his time with Katie Gale. The easy way would not begin to describe this complex man or do credit to his character.

Joseph Gale moved to Oyster Bay in 1878, leaving behind in Olympia a wife, Calista. Calista was a dressmaker some five years older than he. It is possible that Calista disdained what would most certainly be a difficult rural life and said she wouldn't leave whatever home she already had established in Olympia. They had married in 1877, just before his departure for Oyster Bay. It wasn't a big move for him geographically. Oyster Bay was just a few miles down the road by horse and not more than a day's boat ride by water. But the move was big in terms of his ambitions. He was clearly driven by the compelling possibility of finding success and wealth in the oyster business. He was thirty years old. There was no time to waste.

Joseph was born in Illinois in 1847 or 1848 and as a child of five was among the first American settlers in Lane County, Oregon Territory. It is possible the family had friends or even relatives who had already settled there successfully and had urged the Gales to follow.

The new territory, established after the Oregon Treaty of 1846 divided the Northwest between the United States and Great Britain, encompassed what are now the states of Oregon, Washington, and Idaho and even portions of Montana and Wyoming. It was organized and incorporated by the United States by the time of Joseph's birth. In 1848 the first European Americans came to settle and build lives in the area that became the town of Cottage Grove.

Joseph and his family were among the thousands who crossed the country in covered wagons in search of new land and new life. They began their travels in St. Joseph, Missouri, and followed the Oregon Trail to the West.

Joseph's father was Joseph Everitt Gale. He married Elizabeth Garrison in 1831 in Illinois. He came west with his brother William Gale, a former Campbellite preacher and homeopathic physician who was married to the Welsh Rebecca Elizabeth Jones. They had been married in Posey City, Indiana, and subsequently moved to Illinois. James Newton Gale, William's oldest son, was an eager participant in the adventure. Adventure it was, for the Gales were members of the famous and much-written-about Lost Wagon Train.[2] The Gale party had the distinction of being known as the "Rough and Ready" group among the wagoner families, according to Joseph's cousin, Joseph Marion Gale.

Joseph Marion, seventeen when the trek to Oregon began, later served in the U.S. Civil War and became a teacher and newspaper editor. "Although we were Christians," he writes of the trip west, "we kept our powder dry and our 'toothpicks' sharpened. Mine had a buckhorn handle and a fourteen inch blade, heavy enough to cleave the skull of any enemy we might meet, except possibly the buffalo or mountain sheep." They had a couple of near opportunities to test those "toothpicks" but negotiated their way through testy encounters along the way and reached Oregon Territory unscathed. They seem to have found helpful protection through the services of a Sioux man named "Sam Arc."[3]

The Lost Wagon Train was made up of 615 men and 412 women, for a total of 1,027 persons. They were scattered among 215 wagons as they plodded toward their promised lands. With them, they had 3,970 head of cattle, 1,700 sheep, 222 horses, and 64 mules.[4] They set off from St. Joseph, Missouri, on April 1, 1853. Their route took them to Fort Kearny in Nebraska, Fort Laramie in Wyoming, and Fort Boise in Idaho. It was after Fort Boise that things got dicey.

Road commissioners, drawn from among the earlier settlers in the Willamette Valley, were eager to provide a free route to the valley that knocked a few days off travel time as an alternative to the established trail along the Columbia River. They thought the new trail would speed up settlement and also be an enticement to come to their community. Therefore, by 1852 a new, free emigrant road had been hastily surveyed and roughly cut by the industrious, ambitious, already-settled Oregonians. Fallen trees were still scattered along the way and there had been skirmishes with Native peoples while the road was being chopped through woods and mountains. The newcomers, including the Gales, had no idea what conditions they would face on this new road. They were so near the end of their long trek that when a guide showed up to take them to its conclusion along the new, free, and considerably shorter trail, they must have been jubilant.

The cutoff would, indeed, save some 130 miles of travel. The difficulty was that the shorter route, only partially completed and tricky for that reason if no other, would entail a crossing of the Cascade chain of mountains.

Elijah Elliot was sent from the valley to meet the wagons on the east side of the mountains and guide the train. His own family were members of the wagon party. That fact seemed to other travelers to make his leadership more trustworthy. He surely wouldn't put his own kin in harm's way.

He met the exhausted travelers at the Malheur River. A confrontation with Indians in the Harney Basin caused Elliot to take the wagoners and families on a lengthy side trip to skirt Malheur and Harney Lakes. The emigrants ran out of supplies and began to eat their cattle; these poor beasts were already lean and tired from crossing the prairies. One journal recounts that the meat on a cow was barely enough to grease the skillet.

Andrew McClure, one of the wagon party, writes in his journal, "The road is the worst we have found on this side of the Missouri and the worst I ever saw. I think that we have not traveled over one hundred feet of level ground today and the hills are covered with large stones. . . . The road said to have been surveyed across the Cascades is the only assurance."[5]

The water in the lakes they passed was apparently undrinkable and other sources of hydration were few and far between. When there was water, it posed its own problems. Wagons were not called "prairie schooners" for nothing. The so-called Yankee bed on which the bow and bonnet of the wagon were secured was made of hardwood and was at least two feet deep. It could be made watertight with tar and floated over the many river crossings. And there were many crossings.[6]

At one point the emigrants realized the full depth of their predicament. It was October and the first snows were surely not far in the future. Hungry and fatigued to the point of desperation, they turned on Elliot. He was apparently very nearly hung for his seemingly incompetent leadership.

A number of attempts to alert the Willamette settlers on the far side of the Cascades to their predicament were made by sending out advance parties from the wagon train. Some set out to find help and to locate the road they were assured was ahead. Wrong turns were made and horses became mired in mud. (This was a common cause of consternation on the trail.) Near starvation caused at least one would-be rescuer to eat his horse.

As they climbed the Cascades, people got out and walked to lighten the load, for the oxen were nearly depleted of strength. Steep grades were so difficult for the beasts that everyone who could walk, did. Furniture and other treasured belongings, brought so far already, were tossed aside. Of course, this was not an unheard-of practice. Emigrants had probably noticed the discarded heirlooms of many families who had passed before them on the trail long behind them. They would have seen gravesites and carcasses of dead animals. But now, their own loads had to be lightened and survival was the only consideration. Thin and weary milk cows were called into service when oxen could no longer pull.

Back in the upper Willamette, settlers knew the Elliot wagons had taken the cutoff, but now they were weeks overdue. The emigrants soldiered on and the settlers stewed. On October 6, 1853, a party sent out by the wagon train finally found the new, free road and sent word back to where the wagons had stalled, waiting information. A scout rode ahead of the wagon train hoping to find the Willamette settlers and rally supplies and help. He himself had no provisions and, it is said, stopped to cook and eat the stillborn colt his mare had birthed. The smoke of his campfire was visible to settlers in the Willamette Valley, for he had stopped on the 2,126-foot Butte Disappointment for his cookout. According to contemporary accounts, the Willamette folk sent out ninety-four pack animals and twenty-three wagons loaded with bacon, flour, potatoes, onions, and other staples. Wagons and men on horseback dropped supplies all along the route to refresh and sustain the feeble new settlers as they continued their journey westward.

When they finally arrived in the valley, they were mightily welcomed and helped to find jobs and accommodations. Accounts say the emigrants who arrived then doubled the population of the Upper Willamette.[7]

Once in Oregon Territory, Joseph Gale, a little boy who had borne this grueling journey, grew up living amid the excitement, challenges, and novelties at hand and among people who were clearly ready to try their luck at just about anything. They had come through a singular experience that must have in many ways defined their lives.

Joseph's adolescence in the small settlement coincided with a decade of enormous social and cultural upheaval. Abraham Lincoln was elected to the U.S. presidency in 1860, when Joseph was about thirteen. A civil war was declared and fought, ending in 1865, and African Americans were freed from slavery, first by Lincoln's Emancipation Proclamation, then by the passage and ratification of the Thirteenth Amendment to the U.S. Constitution, also in 1865. Lincoln was assassinated that same year. Transcontinental train service began. The Homestead Act was passed and signed by President Lincoln in 1862, offering the many newcomers to the West the opportunity to acquire land. Joseph's family, however, had taken donation claims under the Donation Land Claim Act of 1850.

Joseph didn't need the words Horace Greeley made popular in an 1865 editorial: "Go West, young man, and grow up with the country." Joseph was already there, in the fabled West, and was an ambitious young man. Nevertheless, these words and his family's penchant for risk, not to mention their fortitude, must have seemed to obligate him to some kind of greatness and achievement.

Indeed, the famous "Go West" slogan, originally penned by John Soule in a Terre Haute, Indiana, newspaper, must have fueled many imaginations. But not every young man was so readily poised and situated to take action on it. If Greeley's words weren't enough to inspire Joseph, there were Horatio Alger's stories of success by luck as well as pluck. These were popular reading for boys of the era, and Joseph could have been one of them. It was a decade full of promise for these enterprising young fellows from the East and Midwest of the United States as well as the ones already in the West — at least, it was if you were white. Whatever he read and whatever his influences, Joseph must have been itching to find his destiny.

Of course, not all was joyful for the Gales in their new Oregon homes. There were family deaths, including the death of Joseph's older cousin's spouse. James Newton Gale lost both his wife and two small children. James Newton had shared the journey to the West; the bonds among the family members must have been strong and the sorrow must have been shared throughout the family.

Religion would have been part of Joseph's early life. Discussions certainly would have been many and intense. His grandfather, John Wesley Gale, born in the eighteenth century, was almost certainly from a religious family, and they were undoubtedly adherents of John Wesley. James Newton's father, Joseph's uncle, was a preacher of the Christian or "Campbellite" denomination.[8] He had preached in Illinois. James's mother was the aunt of a "well known revivalist," a Methodist Episcopalian, on the East Coast, Rev. Thomas L. Jones. However, about the time they left Illinois, according to Harrison Kincaid, who wrote an essay dedicated to James Newton Gale after his death, the family became skeptics regarding organized religion. They maintained a belief in God and "a future state of existence" but were "inclined to rationalism and the philosophy of spiritualism." James Newton was known later to be a leader of the temperance movement in Washington Territory and used his publishing career, apparently, to further the causes of temperance.[9]

In 1870 Joseph, a young man of twenty-three, appears on the census roles of Cottage Grove. He is a boarder with the Stewart family and working in a sawmill. He lists the value of his real estate at $600 and his personal estate at $500.

He must have left Cottage Grove and moved to Olympia, Washington, a small town incorporated in 1859 as part of Washington Territory, soon after that census was taken. Washington Territory had split off from Oregon Territory in 1853. It is very likely that it was Joseph's cousin James's move to Olympia that inspired his own travel north. James Newton, associated with other publications and newspapers in Oregon Territory, had moved to Olympia in 1867, apparently "headhunted" by Republican leaders to edit an independent Republican newspaper called the *Transcript*.[10]

Joseph had a "grubstake" from his Oregon properties and, after the move, went right to work in Olympia. He lived in a boardinghouse and listed his profession as "teamster" in an 1875 census. He married his first wife, Calista, there in 1877. From Vermont originally, she apparently had traveled to Oregon, where she married Dustin Sands, who was from Maine, and had moved to Olympia with him by at least 1870 when Dustin got a job in a sawmill. She divorced him the year before she married Joseph Gale and, with a six-year-old boy named for his father, made a home with Joseph. Joseph was about thirty years old. Calista was in her late thirties.

Though Joseph's home may have officially been in Olympia, he was already working and living part-time at least on Oyster Bay by the late 1870s, apparently without Calista's blessing or companionship — and perhaps without informing anyone on Oyster Bay of his marital status. Though still joined legally to Calista, he listed himself as single in an 1880 Kamilche census.

Calista "abandoned" him, Joseph complained in a divorce proceeding in 1881, without his "wish, will or consent." She retorted that he had taken up with another woman on Oyster Bay. A divorce was granted. Calista worked as a dressmaker in Chehalis for a time and lived there with young Dustin. She later returned to live in Olympia with the family of Joseph's cousin, James Newton Gale, called "Newton," who was still the editor and publisher of the *Transcript*. He sold the paper in 1888 when his health was failing. Calista was living with the James Newton Gale family during the months preceding his death in May 1889 and may have been helping the family through the illness. Whatever had transpired between Calista and Joseph, apparently she had become close to other members of the Gale family and perhaps proved a stable, loving friend for Mrs. James Newton Gale after Newton died.

Meanwhile, through the 1880s, as Joseph spent more time on Oyster Bay he learned how to cultivate, harvest, and market oysters. Joseph, along with Abner Smith (also known as A.J. and "Saxy"), his partner and housemate during his first years on Oyster Bay, and David Helser, a married man whose wife accompanied him to help improve their homestead and start their business, organized the Puget Sound Oystermen's Association in 1881. This was just a few years after their arrival on Oyster Bay in 1878.[11] Indeed, the trio's entry into the oyster business marked the beginning of a new era on Oyster Bay.

For Joseph, this period was the launch of a new life as well. He must have met Katie Kettle during his first days on Oyster Bay. She would have been working oyster beds with relatives. And, being without prior experience in shellfish harvest or cultivation or life in a maritime community, he would have needed them and her to gain any foothold in this new world.

Katie Kettle was around twenty years old and was apparently previously or still married to a man whose name doesn't appear in the records. She gave birth to two children, Hattie and Henry, during the early years of Joseph's life on Oyster Bay. We do know that these were not Joseph's children. Their father was probably an Indian man, given what we learn about Hattie later. He may have been older and, given conditions of the time, may have died while he and Katie were together.

Katie's kin had been harvesting and selling oysters for years. They knew Oyster Bay. They knew the weather, the tides, and the currents intimately. They had the strength and the know-how that greenhorns like Joseph and "Saxy" would need if they were to make a success of their business. In addition to their knowledge, they were a ready, available pool of cheap, exploitable labor.

So Katie, along with the Kettles and other Indian people, began working for Joseph shortly after his arrival on Oyster Bay. They soon became lovers and steady companions in a nascent business venture.

Joseph's relationship with Katie and hers with him wasn't unique. In 1879 there were 355 white men in Mason County and only 139 white females. The ratio of Indian men to Indian women in the area was also out of balance. The men wanted and needed intimacy and camaraderie and, literally, helpmates. And the families of young Indian women had been torn asunder by the midcentury war and a damnable reservation system. They were all pioneers of their own lives, willing to explore the strangeness of cross-cultural alliances that seemed to afford some security. According to census data that included counts of half-Indian children by household, there were at least fifteen unions between white men and Indian women on Oyster Bay in the late 1870s and early 1880s. There were probably many more of these not officially recognized and counted as such.

As for Joseph, he was now over thirty, enthusiastic, and positioned to acquire tidelands and make money in the shellfish business. Following the divorce from Calista, he was free to marry again. Katie was there. She was a constant laborer and an intelligent, willing friend.

By the time Joseph and Katie were together and then married in 1886, Katie's position as the spouse of a white man and the position of her children by him were assured and shored up by force of law. The liaison with Joseph and the legalization of their union must have seemed to assure stability in life and circumstance that Katie had never known. That their marriage was recognized and Katie was accepted into public society as his wife, not a "squaw," is affirmed by periodic announcements in newspapers. A child was born to them in 1883. She died sometime after a fourth birthday. Maud, their second daughter, was born in 1886, the year of their formal union. Joseph said later he wished to marry Katie to legitimize this child. On April 28, 1888, the *Mason County Journal* declared that the wife of Joseph Gale had given birth to a son. This was Ray. Two children from Katie's previous marriage were still living and resided with the couple in their Oyster Bay home.

At the age of thirty, with four children to care for and an interest, through her new husband and by her own cleverness, in lucrative tidelands, Katie seemed set for life. So did Joseph.

16 *The Marks upon Her Body*

SOMETIME IN my student days I read that power makes marks upon the body and soul of those on whom that power is exercised.[1] These marks made by power can be as deep and damaging as those inflicted by a bludgeon. I understood from what I studied that physical consequences come from authority and control misdirected or abused. I also learned firsthand, as many of us have, the regretful agony one experiences in a fatally flawed relationship. But I didn't really understand how the use and abuse of power in such a relationship derives its legitimacy from the culture and society in which it is embedded. I didn't understand how culture can offer approval of and make to seem reasonable the mutilation, punishment, and destruction that power works on lives it touches. After my acquaintance with Katie and Joseph Gale all of this was no longer theoretical. I came to understand that which had been beyond me.

In October 2004 my hands hovered above a case file, a folio of papers perhaps untouched since they were first placed in an archival box many years, if not decades, ago.

The Washington State Archives is located on the state capitol campus, not far from downtown Olympia, the capital of Washington State. The procedure for entering the archive is not unlike that employed by any other well-run repository for important documents. One must leave bags, pens, and other belongings outside the main research facility. After one signs in, an attendant provides a locker and key. I usually leave everything in that locker except my laptop and a camera. I keep the camera, allowed in this archive, to take photographs of pages of text, maps, and file covers as I go through materials. Inside the main room where researchers work is a squadron of trim, glass-covered, heavy oak tables. Under the glass are territorial and state maps.

Along the walls of the room, on heavy shelves, are neat rows of directories, law books, and some filing cabinets with microfilms. On one wall is a substantial clock. It is an antique timepiece secured in a wooden case with a pendulum that audibly ticks away the passing time. Incongruously, on one corner bookcase there is a statue of Confucius, a gift to the state of Washington from the Republic of China in 1972, during the period when Daniel J. Evans was governor.

I sit comfortably at one of the long wooden tables, on which I can spread out files I'm studying. I take notes with the pencil and paper provided by the staff. Sometimes I type whole passages into my computer.

This archives is the place I go to find official state or county documents, including legal files and tideland records from the late nineteenth and early twentieth century. All of those official papers collected by courts, state agencies, and thirty-nine (current) counties of Washington eventually make their way into the Washington State Archives. These carefully stored documents may be accessed for legitimate research.

Delving into the past, into people's lives, is a serious project and no one here enters into that work lightly. The staff's treatment of visitors and file boxes is ritualized, almost sacralized. I like this about archives. I know what to expect. I know that at least this part of my work is predictable. When boxes are retrieved, they are placed the tabletop before the searcher. Staff provide the client with white cotton gloves. Like a surgeon, one handles the contents of boxes gently and with swathed fingers. One slips each old paper out of its file with great delicacy. One follows the rules.

Anyone who loves doing historical research will tell you that at this moment, when the cartons full of numbered file folders are before you, in this state of giddy apprehension when you know you are going to discover something important, your heart is in your throat.

On that day in 2004 I pulled a folder from the first box I'd requested. On the opening page of the court record in that file I read this: "[The] defendant has treated the plaintiff as a menial, has never been kind and loving to her and has repeatedly struck her, inflicting bruises and wounds upon her person, and on the 8th day of July, 1893, the defendant struck her in her face with his fist . . . and at the same place, at her home in Mason County, the defendant kicked the plaintiff with his booted feet, inflicting serious and painful wounds upon the person of the plaintiff."[2]

I had long since learned to crave the thrill of the chase. I've spent years doing research, first in Sarawak, Malaysia, where I was a young Peace Corps volunteer. Though obliged by my job to build gardens and pit latrines, I found time to study head-hunting rituals and labor exchange systems. I visited village farms with young Bidayuh friends and managed to evade the very real dangers of major floods, the Brunei Rebellion, and the Malaysian Confrontation. Soldiers I drank Tiger Beer with one night in the bazaar of my little two-block town were sometimes dead the next night, killed on our border with Indonesian Borneo.

Later, my fieldwork as a cultural anthropologist in Kelantan, Malaysia, focused on the relationship between performance and healing in village settings. Then, in the early 1990s, I went to work for the Puyallup Tribe of Indians in Tacoma, Washington, and began a new career focused on the reconstruction of treaty-period culture from largely archival and oral historical materials.

Still, for all the years of living in often-difficult circumstances, witnessing death and horrible disease and even war, and reading documents of a cruel and bitter period in the history of my own region, I hadn't come to terms with the fact that the work I'd chosen to do in my life would often bring me so up close to injustices committed against good and decent people.

In those three or four months after finding Katie Gale's tombstone, I had been looking for "facts" about her. I'd looked at census figures and death notices and had found a few other details. But this document before me told a story I hadn't expected. And it wasn't an easy one to take in.

The defendant, Joseph Gale, Katie continues in her complaint, "is addicted to the intemperate use of Alcoholic liquors and is frequently in a beastly state of intoxication at his home." He is, she says, "violent and immoral in his language and actions while intoxicated." The complaint notes that the plaintiff has "discharged the duties of wife towards the defendant faithfully and to the best of her knowleg [*sic*] and ability."

These words are typewritten on the first page of the July 18, 1893, petition for divorce Katie Gale filed against J. A. Gale in the Superior Court, Mason County, State of Washington.[3] It was not her own hand that set down these words because Katie, apparently, did not read or write. However, she signed her *X* on the document and clearly had good representation in this and every future proceeding.

Why 1893? What was special about this time? Well, lots had happened by 1893 that may have spurred Katie to action. By 1893, Nellie McClure, an Indian woman and Katie's neighbor, had put her own name on an upland patent after her husband died. James Tobin, the spouse of Louisa Tobin, Katie's kin and friend, had received a patent for a ranch site on Mud Bay in 1890. The Tobins eventually did so well that James Tobin was referred to as the "oyster baron of Mud Bay." Mud Bay Sam, Mud Bay Charley, and Mud Bay Louie, all Indians and oystermen and prominent members of the Indian Shaker Church and the Mud Bay community, had applied for and received patents for their upland homesteads much earlier.[4] Thus, the Indian people in Katie's community were making strides in the new economy, defying the ravenous white oyster growers' stranglehold on the shellfish trade, and securing a future for themselves and their children. Those tidelands would provide an income for these families for years.

And there were other factors at work. Katie was not alone in being tired of the abuse. Research focused on Oregon Territory shows that, women were beginning to "expect greater influence over household decision-making, and became less tolerant of physical and emotional abuse." A study of grounds for divorce in Oregon in the 1880s shows that nearly all were due to "desertion or financial-support" or physical and verbal cruelty.[5] Katie Gale's case would not be exceptional nor her grounds unprecedented.

Also, women were doing things to assure their economic well-being. Women from around Mason County had been registering their property with the county auditor because the territorial marriage acts recognized community property and the rights of women to their own holdings.[6] In 1878 Harriet Korter, an Indian woman, made the trip to the county auditor's office in Shelton and listed property bought by "her own labor and personal earnings." She owned, the official record reads, "one red cow, one spotted cow, red and white, one spotted yearling (ears marked with swallow tail), one brindle steer two years old, one reddish brindle bull three years old, one red ox about nine years old, one speckled white ox, about thirteen years old, two red sucking calves, and two beds and bedding."

Women generally had considerable political power and influence in Washington Territory. Between 1883 and 1888 women had won and lost and regained and lost again the right to vote in territorial elections. The suffrage movement was on the move and activist women (and some men) were regularly holding rallies and making news from this period until women in Washington got the vote in 1910, then nationally in 1920.

Washington had become a state in 1889 and the rules of the game, including those that helped to define white and Indian relations, were changing as a result. The disposition of tidelands was prominent in conversations over the state constitution. Would the state turn over ownership to those occupying tidelands or keep the title to this valuable and coveted real estate? The upshot of the new laws allowed for the sale of some tidelands, specifically those at some distance from a city. They were to be surveyed and appraised. Second-class tidelands, those with some improvements on them, were to be surveyed if a person owning improvements applied to purchase. Third-class tidelands were to be surveyed if the applicant deposited enough money to cover expenses incurred in completing a survey and appraisal. Preference rights to purchase the tidelands had to be exercised within a limited time period or otherwise would be sold by sealed bid.[7]

Acts passed by the state legislature, such as the Bush and Callow Acts, provided special consideration for the sale of tidelands on which oysters had been planted. Any person who had planted such beds prior to March 26, 1890, had between six months and three years to apply for ownership before the land could be sold by the state. The Callow Act, approved in 1895, provided that anyone buying land planted with oysters could have the land surveyed at his own expense and be entitled to purchase up to 160 acres at $1.25 an acre over time. To take advantage of these acts, it was necessary to be a citizen of the United States. According to the state and the Office of the United States Attorney at the time, Indians retained no special privileges in connection with these sales, notwithstanding the treaty that explicitly reserved the right of Indian people to continue to harvest in "usual and accustomed" territories.[8] They would have to go through the same red tape as everyone else to claim tidelands. They would incur the same expenses, including the expense of hiring an attorney if need be.

The Board of Appraisers for Mason County noted prior claimants to tidelands, those who had recorded with the county auditor before statehood and in accord with territorial law. These included Indian shellfishmen "Thie" (Tyee) Bob and Jack Slocum as well as Joseph Gale.

Soon after, by 1890, when Mud Bay Charlie applied for oyster tidelands in Mud Bay, Little Charlie (the stepson of Mud Bay Charley), Olympia Jim (who had a homestead on the Thurston County side of Oyster Bay), and Sally, Jack, and John Slocum had done the same. They were followed in 1892 by Mud Bay Tom, Dick Jackson, Mud Bay

Sam, Mud Bay Lewie or Louie Youlouaut, Olympia Jim, and Sandy Wohaut.[9] These were all Indian people in Katie's circle of friends and the greater Oyster Bay–Mud Bay community and people who had, by their actions and declarations, attained the right to buy these tidelands.

In spite of the care Indians took to assure themselves a place in the future of the oyster business, they were largely ignored by the general public or marginalized by other oyster farmers. In June 1893 the *Washington Standard* listed the names of the prominent oyster shippers on Oyster Bay: "Harry Weatherall, Samuel K. Taylor, Joseph Gale, David Helser, Saxy Smith, and several Indians." The Indians were unnamed and gradually forgotten in official histories of the industry.

Harry Weatherall's partner, the woman who worked side by side with him and was seen by others to give him the money to buy oyster beds, Sallie Weatherall, is not mentioned. Katie Gale, equally a partner in business with Joseph, is not mentioned. By this year Indians were a footnote or a sidebar to the business of oystering. Women were less than a footnote, though they had in the past been at least equals in the harvesting and sale of oysters. The "drudgery" of oyster farming, the same article notes, "is borne by Indians and Chinamen. White men shrink from thus exerting themselves, and especially so, when they can hire heathen and descendants of the noble red man to do the work for a nominal price." Apparently Weatherall and Gale placed their Indian wives in the same class, for as they became wealthy, the women still had to labor year-round on oyster beds.

Being left out of the oyster-trade equation and watching the white men grow fat on their labor must have rankled Katie Gale and her community. Still, there were even other events that would have spurred Katie to grasp a chance to establish her economic independence. All was not well in 1893. In February of that year it was reported that the "last cold spell" had damaged oyster beds on Oyster Bay to the tune of at least $30,000. The *Washington Standard* held that it would "take two or three years" for the oysters to get back to their old standing. In March J. A. Gale was reported to be shipping "40 to 50" sacks a week, down at least 50 percent from previous numbers. As it turned out, it couldn't have happened in a worse year.

The oyster shippers were hit hard. And that wasn't all.

The Northwest and Washington State were increasingly linked to a national and international economy. This shared destiny was assured when on January 6, 1893, the Great Northern Railway completed a transcontinental line to Seattle. The Northern Pacific had linked Seattle to Chicago in May 1888.

However, being closely coupled commercially with the world beyond South Puget Sound had its drawbacks. A national economic panic began in the spring of 1893, seriously reducing employment and investment in Washington State over the next four years. In February the Philadelphia and Reading Railroad announced bankruptcy, thus setting off the chain of events caused the Panic of 1893. Many call it the greatest depression to hit the United States until the Great Depression of the 1930s.

And what of Katie Gale in this unstable early poststatehood environment? By 1893 the stage was set for her to make a move. She was ready to make important decisions about her life, her land, her livelihood, and her relationship with her white spouse.

Katie's body had become a landscape of pain, much of it inflicted by her white spouse, who, he said in court, was "reluctant to use force or severity with her," that whatever "ill treatment" he had imposed on her "was occasioned by [her] unbearable provocation." Clearly the beating described in Katie's divorce petition wasn't the first.

The mistreatment Katie suffered in her marriage might have been enough to cause her to seek a separation from Joseph, just as such treatment compelled other women to leave their husband. Economic conditions gave her yet another reason to seek separation from Joseph. This economic panic and its consequences had reached even the people of Oyster Bay. Banks in Seattle had gone under. Loans were called in. Unemployment was rising. And, it seemed, her husband was owed money he couldn't collect and was running their oyster business in the red. She understood that he intended to sell or encumber their property.

Economic downturns had never touched her people before the coming of Europeans and European Americans. They were people who fished and hunted and lived in harmony with the seasons and what was there to be harvested. Only natural disasters, such as fish runs blocked by landslides and earthquakes or heavy, late freezes, could bring shortages. Now Katie lived in a world that was plummeted into near-chaos by the national and even international activities of marketing and finance.

The Gale business was, apparently, overextended. Joseph might do something to jeopardize their holdings and their future. She would manage, as she had before, by taking control. Her friends and kin had found ways to survive so far, and she would, too. She would, she decided, take steps not to lose the land or the tidelands and, at the same time, protect herself from further abuse.

She was Joseph's legal spouse and would have legal standing in a court of law. Washington was a community property state. And she had a supportive community of friends and kin. That included European American allies. Just two months after the panic began and ten days after Joseph's most recent assault on her, Katie Gale filed for divorce.

In Puget Sound the largely white, American hegemony was complete.[10] The stream of immigrants had overwhelmed the indigenous population and had increasingly occupied lands that though in some instances were free of permanent structures were used year-round and maintained by Indian people for hunting and gathering. All the choicest territory, including open prairies and flatlands, burned and kept clear for choice Indian root crops, was now "real estate"; that is, it had become a commodity in the new society.

The land was advertised widely, its qualities touted to potential investors along the Eastern Seaboard to attract even more developers.

Now that the railroad had come, there was nothing to stand in their way. Chief Seattle had predicted this time in the December 1854 speech attributed to him. The time when Katie Gale's ancestors had "covered the land as the waves of a wind-ruffled sea cover its shell-paved floor" had indeed passed away. Even most of the promises of Governor Isaac Stevens and the great "father" in Washington DC were "but a mournful memory."[11]

Occupants of Indian villages throughout Western Washington and Puget Sound had, by force of treaties and the encroachment of American settlements in and around their old territories, nearly all been made to move to reservations by this time. Or they were being assimilated as they moved onto independent homesteads or into boarding schools. On the reservations a "tribe" appellation was used to describe those assembled. There were the Puyallups, the Quinaults, and the Skokomish, for example. Tribes were politically expedient entities — constructed conglomerates of previously independent bands of people who had their own names and places. These past associations with singular names attached to particular places would become less significant if even remembered as the years passed. Any houses left standing in former Indian territories were, typically, burned by white settlers during this period, if not before. The friendly conversations over clam dinners on beaches where whites and Indians sat together were becoming rarer and rarer.

Katie Gale and the other Indian people still on the bay and domiciled on their own homesteads or on float houses around the region were being made invisible as Indians by the 1890s. By 1897 the *Mason County Journal* reported of the Squaxin, in an article about the death of John Slocum, that "the tribe is almost extinct, and the few remaining are scattered about the various bays, mainly engaged in oystering."

The laws of the land and the more subtle devices of colonization had defined whole peoples out of existence. The children of Indian women by European American husbands were being groomed to disappear into the general population. Stevens's treaties, the Dawes Act, the boarding schools, the farms — all programs aimed at suppressing Indian culture and integrating Indian people into the dominant, mainstream culture — seemed to be working their magic. The little acts of rebellion, such as children who ran away from the boarding schools, were put down, quashed, or ignored. Yet Katie Gale and the Shakers and many others all around Puget Sound found ways to fight back, assert identity, and subvert the discourse, at least temporarily and locally.

Katie had been witness to the changes. Specifically, she had watched Oyster Bay, the refuge of her enterprising kin and kindred, become the domain of a few white businessmen who treated her and them as "menials." She, too, though an owner, was treated by her husband as a common laborer, paid as a piece worker like all the rest of her husband's employees. She earned the dollars he gave her from the very land and tidelands that had provided her living for years before she had married Joseph. It must have been a bitter recollection to her that this same land had been harvested for generations by predecessors to the greatly reduced people now collectively called the Squaxin. Her future was in the hands, now, of an abusive, thankless man for whom she had worked since at least 1880 and by whom she had born his only children.[12]

17 *Katie Gale Goes to Court*

KATIE GALE had a loud voice, the record says. I recognize that voice as a voice of resistance. Case records from 1893 say that she quite literally raised a roaring cry — a furious protest — against this European American man and his domination over her, her work, her children, and her life. It was an angry shout heard up and down the bay, across the waters, and over the sounds of gulls and grinding steam engines on the boats carrying their loads of oysters to market. It was a voice heard by the men in their scows and the people on their float houses. Joseph's friends deplored it, pitied him that he had to live with such an insubordinate and insolent woman. They talked about it in their courtroom depositions. They filed affidavit after affidavit in support of Joseph and in disparagement of the impertinent Katie. They deplored an outspoken woman.

Katie didn't just rage and shout. She bit Joseph, so the records say, and yes, she probably pulled his whiskers, just as the stories that still circulate today say. That's what was remembered and written down by some who knew her or had heard of her. That's what has been repeated and embellished upon. "She tied his whiskers to a tree, I heard," someone told me a few years ago. It was a version of the story Cora Chase had heard as a girl and recorded in her memoir. This perhaps sensationalized version of Katie and Joseph Gale's story lives on. Some have told me that "she was ahead of her time." These oral historical accounts are sketchy. They repeat the fiction that Katie was Joseph's spouse by an "Indian marriage," that is, not legally wed to him.

This story, at least, is wrong. She was legally married to Joseph. And that made all the difference in what was to come.

In the early days of their relationship, Joseph and Katie Gale's partnership seemed to have been a more equitable one than it became later. When they were first together, they were both laboring on the oyster beds. Both were scrappy survivors of challenging early childhoods. Both were ambitious and willing to put aside money to acquire property. Both needed a partner to share the load and to improve their circumstances. However, their goals may have been quite different. Joseph clearly wanted to accrue wealth and, perhaps, gain public recognition for success. Katie may have simply wanted a decent home and a good life for her children and extended family. She probably wanted some security in the transitional world in which she found herself.

Now, in 1893, the Gales were wealthy, recognized publicly as such, and Katie realized that nothing was in her name. Though they and thousands of other Western couples were essentially economic partners, the males' names on deeds and business contracts gave them incredible power over women.[1]

By 1893 Katie and Joseph had labored together on Oyster Bay for at least thirteen years. We know this from Calista's comments about the "other woman." Eighteen eighty was the year Joseph Gale registered his first claim to an oyster cultivation bed with the Mason County Auditor. Also, we know from the oyster violation case that Gale was involved with the Kettle family in 1880. We can speculate that he knew Katie then.

The Gales, co-laboring as husband and wife these many years, had obtained through purchase valuable real properties, uplands and tidelands, together. But Katie Gale's name was nowhere to be found on any documents associated with the properties. Katie would probably have a difficult time preventing Joseph from selling the tidelands if he chose to do so.

In 1881 the Gales bought thirty-six acres adjoining Oyster Bay from the Northern Pacific Railroad. Katie said in court that this acquisition was made with money she had given to Joseph. This is quite plausible. We have no record of how much Joseph had left of his grubstake, nor how much, if any, money he had made in the intervening years. But we know Katie had been on Oyster Bay working with her family for many years. Given other evidence of her shrewdness with money, she very likely had put a good sum aside and had not given it all away or spent it. Other women were doing this. We know that Sallie Weatherall saved both her own earnings and her spouse, Harry's so that they could buy land together. There is testimony from witnesses to a transaction on their float house in which she fetched a secreted sack of cash for the purchase of tidelands. Perhaps it was really these Indian wives who saved, kept track of money, and were ready to spend on good investments.

Katie also claimed that it was she who had, in 1887, bought a six-acre oyster claim from Sig Bettman, one that was originally Big Frank's. Though Joseph's name was on the sales document, she said she had given him the cash for the purchase. This bed lay just in front of the upland Northern Pacific property the Gales already owned. It was this bed that the Gingrichs (parents of Cora Chase) worked in 1897. It was this bed that the Gingrich family called "Katie's."

Since their "legal" marriage in 1886, Katie and Joseph had purchased three other beds. These were described as one six-acre and two four-acre plots at $200 per acre. Katie also claimed these as community property in her suit. She also asserted that the sum of $7,200 was owed her, her share of the proceeds of "the oysters taken from the said oyster claim of the plaintiff and appropriated by the defendant since the year 1887." She was, in this portion of her declaration, asking only for the proceeds from the oyster bed she says was bought with her money after the marriage, that is, the bed that was originally Big Frank's. The $7,200 is the sum of stated yearly revenue of $1,200 times the number of years the bed had been in her/their possession. That's money worth fighting for. In 2012 dollars it would amount to something like $180,000. Curiously, she did not request proceeds from other oyster beds she said they acquired after marriage. These surely would have been considered community property. She and her attorneys may have reasoned that it was better to go for the lucrative beds she knew she could get and manage.

She did ask for her share of other assets acquired during the marriage. These included horses, cows, yearling cattle, calves, and the furniture in the house, as well as a portion of 160 acres of improved uplands they owned and had worked together. This latter parcel of land was above the slope behind their house and tidelands properties and well away from the bay. They had bought this land from Ada Hartman. It carried a mortgage.

The 1893 proceedings were not friendly.

Some of Joseph's fellow oyster growers filed statements with the court on his behalf. That Gale, Smith, and some of the other oystermen would support each other in public proceedings is not surprising.

Their statements took the form of written and signed documents. Among those who filed were Abner Smith and the local adventurer Frank Mossman, who had some oyster beds but was known mostly as a "great" hunter of cougar, bear, and wildcat. Mossman and his white foxhound, trained to hunt, were notorious around Kamilche and Oyster Bay. These men, among others who provided testimony on Joseph's behalf, claimed to be shocked by Katie's behavior.

Mossman, for example, in his affidavit writes that he had lived "within less than one half mile of the residence and place of business of the defendant" for nearly five years. He says he once went with Smith to the Gale place to separate the couple during a tumultuous fight. It is unlikely that the pair could have seen or done anything about this rowdy altercation unless they were already on the Gale property or just next door at Smith's property when the couple were in the throes of their dispute. Even then, they'd have to paddle around to the Gale place or walk a fair distance. Mossman continues, "Then Gale and I proceeded out of the gate. Mrs. Gale the plaintiff herein followed us and cursed and abused Gale at every step using as vile language as I ever heard from anyone — ”

In response to Katie’s charge that Joseph was often intoxicated, Mossman writes,

> I have known defendant for this last twenty years and seen him often — he drinks intoxicating liquors — but I can say that I never saw him intoxicated — he is not inclined to be abusive when he is drinking. I never saw him much under the influence of liquor at his place — he usually does most of his drinking when is absent on business — His business (buying selling and dealing in oysters) takes him from home much of his time. His practice with his wife is to pay her for her work such as picking and culling oysters and preparing them for market in the same manner that he pays and at the same time he pays his other help engaged in such work.[2]

The employer-employee relationship described by Mossman and held by Joseph, according to his own testimony, to be appropriate is one that some other European American men would consider a shameful way to treat a woman who was clearly a “wife” and not a “squaw.”

Abner “Saxy” Smith was among those who expounded on the theme of Katie’s unfitness in support of Joseph. He was particularly concerned that Ray, the little boy, was found alone at the homestead on occasion (though Katie would have been down on the bay very near the house and, as we have seen, women often went about on visits and left children at home) and that Katie took the children with her to visit kin. Apparently she could neither leave the children nor take them with her without eliciting judgmental comment from some. Smith worried that if the children were to stay with Katie, “according to Indian customs,” she would “teach the children to hate the whites” and “disrespect their father.” Perhaps he had harbored these anxieties regarding his Indian wife, Louisa, and their own children.

Underlying these testaments was a not-so-subtle appeal to the judge. Women don’t act like this, do they? Shout? Bite? Pull whiskers? Leave children home alone? This did not match, they seemed to say, their dominant-culture expectations of a woman. And it certainly didn't jibe with their stereotype of the Indian wife who was expected to wait hand and foot on her European American mate.

Of course, the men were dissimulating, for few of the women, Indian or white, that these men knew would have been wilting or willing stereotypes of Victorian women or stay-at-home mothers. This was a rough life and it took women of spirit to endure it.

The men may have felt a little pushed to the wall and loaded for bear, so to speak, by the time Katie Gale brought her suit. The picture they painted of her behavior may have been exaggerated by their own fears of the growing power of women in the United States. Susan B. Anthony had visited Olympia. She addressed the territorial legislature in October 1871. She and others toured the state promoting women's suffrage and organized the Washington Equal Suffrage Association. A suffrage bill was introduced that year in the territorial legislature but failed. Still other bills were introduced and some gains made over the ensuing years. The suffragettes had won a limited victory in 1890.

It would be a mistake to think that Katie Gale, Joseph Gale, and their associates lived in a vacuum, isolated from these political developments. We know the people on Mud Bay and Oyster Bay followed politics and court decisions. There is no question but that Joseph and his friends, business associates, and lodge brothers would have been reading about the "women's question" with interest if not a little fear and disdain for what a victory for women's suffrage would mean for them. The temperance movement was closely allied with suffrage. Joseph's own cousin, the Olympia newspaperman James Gale, was an outspoken leader of that cause, and his words were being read throughout the state.

Like James Gale, some men were either supportive of the women or at least neutral. A farmer, L. K. Cogswell, wrote a letter to the Washington territorial governor, Eugene Semple, in January 1888 from his farm in Chehalis, a few miles south of Olympia and Puget Sound:

I am very glad you did not heed the great clamor that has been made lately for a veto to the suffrage law. Mrs C. says she does not want to vote, nor the right to vote & that women generally do not wish to vote. & if she did it would be the same way I voted. But all that does not alter the plain fact that a woman should have just as good a right to vote as a man. It is her option to vote or not as she pleases. The great fuss, that the law will injure our country is without foundation. I have been five time across to & from the valley of the Mississippi by different routes & our Territory is pointed out with pride as having liberal and advanced laws. & it will be an inducement to many families to join us in the near future.

To my mind one sex has as good a real right to vote, hold office, or anything else as the other. With one exception it seems proper that women should be excused from jury service.

Hoping that our territory & future state will be a leading one in liberal, concise & wise laws & swift, firm, sure, & economical in their enforcement.

I am Yours Obediently
L.K. Cogswell.[3]

Cogswell apparently had been a breeder of Red Poll cattle in Wisconsin before making his journey west. The letter to the governor was handwritten on his colorful Wisconsin stationary, which sports a letterhead with the etched likeness of an elegant cow named "Ocean Maid." She stands before a barn, feet in lush grass, clearly ready to be milked.

Still, though men like Cogswell were in the area, those who enjoyed their whiskey would have been ruffled by the prospects of Prohibition and might have been as well by women's suffrage.

In short, the alarm the men of Oyster Bay expressed and the hyperbole they employed in describing Katie Gale was not unique to them. Men all around the country who didn't like what they heard and saw of women's politics employed fiery language to frame these stereotype-defying activists. Words like "jezebel" had been used to label some of the leaders. Some had been pelted with eggs or stones and jeered at.

Language used by some men in testimony in the Gale case was clearly a response to the disturbing fact that a woman, and an Indian woman to boot, had the mutinous gall to rail against the prerogative of white men and the order they had sought to impose on the raw land and once-thriving indigenous cultures. They had thought their work of subduction complete. They were wrong. Katie's body had suffered Joseph's blows and kicks, but her mind was not colonized. And her shouts, like the shouts of many other women in 1893, proved it.

However, statements by men about Katie were not all damning. They described her as a hard worker. That Katie was a solid and reliable laborer was clear even in comments of those men who testified on behalf of Joseph. Mossman, for example, calls her an "industrious woman" and, he says, by her labor she had earned a substantial sum from Gale.

She wasn't, of course, the only "industrious" working woman on the bay. Harriet Korter went to work in a saloon in Kamilche when her husband died in 1888. She probably had engaged in outside employment before his death, given the extent of her personal property. Jennie Krise worked side by side with her husband and was also a midwife. One of the Sherwood women, the daughter of Joseph Sherwood, was occupied as a house servant. Other Indian women continued to pick and cull oysters, working for or with either Indian or white growers. European American women also worked at a variety of occupations in and outside the home. For example, one of the Simmons girls, Annie, owned cattle, registered her own brand, and listed her occupation on a census as "cattleman."

All the women, white and Indian, had the formidable task of maintaining a household, gardens, and cows and raising children under what today would be thought burdensome. Illnesses and accidents took their lives and the lives of their children sometimes suddenly and overnight. Otherwise healthy babies died of "spinal complaints."

In the spring and early summer of 1891 four young children died on the Skokomish Reservation alone. Colds turned to pneumonia and consumption often followed. Babies who were left for only moments got too near wood stoves where their clothing was vulnerable to dancing sparks and they were burned alive, engulfed in the flames of their own homespun garments. In one tale of horror, a woman preparing an alcohol-laced medication on the stove was fatally burned when it exploded. In another macabre story, a mother with a young babe in arms knelt beside the grave of a child she had buried two years previously. A rotten tree fell and crushed mother and infant. There were drownings or near drownings. There were fatal buggy accidents and murders. And there were suicides.

But amid it all, women worked hard, as hard as the men, and many of them were becoming accustomed to asserting and claiming their fair share of the profits of their labors.

Katie Gale and the others were "industrious" women, to be sure. All the women of the bay would merit that description. The allusion in Mossman's affidavit, however, might have been to the "industrious women" glorified in Old Testament verses. These men would know their Bible and certainly knew what their religion required of women. An "industrious woman" was one, it seems, who ran her household well, provided for her family, and enhanced the status of husband and children in the eyes of the world. If Katie was an "industrious woman" she was certainly not all bad in the eyes of Joseph's peers, in spite of their churlish words about her.

Joseph was served his court papers on July 20, 1893, not long after the national economic panic began. He was given twenty days to defend the action.

Joseph, of course, fought back. If Katie's goal was to keep the land and the oyster beds that were hers and to provide for herself and her young children — Maud, seven, and Ray, five, plus Henry and Hattie — Joseph's was to hold on to the land and tidelands for himself, sustain his business, and gain sole possession of the Gale offspring.

Joseph asserted that the value of the land they owned had dropped considerably. "My own business is now a losing business," he says, suggesting that Katie had had nothing to do with it and in contradiction to the newspaper report of that same year that portrayed him as a wealthy landholder. He was, he says, "short of ready money," though he had been in the oystering trade for many years. He had "considerable sums due him" but at the time it was "impossible to make collections," no doubt due to the shortage of cash and credit throughout the flailing banking system. All businesses were suffering with the "panic." Joseph had been shipping oysters to key buyers around Puget Sound in 1893, but now perhaps orders were not coming in or perhaps due to the winter ice losses he could not fill them. He had an agent in Seattle, where the economy was particularly sour. It is very likely true, given the economic depression and the losses from the previous winter, that the Gales' business was in trouble and that the Gales' had few or no liquid assets and a real lack of ready capital.

Nevertheless, Katie asked, and the court agreed, that Joseph would pay for her attorney and court costs and provide Katie with the sum of thirty-five dollars at the first of every month until the final hearing and disposition of the case. Joseph was ordered to continue to conduct business but was restrained from selling or encumbering any property described in the complaint. This ruling, at least, would keep the property in the family for the time being and prevent Joseph from transferring their jointly acquired real estate.

Still, Joseph claimed, offering little or no proof, that all the property the Gales owned was either purchased with his own money or purchased before their marriage. His friend and partner Abner Smith declares in his letter to the court that Joseph had filed all his claims, except the Bettman one, in 1880 and 1881. However, this was during the time that Joseph and Katie were probably already together. Thus

Joseph mustered little to defend himself against Katie's assertion that these assets were acquired together and with her money and labor as much as with his.

Instead of offering evidence, Joseph responded to Katie's petition and claims by attacking her honor, temperament, ethnicity, and fitness. She was not a proper wife or mother to his children, he asserts. His was not only an ad hominem argument but one called an "argument by generalization," that is, one against the morality and fitness of Indians in general.

The court, however, held him to the point and he was made to answer. Joseph does not dispute the fact that he and Katie were legally married and had been since 1886. He admits that they had had "relations" before that and that Katie was his "employ." He married Katie, he says, to legitimize their children and notes that the first of their children, Elizabeth, or Lizzy, born in 1883, had died.

In the statements he filed with the court, he continues to assert that all the land and tidelands that Katie claimed as joint acquisitions were paid for by him before their marriage or procured with money he had accrued before the marriage. He does admit that the "cows horses yearlings household furniture" were "community property."

He dismisses the charge that he treated her like a menial. He proudly reports that he "always paid plaintiff for her labor and assistance in affiant's business." During the past year, he says, he had paid her more than $700 (around $17,000 today) and owed her $16 for picking eight sacks of oyster. The going wage that year, apparently, was $2 a sack. "I allow her to pick oysters on my own oyster beds and I then buy them" and "[give] her the regular market rate or price I would give Mossman Taylor or Smith or any other person of whom I would buy oysters."

If she couldn't support herself with the money he paid her, he suggests, it is because she behaved like an Indian. That is, she worked until she received payment (and this was true, he added, before they married), "then she would go off and stay with the Indians sometimes for months." He complains that she would "get up in the night" and be gone for days. He claims she was "running with Indian men." He portrays her as erratic and unpredictable. He denigrates her work habits.

Dismayed by her behavior, he complains that "she usually returned broke and affiant would give her employment again." She had, he says, "wild Indian ways." All this in the face of his own friends' characterization of her as an "industrious woman." She squandered her money, he says, giving it to her "tillicum and kindred." That is, she gave money to help support and enhance the lives of family members.

Then there was her temper, he continues. "She is an Indian woman of vulgar taste violent and unruly temper and has often made life a burden" for him, he says. Joseph portrays himself as the victim of Katie and her "large daughter Hattie Kittle," who was fourteen (or sixteen, if the 1889 census is correct) in 1893. Earlier in the month he was, he says, "eating supper at the table." He asked Katie about her trip to Tacoma over the Fourth of July. Katie mentioned her friend Lucy. Joseph asked, he said, if this was "blind eyed" Lucy. Katie became furious that he referred to her friend in this way. Joseph left the room and "lit my pipe."

Hattie and Katie stayed in the kitchen, talking in "Indian," Joseph says. Joseph understood enough, he says, that he knew that Hattie wondered why her mother allowed Joseph to speak about her "tillicums" (friends) in this way in her house. Joseph went outdoors, he says, to go feed his horse but was followed by the angry Katie, whose indignation was fueled by that of Hattie. She was "in a perfect fury" and, being the "most fleet-footed," seized his "long beard" and pulled with both hands. She was "raging like a mad bull" and he was "compelled to strike her," using "no more force than was necessary." Katie retreated with "a large quantity of affiants whiskers."

Studies of court cases during this period have shown that a "far greater level of violence was tolerated from men than was permissible for women."[4] It was not acceptable for a woman to strike her husband, because to do so challenged the man's position as head of household. However, some form of resisting or challenging husbands was not, apparently, uncommon within "frontier" marriages, though perhaps physical challenges were rare. A challenge from a wife was considered to be a particularly egregious act if the challenge was made in the company of a husband's male colleagues.

Joseph's cronies supported his complaints and offered more witness to Katie's temper. Mossman says he saw Katie biting Joseph's arm. "She cursed and abused Gale," Mossman says, using "as vile language as I ever heard from anyone." She talked partly in Chinook, according to Mossman. Mossman also says that Katie told him that Joseph didn't like her going to "the Indian house" (probably the Shaker Church) but that Joseph was "not as good as an Indian."

Abner Smith, Joseph's old friend of twenty years and partner with whom he had moved to Oyster Bay, supported Joseph's claim that all land and tidelands were purchased before the marriage and then added his own concern that Katie went off to the "Siwash or Indian Church" down the bay and on other excursions, usually taking the children with her.

Smith was troubled by Katie's visits to her Indian relatives, "of which she has a number," and asserts, in agreement with the other depositions filed on Joseph's behalf, that she was not a fit or proper person to have care of the children. Maud, he says, was under her control, and Ray, he claims, was "afraid of her." Smith claims he had never seen Joseph abuse Katie nor be "drunk at his place," a questionable assertion, given other testimony regarding Joseph's habitual use of alcohol.

There was drinking to excess at parties around Oyster Bay; one memoirist noted he was sick for days after an all-night gathering. Joseph's reputation as a drinker was recalled by Adolph Johnson in his memoir and by other white men in later, 1898, court files.

Smith's testament to Joseph's sobriety loses some credibility even in his own version of Katie's July assault on Joseph. Smith and Joseph had "a bottle of beer," he says, when Hattie and Katie and Maud came home from Puyallup, Tacoma, and Olympia on July 6.

The "Siwash or Indian Church" and the "Indian house" were probably references to the Shaker Church at Mud Bay or the Shaker Church built at Dick Jackson's homestead across and down the bay a bit from Katie's home.[5] Katie apparently was an adherent of the relatively new religion. She went to Dick Jackson's church and probably sometimes to the Mud Bay church for gatherings. Many of the Mud Bay and Oyster Bay Indians were Shakers and some were ministers. The use of alcohol would be offensive to Katie if she were following the founding principles of the church and the preaching of John Slocum and his followers. The Shakers are sober and meetings could last for hours or days; thus she would be absent from Oyster Bay in order to take part in church meetings.

John Slocum was an Indian logger who was well known around Oyster Bay, Mud Bay, and the Little and Big Skookum communities. John Slocum and his family lived on Big Skookum Inlet, reportedly at the mouth of John's Creek. Florence Howard, who conducted an archaeological survey of the area in 1949, was told that there had been an "intact" longhouse on the site until 1867. She was told that six families had occupied this house and that there was a row of other detached, smaller houses. The Slocum family, she was told, used the site even after the longhouse was demolished. There was a large, still-obvious shell midden at the site in 1949.[6] This is no doubt the longhouse and the same families who dined on shellfish with some of the European settlers referred to in a memoir of the Oakland area described in chapter 14.

Slocum and his family were friendly with Katie Gale. His son, Jack, had oyster beds close to Katie and Joseph Gale's and Jenny, his daughter, witnessed Katie's will in 1898.

In 1881 John Slocum had a logging accident that rendered him unconscious. He was, seemingly, dead. A coffin was sent for. Slocum, however, regained consciousness with a vision for a new life and a new church. The church he founded called for a cleansing from old habits, including drink and profanity. It incorporated some elements of indigenous practices and beliefs as well as bells and crosses and other elements from Christianity. The religion spread quickly around Puget

Sound and beyond and is still a viable, important institution that has many members among Indian people in the United States and Canada today.

The young Shaker Church, as it attracted membership from around the region, often met in defiance of Indian agents and missionaries. It gained new footing after its incorporation in June 1892.

The church's charter meeting was held at Mud Bay. Attorney James Wickersham of Tacoma was engaged by Mud Bay Louie and other South Puget Sound Shakers to help them to establish their rights and immunities as a religious community, a necessary move to get out from under the thumb of the harassing agents and people like Edwin Chalcraft on the Chehalis Reservation, who discouraged Indians under his administration from attending Shaker meetings.

The road to incorporation was one of the unintended consequences of the 1875 Indian Homestead Act. A number of prominent church members had applied for and received land off reservation.[7] The act extended the benefits of the Homestead Act of 1862 by allowing Indians to apply. Section 15 provides that "every Indian born in the United States, who is the head of a family, or who has arrived at the age of twenty-one years, and who has abandoned or may hereafter abandon his tribal relation, shall, on making satisfactory proof of such abandonment, under rules to be prescribed by the Secretary of the interior, be entitled to the benefits of the Act entitled 'An Act to secure homesteads to actual settlers on the public domain.'"

The landholding, off-reservation Indians in the Mud Bay, Oyster Bay, and Chehalis areas apparently considered themselves, as the act stipulated, unattached to their "tribes." At least, they were willing to apply for Indian homesteads and declare themselves to be "unattached." The meaning of "unattached" was apparently vague enough that being considered such for legal purposes did not interfere with their daily lives and relations with Indian kin and friends. As holders of Indian homesteads, they were eligible for all the rights and immunities of citizenship.[8] Thus the legal status of these landholders and church leaders under the Indian Homestead Act allowed them to establish a corporation within the laws and statutes governing the state and Thurston County.

Wickersham met with Shakers at the house of Louis Yow-a-luch, or Yowaluch, known as "Mud Bay Louie," on July 7, 1892. Present were John Slocum, the church "seer"; John Smith of the Chehalis Reservation; Jack Simmons of the Puyallup Reservation; and Bill James of the Puyallup Reservation. Both Jim and Charlie Walker were present at this meeting. All of these men were elected to be elders of the newly organized church. Ministers appointed included Slocum and Yowaluch as well as James Tobin and Dick Jackson.

Wickersham was a city attorney for Tacoma who became a member of the Washington state legislature in 1894. These were two among other posts he held in his life. In 1891 he had argued a defense for a white man accused of selling liquor to an allotted Puyallup Indian. He forwarded a defense based on the Dawes Act. The act, he said, had, in assigning the man an allotment, granted the Indian man citizenship and therefore he had no special status that would prohibit the sale. The win was double edged. Wickersham was involved with men who argued that because Indians were landholding, allotted citizens, there was no longer a Puyallup tribe and non-Indian investors could deal directly with Indians on land matters without the interference of the Indian agent. In addition, unallotted land, they argued, reverted to the government and was available for purchase. This argument, carried to its conclusion, would certainly have led to the dissolution of the Puyallup tribe and rendered many tribal members poor and landless. The Dawes Act certainly furthered the goal of dissolution of tribes in many instances, the Puyallup instance aside.

Wickersham, however, in spite of Puyallup controversies, has been portrayed by those who have studied the Shaker Church as a defender of Indian rights.[9] Homer Barnett, whose book on the Shaker Church is considered a classic, notes that Wickersham was a "vigorous" supporter of the church and the rights of its Indian citizen members.[10]

Others, notably George Castile, dispute this benign interpretation of Wickersham's motives and actions.[11]

James Tobin was already a Shaker minister before being named such in the original church charter. Tobin became a respected member of the church after he and Louisa Tobin acquired land in 1890 and moved to their Eld Inlet homestead permanently. Then, after the church was officially chartered, his role was central to the continuing development of the church and its recruitment efforts. Dick Jackson, a farmer on Oyster Bay, was another early and important member and minister; he built a small church building on his land just down bay and across from Katie's house.

Myron Eells, the superintendent at the Skokomish Reservation, called the Shakers "earnest." They were known to be "moral in character." R. E. L. Newberne, in an 1896 report to the Commissioner of Indian Affairs, says that "Shakerism" was the "principal and most helpful religion" the Indians had. Its adherents, he writes, "have done much to discourage intemperance among the Indians." "It is," he adds, "the only religion, so far as I know, that will keep an Indian of Western Washington sober if he is inclined to get drunk."

Yet the Shakers were constantly harassed and even jailed for practicing their religion, including curing or healing rituals that involved deploying a "shaking" movement over the ill person.

Even church members' mobility was restricted. In 1884, for example, the Court of Indian Offenses on the Chehalis Reservation passed the following set of orders aimed at keeping the religion from spreading:

> All Indians visiting the Reservation shall go directly to the Head Chief, Jim Walker, or the Superintendent, for permission to remain, which shall be given in writing.
>
> No Indian belonging to the Chehalis Reservation is to leave the Reservation for any purpose, without a written Pass, signed by the Head Chief, Jim Walker, or the Superintendent.
>
> The giving of "shakes" to sick people, in treating them for sickness,

> is in violation of Rule 6, in "Rules Governing Courts of Indian Offences" and is prohibited, but if an Indian begins to shake and cannot stop doing so, he must not have any other person present, unless it be his wife, or the husband, as the case may be. Children shall not be present.
>
> No one shall offer to give another Indian the "shakes," but if an Indian requests it be given to him, it may be done, providing they apply to the Head Chief, Jim Walker, or the Superintendent, in advance, so that both may be present to see that no Government Rule is violated.
>
> Any violation of this Order, and punishment for the same, will be determined by the Police Court on this Reservation.

Edwin Chalcraft (the superintendent referred to in the orders) signed this document on April 14. He wrote, cynically, that it was "safe" to require Jim Walker's signature on the orders because he was "loyal to me" and couldn't write and therefore couldn't "sign his name to a pass." Thus, apparently, was some business accomplished in reservation life of the 1880s.

By the time the church was chartered, of course, Jim Walker was a Shaker himself. But in 1884 Chalcraft thought he had a dupe. The contempt for and effort to control the Shakers were all part of the government's and non-Indian churches' intention to colonize and assimilate Indians physically, mentally, and spiritually and to eliminate any vestiges of Indian religious and healing practices. Missionaries, operating in accord with Grant's Peace Policy, were active throughout the region, including Catholics and Presbyterians on the Puyallup Reservation (with the Presbyterians also offering occasional services on the Nisqually and Chehalis Reservations), Episcopalians on the Quinault Reservation, and Congregationalists on the Skokomish Reservation. Thus Shakerism was in competition with established and well-connected denominations for the hearts and minds of the local American Indian population.

One anecdote from the period tells of a sanctimonious white Olympian who rebuked a Mud Bay Shaker for the strange beliefs and rituals of his sect. The Indian man pointed out that he had seen the white churchgoers draped in long, white garments, singing and walking into the waters of Budd Inlet to be "baptized." What could be stranger than that? he asked the white man.[12]

Long and frequent Shaker meetings could account for many of Katie Gale's alleged absences from her home. Her membership in the Shaker Church, no doubt, bears heavily on how she lived her life after the early 1880s and why she may have grown to dislike some of her husband's ways and think of Indian men as his "betters."

Fear of and disdain for the Shaker religion could account for some of the concerns expressed in court that an Oyster Bay woman, the spouse of a prominent oysterman, was a follower. Claims that Katie Gale was "unpredictable" may have been expressions made out of ignorance of the church itself and the uncertainty of the times generally. Stories of the Ghost Dance religion and the massacre at Wounded Knee (1890) were fresh in people's minds. Sitting Bull had been captured and was shot dead in 1890. There were still what European Americans called "savages" in the land, and not all of the Mud Bay and Oyster Bay Indians were "civilized" according to white standards. Though the maritime community had a history of peaceful relations, intermarriage, and cooperation, the post-1870s settlers, many of whom were entrepreneurs with different goals from those of the first, farmer immigrants, seemed a different sort. And the times had changed. National policies and military action might seem on the surface to have settled the "Indian Question." But the fight between Indians and whites was still being fought in some homes and harbors where people did not or would not understand one another or were determined to maintain ascendency over resources and the future of the region.

The defense brought forward by Joseph Gale against Katie Gale's suit boiled down to this: Katie is not fit to be the mother of Maud and Ray because she is an Indian. Her behavior was outside the norms of white society and the expectations for a woman in the Victorian age. He, Joseph, was well within his rights to expect more and to have punished her for her behavior. Oh yes, she may have had legal standing in the court. She may have been a citizen. But she was culturally and behaviorally, decidedly, still an Indian. That was, he argued, cause enough to take her children away. Maud and Ray Gale, the children of Joseph, deserved to be white and to be brought into the white society outside the influence of their mother, her kin, and her friends.

Joseph brought two more European American oystermen to his defense. The first was the oyster farmer Samuel K. Taylor, who had no idea, he said, what Katie said to Joseph because he couldn't understand Chinook. Less harsh in his affidavit than Smith, the major concern expressed in Taylor's testimony was seemingly a hypothetical. The children should be with their father because he would send them to school. The Gale children were five and seven years old during this proceeding. It is likely that there had been no occasion to know whether Katie would or would not send them to school. No evidence was brought forth to support Taylor's worry. On the contrary, some of Katie's relatives were educated and many younger children in mixed families were going to school. It doesn't seem likely she would have deprived them of any opportunities to learn. Taylor was also distressed about Maud. Maud had apparently been injured from a fall and was required to walk with crutches as a result. Joseph's allies and witnesses complained that Katie had not allowed proper medical treatment.

Dennis Hurley, another oysterman who came forward in support of Joseph, did not, he said, understand Chinook or "Indian" either, so he didn't know what Katie said to Joseph when he witnessed her "abusing" him or being "rude" or "very violent." Her tone and manner, apparently, were enough to cause Hurley to judge her unfit.

Joseph Gale's last two witnesses were Chinese employees, men who had worked for him three years and one year, respectively, and who lived in a float house in front of the Gale homestead. They were there to defend against Katie's accusations of Joseph's cruelty. The men said they'd never seen Joseph strike Katie, nor had they seen Joseph drunk. There was no mention of what they could or could not understand of Katie's "Chinook" or conversations between Joseph and Katie.

In Joseph's final "answer and cross complaint," he further developed the central theme introduced by his witnesses: Katie is unfit to have the children. The plaintiff, he said, "endeavors to teach [Maud] disrespect for defendant and for the White race. She teaches her the Superstitions of her race — That plaintiff teaches said Maud immorality. That plaintiff associates with Indians against defendants objection frequents immoral company. She is irregular and wild in her habits. She is now with her Indian relatives or tilicums as she styles them."

He reiterated his complaint that Katie had given her money to "Indian relatives and Tilicums" instead of saving it for her own and the children's sustenance. In the end, Joseph asked for "absolute control of said children that he may have them properly trained and educated free from the influence of the plaintiff."

He asked that the plaintiff take nothing from her suit and that the bonds of matrimony be annulled and dissolved. In exchange, he suggested that the property alleged to be the separate property of the defendant be so decreed and that the livestock and household furniture be divided equitably.

18 *Turn Around*

ON SEPTEMBER 6, 1893, Joseph Gale filed an astonishing sworn statement with the clerk of courts in Mason County. In it he says that the "plaintiff and defendant have settled their property differences as shown by the annexed exhibit," the plaintiff has "entered into possession of the property granted to her," and that there is "no necessity for the continuance of said order for alimony or restraining order."

In early August the court had required that Joseph stay away from Katie's property and that he mortgage the property acknowledged by the court not to be at issue so that he could begin to pay alimony to Katie. Joseph said the court orders would prevent him from doing his business. This "hardship" apparently motivated him to find a solution that would cut his losses. By August 29 he had arrived at an understanding with Katie. Their agreement took the form of a typewritten contract between them. It was attached to the sworn statement delivered to the court.

In the agreement Katie received title to a strip of land 210 feet wide on the waterfront bordering the east side of Lot 1, Section 21. It was approximately six acres. This was presumably the land on which her house stood. She also received the west half of the northwest quarter of Section 21 in Township 19 North, Range 3 West, a total of eighty upland acres. That was the property they had acquired from Ada Hartman. She also received the Bettman claim, the tidelands in front of her waterfront property.

Joseph had also agreed to convey to her six acres of oyster ground across the channel, part of the other Gale claim. Joseph agreed to buy eight-plus acres for Katie from this claim, meaning that the claim alone did not allow him, given the rules of the state, to assure her ownership. He was not to pay more than twelve dollars an acre for these lands, according to the agreement.

Joseph was also to pay for the costs of a divorce ("which may be hereafter obtained between these parties" and "not to exceed one hundred dollars") and to be allowed to send the children to "some good school." He was to bear the cost of their "custody and expense of maintenance." Katie was to retain her sewing machine and all the household goods except for Joseph's personal items. She was also to retain half of all the livestock except the "two fillies" that belonged to the children. Joseph retained all the rest of the property, the bulk of the oyster claims.

This agreement secured Katie Gale's future and assured her the life of a well-to-do woman or, at the least, one with a steady income. Joseph may have been mean and he may have been cruel and abusive and he may have been desperate, but this settlement was the act of an honorable man who acknowledged his wife's role in accruing their wealth.

The agreement was witnessed by James Wickersham (the attorney for the Shakers), George T. Reid, and Jack Simmons, an Indian oysterman, and signed by both Joseph and Katie Gale. (Katie marked a cross above her name, asserting thereby that the document had been read to her and met with her approval.)

Wickersham's name does not appear on the earlier court papers. Katie's attorney of record in that proceeding was J. E. Sligh. That Wickersham's name appears here on the agreement is significant. Was Wickersham watchdogging Katie's courtroom dealings? Was she acquainted with him through his support of the Shaker Church and among those to whose rights he was attending? Did Shaker Church members, including Dick Jackson and James Tobin, and Wickersham help her to understand her rights and even encourage her action?

This agreement was a victory for Katie. She was awarded essentially what she asked for, including the land and tidelands she claimed to have paid for. Katie was now a landholding Indian citizen with the means to support herself and her children.

But the victory was also one for Joseph. He had negotiated to have his children educated away from Katie's influence. And he held on to most of their valuable oyster lands, the center of his industry and the business upon which he was building his reputation in the white economic and political world.

As vituperative as the 1893 proceedings were, Joseph and Katie Gale did not complete the paperwork that would have finalized a divorce or an annulment after the settlement. What happened? Though Katie wore the scars of Joseph's beating on her forehead and had achieved virtual financial independence from Joseph with the division of the property, she agreed that they would stay together as a couple, at least legally. Maybe she wanted to retain her relationship with the children and felt that would not happen if they divorced. Maybe Joseph needed her support in the business and rights to use her shoreline for his business. Katie said in court papers that she had forgiven Joseph's earlier abuses. She and Joseph had (and community people who knew them concurred) assumed some form of marital relations again after the 1893 agreement that ended the first suit was signed. It was a reconciliation of sorts.

The children did not leave the home but attended the Oyster Bay district school in Kamilche instead of being sent away from Katie and their home. Joseph went about his business, which required, apparently, that he spend most of his time away from Oyster Bay, and Katie continued her labors on the oyster beds. She was, from this time on, running her own, parallel, business with her own employees, sink float, and culling house.

However, this new arrangement did not last long.

In January 1898 it was Joseph who filed for divorce. He renewed his bitter complaints about Katie in the courts and made it clear he was determined to be rid of his spouse. He again asked for sole custody of their children.

By 1898 Henry and Hattie, Katie's elder children, had both died of tuberculosis, in 1895 and 1897 respectively. Katie had the disease as well and must already have been displaying some symptoms of it. As early as 1893 there was a newspaper report that said she was too ill to get out of bed. During the late nineteenth century about one in seven deaths in the United States were caused by tuberculosis. There was no cure and no real treatment. The best one could do is travel to a better climate or to a sanatorium. Better perhaps to die on top of Thomas Mann's Magic Mountain, rugs pulled around one's knees and lounging in the pure air, than at home. That kind of treatment and retreat, however, took money that working people didn't have. Katie possessed a bounty of oysters, land and tidelands, kin and family, but not the wherewithal or proclivity to travel to a spa or tuberculosis clinic.

Disease shortened many lives in the 1880s and 1890s. Hattie and Henry died young, but so did little Lizzie.[1] That child lived barely six years. Katie's near neighbor Louisa, the wife of Abner Smith, died of tuberculosis. Louisa's two children, both afflicted, were sent to Yakima, where it was hoped the drier climate would heal them, according to Tim McMillan, whose family have been associated with the Olympia Oyster Company for generations. Katie's neighbors on the north side were the McClures. The McClure homestead was right above Katie's oyster beds. Nellie McClure labored on the homestead after her husband died, probably of tuberculosis or other lung diseases. Nellie remarried Emmet Sutton but succumbed to the disease herself not long after. Harriet Korter's husband and two children died during the same period.

White women born in 1850 could expect to live to about age forty in the 1890s, and white men to about age thirty-eight, on average. The figures for American Indians and other racial groups in the United

States during this period are less reliable, though living past childhood and into one's twenties increased the probability for a relative long life.

Katie Gale, over forty, had already lived a fairly reasonable lifespan given all she had endured and been exposed to.

One can only imagine what instigated Joseph's renewed, 1898, attack on Katie's character, desire for divorce, and interest in the children. He claimed that he wanted to prepare the children, Ray and Maud, now ten and twelve, "for the station in life they are entitled to occupy." There is no indication that he had made much effort in this direction during the previous five years. He had been given by the court in 1893 the authority to send them to any school he wished. In fact, they were attending the local, public Oyster Bay school, along with all the other white, Indian, and mixed-race children on the bay. Witnesses brought to testify for Katie declared he had contributed nothing to their care for the previous six months to a year.

Perhaps Joseph was under pressure from his twenty-seven-year-old mistress, Lillian, to divorce. Lillian McDonald, with whom Joseph had spent a great deal of time after 1893, was from Scio, Oregon. The two may have lived together when Joseph was on those long trips away from Oyster Bay.

Joseph was almost exclusively in Seattle now, doing business in the burgeoning, postdepression city that was about to be delivered a miracle boom. Joseph couldn't have known this when he became a wholesale dealer in oysters, crabs, and clams on Commercial Dock at the foot of Madison Street. What an exciting and different life that would have been for him compared with the life on little Oyster Bay!

Joseph's life in Seattle must have made the years of struggle and neglected duties on Oyster Bay seem a perhaps avoidable misery. The future looked bright and promising once again. Joseph had turned fifty. Perhaps he felt it was time to act before life got away from him. And then the possibility of a fortune was placed right in his lap.

19 *Joseph's Complaints*

IN 1889 much of the downtown business district of Seattle had burned to the ground. But undaunted, leaders of the city rallied and immediately began rebuilding. Mainstays of Seattle retail commerce for years to come, such as Bartell's drugstore, Frederick and Nelson department store, and the Bon Marché department store, opened their doors for business. Todd Shipyards was not only doing business but delivered more than two dozen vessels to customers by the late 1890s. There were electric trolley lines. The transcontinental railroads had been making trips to Seattle throughout the decade. Things were looking good, even though the depression of 1893 had slowed things to an almost halt for a while.

Then, in July 1897, this city of about forty thousand had been visited by a miracle. It was called the steamship *Portland*, a steamer running full-tilt with a load of very excited, rough-and-ready passengers on a return trip from Alaska. It unloaded at Schwabacher's dock on the Seattle waterfront. Its cargo wasn't food or goods from Asia or even ordinary travelers or entrepreneurs come to see this relatively new Washington State and the Pacific Northwest for themselves. No, indeed. The steamer *Portland*'s passengers were sixty-eight Klondike miners on their way from St. Michael, Alaska. They had struck it rich.

The rush was on, and word spread via telegraph after the gold and the ship landed. Thousands of Seattleites left for the north as soon as they could book passage. The Pacific Coast Steamship Company had begun carrying passengers and freight from Seattle to Juneau in 1889. Now it was commissioned to carry gold seekers on the "poor man's route," which would drop enthusiasts in Skagway, there to make their arduous way to the Klondike. The Pacific Coast Company's ship, the *Willamette*, left from the Pacific Coast Steamship dock on August 7, 1897, already loaded with four hundred people from Tacoma.

As time went by, people came from all over the state to board other, later steamers at the docks. Some of them brought baggage on pack trains. One observer wrote that people brought the things they would need to make money, including mining apparatus, gaming tables, and bakery appliances. The observer noted that there were physicians aboard as well, pledged to go for gold if not patients. "Over twenty steamers were . . . due to sail before September 1st."[1]

Prospectors and entrepreneurs rushed from all around the country to Seattle to get supplies for their Alaska journey and book passage to the north. The Canadian Mounted Police required that each person bring a year's supply of food and equipment. That meant a big opportunity in Seattle to sell to the eager would-be miners, off for an adventure of a lifetime. The businesses already in Seattle flourished, and many others came to the city to start new businesses or cash in on the work the rush would support. Seattle and its citizens were well positioned to make a bundle from gold fever.[2]

Joseph Gale would have to try hard not to make money in the current Seattle atmosphere. His business was located on a dock just between Colman Dock (Pier 52, the main ferry terminal in Seattle in modern times) and Schwabacher's dock (Piers 57 and 58). Northern Pacific Railroad lines ran conveniently right in front of the docks. Schwabacher's already had a reputation. It had been the site of the docking of the Japanese ship that heralded the opening of a modern trade with Asia in 1896. Now there were the gold miners. The economy was booming, with adventurers eating, drinking, buying supplies, and spending their good fortune, or hopes for same, in the streets of Seattle. Joseph was right there.

Joseph was also serving as Washington State's deputy fish commissioner. He had amassed more wealth and stature in the years since the first divorce lawsuit. An Indian wife must have seemed to him a growing burden and an inconvenience to his rising status and ambitions. He was, observers on Oyster Bay said, busily engaged and seldom at home with Katie or even seen on the bay.

However, in spite of all his dealings in the robust Seattle economy and success in the political world outside Oyster Bay, he was, he told the judge, broke. This was his response to three separate contempt charges issued by the judge in the 1898 divorce case when he refused to follow a court order to supply Katie with the money to defend herself. He had lost money, he said, operating his wholesale business. There are no records in the court files to support or refute this claim. He asserted that not only had he lost money in business, but he had gone further into debt to buy considerably more land and tidelands in the five years since the 1893 proceedings. Perhaps this survivor of the Lost Wagon Train just didn't have a head for business.

Furthermore, he claimed, he owed Richard Sandam for an oyster bed. He owed Gilbert Ward, Dick Helser, and "Madam Coulter" for oysters purchased from them for resale. His taxes on land in Mason County were three years in arrears. He owed merchants in Shelton "$40 or 50 so dollars" for household supplies. He owed $300 to Tom Kee, a Chinese-Umatilla man whom he had left in charge of the Oyster Bay harvesting operations. "All the money I possess on earth at this time is $5.00," he lamented in answer to the judge's rulings against him.

He was poor, he said. But cash flow wasn't his only problem. He complained to the court about the "hardships attendant upon" the daily and nightly labors involved with oyster gathering. He had, he said, consulted with a Dr. Hugh Wyman, who told him that he must "never again go upon the oyster beds or superintend gathering." The doctor had told him to "never again put on gum boots" or he could not "answer for the consequences." He had had to, he said, "content myself with contracting the gathering of oysters." The evidence is that he seems to have been doing just that for several years.

The fact that his wife was consumptive yet had to continue to harvest to support herself and their children was not mentioned in his complaints or anywhere else in the court record until the very end of the proceeding.

Witnesses attested to the fact that Katie and Joseph indeed continued to live as husband and wife after their "reconciliation," though not often in the same house. Joseph seemed to believe that the division of property in 1893 freed him of any responsibility for the family. He complained that as a result of the settlement in 1893, Katie should have an income equal to his and adequate to her needs. He had not, he said, anticipated that he would be required to pay her anything ever again after the agreement.

Still, Joseph wanted a divorce now and he wanted his children. He again raised his objections to Katie's fitness as a mother. In Article VI of his written statement, he said that he was a "white, native born American, and the defendant is a full blooded Indian person." It was for this reason, he wrote, and their incompatible temperaments, that he could not continue marital relations. "Said children should be awarded to this plaintiff," he asserted, "for the reason stated and for the reason that the plaintiff alone is able to properly care for and educate them for the station in life they are entitled to occupy."

His declaration clearly contradicted his statement that Katie, after the 1893 settlement, should have property and money equal to his. She should, according to his own statements, be able to properly care for and educate the children as well as he. It is, of course, that she was an Indian that was really his problem. At the end of the day, Joseph believed that Katie could not prepare "his" children for polite European American society nor groom them to be the children of the successful public figure Joseph Gale.

Katie just can't learn, he says, echoing the sentiments expressed by Judge Greene when he instructed the jury in the Mud Bay murder case. She can't change. He says he had tried to educate her. In spite of his efforts, he complains, she remained an "uncivilized, ignorant character, and given to the same superstitious acts of living and general demeanor of the uncivilized members of the race from which she springs." She would not, apparently, assimilate. And unless she were assimilated, Joseph could not rise further in this world with Katie by his side.

Katie, in her own reply to Joseph's crude, racist depiction of her, "admits" that she is an "Indian woman." This is not to be read as a self-deprecating comment but an acknowledgement of the truth of her identity. She is an Indian, yes. She is not a pretend white woman. However, Joseph was dead wrong when he used her ethnicity to argue that she was not fit nor able to be a good wife and mother. She had never turned her back on kindred, her beliefs, and her ways. And there was no need to. Because, she says, though she is an Indian woman, she "appreciates and realizes the duty of a woman to her husband and has the feelings common to womankind regardless of race."

Katie's old friends from Oyster Bay, highly respectable European American people she had known for years, came to her defense. Frank Gingrich, William Krise, Christopher C. Simmons, and Joseph Kullrich all stepped forward to file affidavits on her behalf. Krise and Simmons were more farmers than oystermen, though Krise had had some beds. They had been among the first wave of European American homesteaders to the area. They were of excellent reputation and character. As farmers and part of a generation that had preceded Joseph Gale and the oystermen to the area, they seem to have had a different relationship generally with Indian people. Simmons and Krise lived in the Kamilche Valley area on land adjoining Franklin and Anne Kennedy's homestead. They'd known Katie for over twenty-five years and as neighbors they'd watched the Katie and Joseph drama unfold, helpless to know quite what to do. Nevertheless, when opportunity came to defend Katie in a court of law, they all stated unequivocally that Katie was a virtuous woman and a good wife who supported her children by herself.

Stories about Katie Gale from those families who saw the good in her live on to this day. Justin Taylor, a longtime local shellfish grower, remembered his mother saying positive things about Katie Gale. His mother was born into the Waldrip family in 1892. Though she was young, she remembered later that she "liked" Katie Gale and thought enough of her to pass that recollection to her son. This one brief story remembered by an elder oysterman and passed on to me in 2010 told me more about Katie Gale's position on Oyster Bay than I could ever gather from court archives.

The affidavits, however, contain rich detail. Katie's children, Christopher Simmons declares in court documents, were "unusually bright and well taken care of." Simmons says that it was "generally known" that Joseph was living with another woman. Both Simmons and John Leslie, a well-educated Indian man, supported Katie's contention, first made in 1893, that Joseph was a heavy drinker.

Sometime in February, while his complaint was making its way through the courts, Joseph forcibly abducted his children. He smashed Katie's door, tore it off its hinges, and grabbed the youngsters. John Leslie, who witnessed the attack, thought he was probably drunk.

Leslie was a particularly compelling member of Katie's inner circle of friends and supporters and a trusted observer and witness. He was the son of Elizabeth John, born in 1838. She was spouse of James Leslie. Elizabeth was known also by her first name, Paw pi ished or Pam-pi-i-she, according to Squaxin census roles. She died in 1917, at age seventy-nine.

As a student John Leslie was known to Edwin Chalcraft. Chalcraft had moved on from the Chehalis Reservation to take over the superintendency of the Puyallup Indian School. He praised Leslie's work and intelligence. After Puyallup Indian School, Leslie was sent to Carlisle Indian School in 1892. He began working as a photographer while there and even made a trip to New York to take "snap shots of the foot-ball game," the November 1895 *Indian Helper* school newspaper reports. He took long bicycle trips with friends. He was a generally athletic, lively young man who took his camera with him everywhere and was liked immensely. At the time of the 1898 court proceedings he had been out of Carlisle for two years. He had left suddenly in March 1896 without graduating. The school paper reports that "he went without saying good-by to some of his best friends who awoke on Friday morning and found him gone. It was not a run-a-way, but only a sudden ending of a plan contemplated for several weeks." His photography mentor, Mr. Andrews, said, "There was a gloom all day in the gallery."

Leslie worked around Olympia as a photographer before becoming a deckhand and later a fireman and engineer on the little steamers that traveled the waters of Puget Sound. At the time of his deposition on behalf of Katie's defense, he was working on the *City of Shelton*. He seems to have garnered quite a positive reputation around the South Sound. He was handsome and seemingly universally admired. Pictures show him in a dark shirt, dress coat, and wearing a dark hat at a rakish angle. He might have known Katie Gale through Squaxin family connections or even through people they both knew on the Puyallup Reservation. He would have given her a hand when she caught the *City of Shelton* at its New Kamilche/Little Skookum stop. He'd have helped with the children, her baggage, and sometimes, some bags of oysters bound for Olympia.

John Leslie deplored what he had seen happen the day of the abduction and asserted that the children had always gone to the Oyster Bay district school and were "excellently educated and trained." Leslie, a conscientious student and dutiful reporter, would know. What is the problem? Leslie seemed to wonder. "The little girl cried and screamed and did not desire to leave her mother," Leslie testified.

Maud was taken to a place "unknown" to Katie. Ray was, presumably, kept with Joseph. Katie was distraught. The children had always been with her, she said.

Maud then made her only courtroom statement, by way of written testament. Her father, it seemed, had placed her with Providence St. Amable Academy in Olympia, where indeed there are records of her attendance from February 1898 through June of that year and again from September through November. Records show that she was enrolled again during the year of 1899 and for the first two months of the school year 1901.

In her deposition, she declares bravely that she wanted to be with her mother but that her father had "ordered me not to go back . . . and I am afraid he would whip me if I did." "I am," she says, "in control of the sisters. . . . I know nobody here." She asserts that she read in the "fourth reader" and had "studied in arithmetic and geography and always go to school when there is school in my district." Yet St. Amable's kept her away from her mother and other Indian kin and this was what her father wanted for her.

After the abduction was reported, the court allowed Joseph to keep Maud with the Sisters of St. Amable but ordered him to pay all costs. Ray, in the meantime, went back to stay with his mother. Ray was certainly in the Oyster Bay district school until the end of the 1898 school year. His name appears as one of the student speakers on the school's spring program. It was from these Oyster Bay School years, apparently, that his friend Adolph remembered him and his mother.

Joseph was relentless. Even though he had by force usurped at least partial control of the children, he was not satisfied. In July 1898 Joseph filed another complaint against Katie. She was, he says, "continually in the habit of visiting the minor girl child [Maud] . . . and upon various pretexes [*sic*], taking said child from said school and keeping her out of the same for hours at a time at which time she is allowed to consort with Indians and indian [*sic*] women of disreputable character." He asked the court to order that Katie be prevented from removing Maud from the school and that she be allowed to visit Maud only if unaccompanied by other Indians.

In December 1898 Joseph, still defying the courts and resisting paying any court-ordered support funds to Katie, acknowledged that Katie was dying. In a show of concern and sympathy, he allowed Maud to leave the Olympia school so that she could be at "her mother's bedside to there care for and attend upon her mother." This must have eased Katie's last days and brought some joy and relief to the young girl, Maud. Joseph also asked that the divorce proceedings be dismissed. Perhaps he supposed it would be to his advantage economically not to be divorced from Katie at her death, given her property holdings.

He added that he hoped to be discharged from paying the court-ordered attorney fees incurred on Katie's behalf. His final bill from the superior court was for $35.80.

These last entries in the 1898 divorce file speak volumes as to the complexity of the relationship between Katie and Joseph Gale. Joseph was capable of perhaps generous, compassionate gestures and seems, from what we know, always on the verge of redeeming himself. But his stinginess and trifling over money seemed never to end.

20 *The Oyster Bay School*

IT WAS not only her father who would exhort Maud to leave her mother and mother's people behind and attach herself to a European American worldview. Maud's books, the readers used in that time by children all across the United States, were full of moralistic teaching tales such as "The Boy Who Cried Wolf," "The Goose That Laid the Golden Eggs," and other parables and fables that were intended to inculcate values and teach principles held to be proper by the dominant culture. Maud read about the Pilgrims and read the poetry of John Greenleaf Whittier and Henry Longfellow. Her geography book was no doubt very like the one on my bookshelf that was used as a text by my schoolmaster great-grandfather in his Ohio one-room schoolhouse. The lessons in that publication would have taught her that "in early times people lived in caves or trees; ate only such things as roots, wild fruits, insects and the fish or wild animals they could kill. They wore no clothing but skins of animals; had few weapons except clubs, wooden spears, and bows and arrows; and only such tools as they could make out of stone, bone and wood." She would have learned that "Indians in America have scarcely made more progress" since that period. "Such people are called savages," she would have gathered from the text, "and their manner of life is called savagery." On the other hand, she would come to understand that Europeans have "practically taken possession of North and South America and Australia, and are rapidly taking possession of Africa." The Europeans, she would read, are "the most civilized of all races." Her father, the man who abducted her from her home and whom she feared, was clearly doing all he could to convince her of that fact. The schools and books were doing their best to help out.

The Oyster Bay School was the primary instrument used to further American consensus culture and its values in the small, culturally pluralistic maritime community. Joseph and Katie Gale's surviving children, Ray and Maud, at one time or another attended this simply constructed one-room schoolhouse with other children from around the bay.

It was a neat, wooden, twenty-four-by-forty-foot gable-roofed schoolhouse, painted inside and out. It had one potbellied stove and enough desks for twenty students, though more could be squeezed in if the small ones shared. There were three eight-paned glass windows on each of the building's long sides. At one end of the rectangular room was a large desk fitted with a bronze handbell and a large globe of the world. The school even had a pump organ, bought and paid for by local fund-raising programs. The school was used for various community functions, including meetings of the Oyster Bay Literary Society. Out back, on the bay side, was an outhouse and tall wooden spar on which the children ceremoniously hoisted an American flag each morning. At the end of the day the flag was carefully lowered and neatly folded and tucked so only a triangular field of stars was visible.

The school population in the late 1890s was composed of Indian, Caucasian, and "mixed" boys and girls, with complexions ranging from the fairest Nordic to the deepest, richest caramel brown. Some children were quite handsome in their suspenders and suit jackets enhanced with printed, colorful neckties. Other youngsters were resplendent in large, handmade lace collars and calico dresses. A few boys even sported up-to-date, fashionable, floppy bow ties worn around and under the broad collars of white shirts.

Miss Frances L. Galusha held forth at the school for only a couple of terms and then left to move back east and marry. Miss Galusha was a graduate of Kansas State Normal School with an emphasis on elementary education. She considered her move west to be an adventure of a lifetime, as did many young female teachers of her day. She was a sweet-faced, earnest woman with a halo of thin, straight brown hair worn up in a high bun at the top of her head. She had lovely deep-set eyes. Her manner of dress followed the style of the day. She wore fashionable, puffed-sleeve, high frilly necked, figure-fitting garments. Achieving her always-fetching presentation each morning was not easy. Her boardinghouse room was rough, its light dim, and the availability of a hot and private bath unpredictable.

She adored her mostly cheerful, ruddy charges and conveyed many uplifting messages to them as humbly and kindly as she could. She was a passionate professional with progressive ideals. She was well trained to teach children spelling, penmanship, science, literature, history, geography, and mathematics up to grade eight.

Discipline was rarely a problem, but then her adult helpers, including a rough and stout matron who cooked luncheons for the children on site, put up with no nonsense and intervened when necessary. The matron had the voice of a Foghorn Leghorn and the personality to go with it. Still, she settled any unruly children. They responded to her command presence, and the pancake turner she brandished, with instant obeisance.

Joseph Gale himself served as the school's director at some point. His job was to oversee the budget and make reports to the state of Washington as necessary. He insisted on a rigorous, always practical approach to dealing with mixed and Indian children. His goals were strictly in line with the dominant culture's ideals of total assimilation. These children must be cut no slack when it came to language. Though many of these Oyster Bay children were brought up by mothers who spoke Twana, Chehalis, Quinault, Southern or Northern Lushootseed, Yakama, German, Finnish, and other languages, and were at least bilingual, only English was allowed in the school. Indian languages and ideologies were particularly frowned upon. Any foolish ideas that children brought into classroom conversations that might represent something learned from their mothers' heathen cultures must be quashed. Miss Galusha, though often put off by Mr. Gale's rough manner and domineering demeanor, did her best to abide by his requirements.

The year before Katie Gale died, on May 30, 1898, Miss Galusha, with her pupils, "rendered an excellent program, including many patriotic pieces and songs."[1] Miss Galusha herself held forth on the school's organ, pumping vigorously at its foot pedals and offering a stirring if somewhat erratic version of "America," to which the students sang all verses. Miss Galusha's bosom swelled, tears filled her lovely hazel eyes, and her pumping became more energetic as the students sang the fifth stanza:

Our glorious Land to-day,
'Neath Education's sway,
Soars upward still.
Its hills of learning fair,
Whose bounties all may share,
Behold them everywhere
On vale and hill!
Thy safeguard, Liberty,
The school shall ever be,
Our Nation's pride!
No tyrant hand shall smite,
While with encircling might
All here are taught the Right
With Truth allied.
Beneath Heaven's gracious will
The stars of progress still
Our course do sway;
In unity sublime
To broader heights we climb,
Triumphant over Time,
God speeds our way!

The Reverend Samuel Francis Smith wrote this wildly patriotic hymn in 1831 while he was a student at Andover Theological Seminary and now children all across the United States learned and sang it to their appreciative parents.

The program continued, featuring performances by the school's students. Jane Burr sawed her way through a violin solo. The audience of parents and community members must have politely applauded her efforts. Two little girls sang Thomas Moore's "Those Evening Bells":

Those evening bells! Those evening bells!
How many a tale their music tells,
Of youth and home and that sweet time
When last I heard their soothing chime.

A fair amount of humor was built into the program, with stories of foolish or runaway boys and set-upon school mistresses. Two children recited stories involving kittens. Five sang the tale of "Birds in Summer."

One boy offered a piece called "The Mortgage on the Farm," something parents in the audience would know about, many having survived the 1893 economic panic that hit the country. Also, just two years earlier, Helga Estby and her daughter, from the Spokane area, had walked across the United States in a quest to win a $10,000 prize offered by a clothing manufacture for such a journey. Estby's hope was to win money and save the family farm, where her husband and children languished awaiting their return. Newspaper reports appeared regularly in local columns as the women made their seven-month trek. Helga completed her journey, only to be cheated of the prize by some technicality invoked by the sponsor. Meanwhile, at home, tragedies greater than the loss of a farm had diminished the family waiting. Helga's bitter remaining children never spoke, nor allowed her to speak, of the folly of the pursuit again. The story of the trek itself was widely published at the time and discussed.[2] Oyster Bay families would have been familiar with Helga's trek and understood the tragedy of loss.

One child held forth on the meaning of the word "persevere." Jo

Simmons offered a little ditty called "Grandpa's Spectacles," which included a finger game. John Bloomfield, on a more serious note, discussed the "Cuban Crisis."

Cuba and the Spanish-American War was a topic on everyone's mind. Just a few months before the end of the school year, in January 1898, riots had broken out in Havana and the USS *Maine* was sent there to protect the interests of the United States. The *Maine* was 319 feet long and 57 feet at the beam. According to surviving documentation, it had four ten-inch guns, six six-inch guns, seven six-pounders, eight one-pounders, and four fourteen-inch torpedo tubes. It was not especially fast, moving about seventeen knots at top speed. It arrived in Havana harbor toward the end of January 1898, and on the evening of February 15 a huge explosion sank it and killed 266 men.

Newspapers in the United States blamed the Spanish in Cuba for the deaths. The conflict that became known as the Spanish-American War was fueled by newspaper owners like William Randolph Hearst. Even the president, McKinley, and many in the business world opposed a war. Nevertheless, U.S. troops were sent to Cuba in April. Resolutions in Congress supported Cuban independence and demanded Spanish withdrawal from the island state. John Bloomfield discussed these events in detail for the edification of his audience of parents and other students. Commodore Winfield Schley had not yet performed the feats that caused the Oyster Bay post office to be renamed in his honor.

When it was his turn to take the stage, Ray Gale recited "The Drummer Boy of Waterloo." Though serious writers and reviewers dismissed its author, Julia A. Moore, the sentimentality of her verse was bravely patriotic and undeniably American.

Young Henry was as faithful boy
As ever stood on the American soil
And he did enlist, without a doubt
When the rebellion was broke out.

He was his parents' only son
And only child he was but one,
That was a girl aged seventeen,
Henry called her his May Queen.

Young Henry said, "Dear sister May,
What do you think my friends will say?
For now my name is on the roll,
And I down south will have to go."

"I hear my country's call," said he,
"For all her sons of liberty,
And I, forever, will prove true
To that dear old flag, red, white and blue."

There are eight more stanzas and Ray recited them all, much to the delight of his proud mother, Katie Gale, who brought her creamed salmon and biscuits to serve at the covered dish supper that followed the performances.

At the end of the program, Miss Galusha gave each of her charges a small gift as a "reward for their good behavior and diligence."

Katie stayed clear of Joseph during the supper and mixer that followed the formal congratulations to the children.

It may have been the last time Katie enjoyed the fellowship of community. She was still mourning her elder daughter, Hattie, who had died the year before. Henry had died just two years before that. Joseph had begun divorce proceedings in January. Maud had been abducted in February and removed to St. Amable's. Katie was quite ill herself. Yet this day must have affirmed for her that the love and attention that she had given her younger offspring was preparing them to live successfully in an ever-changing world now hurtling toward a new century.

21 *Katie Gale Died under a Full Moon*

WHAT DOES a woman who is dying dream about? What goes through her mind as it muddles through the mists of a high fever? What does a woman who has set things right, made certain her children are to be cared for, and settled all her accounts think about as she prepares for a final sleep? I can only imagine how those last hours must have seemed for Katie. I can only ask her from the depths of my own dreams and what I imagine of hers. And dream I did in the first months that I worked to understand and recount her story.

I dreamed sacred boxes, deeply carved, stacked boxes lacquered with wallpaper flowers, filled with tea and dog-eared, fading photographs of children. I dreamed tiny rosebuds in crystal vessels. The vases with the roses were filled with oil and hung on delicate golden chains. They swayed over gentle flames and released a pleasant fragrance. I dreamed baskets of cedar and bear grass. I dreamed the distant mountain, a bright cone across the bay. The mingled smell of summer grass and wild ginger made my head light. The photographs made my heart ache. A rosewood parlor guitar rested against a gateleg table as I dreamed and dreamed about Katie Gale.

Katie died under a full moon. Mars, Jupiter, and Saturn trooped across the western sky during the early morning hours of August 6, 1899. Venus was to rise, bright, in the east just before the glare of the summer disk of the sun. Katie was gone before the little planet had cleared the horizon.

It was highly contagious, the disease that killed her. It spread easily from child to child in one-room schoolhouses and from adult to adult in the close winter quarters of the small houses on the bay.

That Katie would succumb was almost inevitable.

First the bacilli invaded and lodged in her body. Her breathing was weakened and a persistent cough began. Perhaps, in the early stages, she had a slight fever, and the weakness and the cough were taken to be a mere cold. Perhaps the finality of tuberculosis was mistaken for bronchitis. Probably these alternative diagnoses were only a passing, feeble hope, for the characteristic symptoms of the disease and the relentless path it took were well known to her.

She could not see the grey tubercles as they formed in her inflamed lungs. It didn't matter. They did their work. Her body became weaker, the coughing spells increased to constant hacking. The spells were painful and caused her to nearly double over or sink to her knees. The sputum was bloodstained, and as the disease progressed it was copious. Perhaps Katie had been cautioned to spit into a paper bag or into rags that then were burned. This would in no way prolong her life, but it might help stop the spread of the infection to others who shared her household. She did not want two more children to die early deaths.

The warm July and early August days were torture. She had chest pains. Now, with each cough, she thought her ribs would surely break. The muscles that lay over her midsection ached. Her body began to weaken even more. And treatment? The doctors of the day recommended fresh air. Stay outside as often as possible and keep your windows open. A stuffy bedroom where many people slept, a commonly consulted handbook read, would mean deterioration in the health of the patient and spread the disease to other family members. Only the rich, the author admitted, could afford sanatoria, sea voyages, or a move to New Mexico, Canada, Madeira, Algiers, or Bournemouth, all places where the patient might thrive, or, on the other hand, die among strangers.[1]

By now she knew, of course, that she was dying. Far too often she had witnessed the ceaseless, merciless way of this hideous disease. Thus she had arranged for a will to be written. Her plans for the disposition of her property were made in November 1898, the month before Joseph dropped divorce proceedings.

Though she was ill she sent word for the attorney, Preston M. Troy, to come to her house. James Tobin carried her message to Troy's Olympia offices. He told Troy that Katie felt she wouldn't live long and wanted to be sure her children were taken care of after her death.

In his early thirties, Troy had established himself and his firm, Troy and Falknor, on Seventeenth Street in Olympia.[2] Troy drove to Oyster Bay by buggy with his friend, Mitchel Harris. Mitchel worked for his father's dry goods stores in Olympia. Harris's father, a Russian-born Jew named Isaac Harris, had, by his hard work, created a firm foundation for the family in Olympia. In a few years Harris would become a four-term mayor of Olympia and president of Harris Dry Goods. He also became a director of Capital National Bank in Olympia. He was known as a highly ethical young man, and because he undoubtedly knew Katie's brother-in-law, James Newton Gale, and from him the story of Joseph's life and what Katie had suffered from him, he was eager to help protect the interests of her children. Not only would Mitchel have known James, the editor and publisher of temperance newspapers, from his neighborhood (they lived near each other in Olympia), but he also would probably have been acquainted with Joseph's former spouse, Calista, who had lived with the Newton Gale family.

The route took them to Kamilche, then looped back up toward the store on Hard Scrabble, then on, along a rough track, to the Gale place. The men arrived at Katie's Oyster Bay house and entered the kitchen. Maud was there, as were Jenny Slocum and Louisa Tobin and Jenny's future mother-in-law, Jennie Krise. Louisa and Jennie Krise tended to Katie almost daily. Others from around the bay visited her as they could, including Dick Jackson and John Leslie. She would live until the next summer, but she needed help with everything: the wood, the baking, the chickens . . . all that she had done on her own and couldn't now.

Harris and Troy talked quietly with the women in the kitchen area for a few moments, then Troy and Jenny Slocum went into the bigger bedroom, where Katie sat up on pillows, weak but fully competent and in conversation with James Tobin. She was eager to get on with it and told Tobin to go out and close the door behind him. Jenny stood holding Katie's hand and Troy sat on a small wooden chair near the foot of the bed.

Katie began telling Troy, who had a pad of legal-size paper on his lap and a fountain pen in his hand, what she wanted. He was ready to record her wishes. He had an extra bottle of ink in the leather bag he carried with him. The fingers with which he held the pen were stained black—his pen often leaked. Its nib was somewhat splayed and he had to take care not to use too much pressure as he wrote.

Katie told Troy the story of her life with Joseph at some length, with particular attention to the last few years of neglect and abuse she and the children had suffered. Troy had already heard most of this. She said she wanted it written down that the children would get her land and other properties and let there be no doubt that she did not wish Joseph Gale to administer the children's bequest or benefit from her death. She was very clear on these points.

In a large, flowing hand, Troy began to draft the will:

> I Katie Gale, of Kamilche, Mason County, Washington, being of sound and disposing mind and memory, and having in mind the uncertainties of human life, and not acting under duress, menace, fraud or undue influence of any person whatever, do make, publish, and declare this my last will and testament, in manner following, that is to say:
>
> *First*: I direct that my debts be paid

> *Second*: I direct that I be decently buried, and that the expenses of my last illness be first considered of my debts,
>
> *Third*: I give and bequeath to my husband, Joseph A. Gale, the sum of one ($1.00) Dollar, which I direct to be paid out of the proceeds of my estate:
>
> *Fourth*: I give, bequeath and devise all the rest, residue, and remainder of my estate, both real and personal, of every kind, name and nature, whatsoever, owned by me at the time of my death, to my beloved children Maud Gale and Ray Gale, share and share alike and equal.
>
> *Fifth*: I hereby nominate and appoint Mitchell Harris of Olympia, Thurston County Washington, executor of this my last will and Testament

Harris was to carry out the provisions of the will "without the further interference or process of the court." In conclusion, "I have herewith set my hand and seal this seventeenth day of November in the year of our Lord one thousand eight hundred and ninety eight."

Troy called Harris into the room, at which point this draft, based on a template, was "carefully read" to her. She said it was "just as she wanted it" and "then and there by taking hold of the pen used made the cross mark appearing within her name: Katie X Gale." Preston M. Troy then signed as a witness, followed by "Jennie Slocum, residence, Kamilche, Washington."[3]

Katie Gale had chosen her attorney, executor, and witness well. Like Harris, Troy was a well-thought-of young man. A former prospector and miner in California and the Rogue River Valley, he subsequently earned his law degree at the University of Michigan in 1893. Later he became city attorney and then prosecuting attorney of Thurston County. He took on many other civic responsibilities and by 1914 was president of the Olympic National Bank. He was an active Democrat and one of the organizers of the Woodrow Wilson League of Washington. He also became a trustee of the Thurston County Pioneer and Historic Association.

It was no doubt Troy who insisted that the third article, "I give and bequeath to my husband Joseph A. Gale," be inserted in the will. Katie did not wish to leave Joseph anything. Leaving a single dollar to someone in a will is a convention to indicate that the omission of a larger bequest is intentional, not due to forgetfulness. This presumably protects a will against challenges and helps to establish the mental state of the deceased at the time the will was written.

Jennie (Jenny) Slocum, the witness, was Katie's friend and ally and a member of the highly respected Slocum family. She was the daughter of John Slocum, the founder, along with his wife, of the Indian Shaker religion. She lived on Big Skookum (Hammersley Inlet) west of Squaxin Island.

It was good that Katie had taken these steps to put her mind at ease about her children's futures because the fevers increased in frequency after December and throughout the early part of 1899. She became even more incapacitated. In fact, there was little she could do for herself or anyone else. This was an unaccustomed and unwanted release from chores. Her temperature, especially in the evening, became elevated, toward the end oscillating between 100 and 104 degrees. Her nights were impossibly miserable, filled with coughing and the sweats, and the pain. She slept very little and sat up in bed to ease the pain and assuage the coughing spasms.

At the very end, she was too weak to care much about anything. She must have been satisfied that she had done what she could in life and was ready for whatever was to come next. Her Shaker Church friends and many others were close by, easing the transition.

Katie, age forty-three, died under what many Puget Sound Indians call the salal berry moon. Maud was certainly by her side. Ray was probably there too.

Katie's death was reported in the *Morning Olympian* of August 10,

1899. She was described as "wife of Joseph Gale, the well known oyster man." The *Mason County Journal* noted that she died of "consumption" and that her health had been "failing for some time" and her death was "not unexpected."

Joseph arranged for her burial at the site near where Hattie and Henry had been interred. It was a good place, high on the hill above her house and barn. From the grave site a person could watch the sun rise and see the magnificent cone and white cap of Mount Rainier on a clear day.

She was buried in a casket common for the day. It was made of cedar with a glass viewing window and brass handles, two per side. Her estate paid for the services of D. C. Bates, the undertaker. The casket cost eighty dollars. However, it was not until Joseph was dead that Maud and Ray ordered and placed the tombstone we found that first day in the woods.

The contents of Katie's will were reported in the local papers. "She Left Valuable Oyster Lands to Her Two Children," a headline in the *Mason County Journal* reads. "The estate," the article says, "consists of 80 acres of first class oyster lands, which is said to yield about $1,500 per year revenue and is valued at from $300 to $400 per acre; also about 40 acres of upland real estate of lesser value."[4] The article is in error concerning the number of acres of oyster land Katie held. It was about 8.8 acres, the amount settled upon in the 1893 agreement. Her upland holdings totaled 86 acres, including a strip 210 feet wide at the water and another 80 upland acres. "Although of Indian birth," the *Journal* article concludes, "she made the best of her opportunities and was a good mother to her children."

Joseph's efforts to control Katie and the children did not stop at her death or with the probating of her will. On September 21, 1899, Joseph petitioned the Superior Court of Mason County to be named guardian of the persons and estate of Maud and Ray Gale, aiming to wrest control from Mitchel Harris. He claimed he had two witnesses who would attest to the fact that Katie, on her deathbed, wanted Joseph to administer the trust for the children. The records do not show who these witnesses would have been. Perhaps Joseph was ready to compel Maud and Ray to provide this evidence. It is hard to fathom who else might have been with her and willing to testify on Joseph's behalf.

The court granted Joseph his request in January 1900, though he, Abner Smith, and J. H. Scott were required by the court to post bond of $3,000, to be voided if there were problems, and on the condition that Joseph "discharge the office and trust of such guardian according to law" and report to the court from "time to time."

In July 1901 Joseph petitioned the court to pay all the expenses of his children from the proceeds of their estate, that is, the oyster lands they inherited from their mother. This he sought though the agreement of 1893 had ordered him to be responsible for their custodial expenses. Nevertheless, the court adjudged that the sum of $930 per year be allowed for their "support, education and maintenance," from the proceeds of the property their mother had left them.

Joseph himself had not been idle in that previous year. In November 1899, just three months after Katie's death, a marriage license in the names of J. A. Gale of Kamilche and Lillian McDonald of Scio, Oregon, was filed in Mason County. Lillian was twenty-eight years old. Her parents, too, had been emigrants to Oregon Territory from Maine and Iowa. So they had that in common. Joseph was fifty-two. He quickly had a fine new house built for the two of them. A special edition of the *Mason County Journal* touted the grandeur of this new home and its brilliant Oyster Bay setting. The children were in schools in Olympia. Joseph had control of their tidelands and upland properties as well as his own. He had no expenses for the care of Maud and Ray.

Joseph seemed to have it all, just the way he wanted it.

22 *A "Broad and Liberal Man" Meets His Death*

IT WAS four o'clock on the morning of September 23, 1901. Lillian and Joseph Gale, still newlyweds, having exchanged vows in November 1899, had been partying all night with other Kamilche-area folk at Carr's hall, up the road from Old Kamilche and a short buggy ride from the Gale house on the bay. These not-infrequent gatherings were always occasions for many toasts. They were also an excuse, much anticipated, for lots of dancing. The local folks enjoyed waltzes, polkas, quadrilles, and even schottisches. Some of the youth loved the new ragtime two-steps the piano player introduced during the evening. There was always a bounty of music at these gatherings. Someone commanded the piano, usually offering popular numbers learned "by ear," while another self-taught musician played the fiddle. Sometimes a harmonica joined in. Those who knew even a few words sang along and hummed the rest.

That night, while the women chatted about their children and the new school year over punch and cookies, the men's conversation was dominated by the news of President McKinley's assassination just days before at the Pan-American Exposition in Buffalo, New York. Though he had been shot on September 6, he hadn't died until September 14. His wounds were not attended to properly and it was gangrene, not the bullet, that had killed him.

The anarchist who shot him was in jail. "A foreigner," Joseph noted repeatedly to the others during the night. He was Leon Czolgosz, son of Polish immigrants and a devotee of Emma Goldman, who is said to have told him one day during his political infancy that "if the life of a tyrant is in your way, take it. The world will applaud your act."

Teddy Roosevelt, the Rough Rider, had been sworn in as their new president at age forty-three. The men admired Roosevelt and liked what they'd read in the paper about his speech at the Minnesota State Fair earlier that month. Something about speaking softly but carrying a stick. So McKinley was out, Roosevelt was in, and Queen Victoria had died the previous January. It seemed to be not only a new century but the end of a way of life, even on Oyster Bay and certainly for Indians all over the United States. Soon to come, for example, was Roosevelt's December 1901 speech to Congress in which he trumpeted the assimilationist views of men like Joseph Gale and ballyhooed the successes of the General Allotment Act: "In my judgment," he said, "the time has arrived when we should definitely make up our minds to recognize the Indian as an individual and not as a member of a tribe. The General Allotment Act is a mighty pulverizing engine to break up the tribal mass." In his 1902 State of the Union speech he asserted (and enlarged upon this assertion) that the aims of national policy toward Indians should be "their ultimate absorption into the body of our people."

It was still dark, early in the morning, when Joseph stumbled out toward the barn. He was humming the tune of the song always played at the end of the dance party evenings these days, "After the Ball." The Gale horse was there in that dark barn, the animal drowsy and silent, waiting his master's return. The carriage had been left just outside in the care of some boys who would watch the horses and hitch horses to carriages when the adults were ready to go home.

Lillian waited in the hall. She knew Joseph would call her when the buggy was ready. He and Lillian would tuck a blanket around themselves and drive the mile or two back home along the still fairly dry, rough roadbed. The fall rains had not yet begun.

A waning half-moon shone in the sky. It wouldn't be light for two or more hours. It was chilly, but not freezing. Still, Joseph could see his breath in the damp fall air. No need to worry about the children wondering why they were gone so late. They weren't at home. Maud, sixteen, and Ray, thirteen, were boarded in Olympia schools now.

The Gales' new home overlooking the bay was a showplace worthy of a man who had made quite a name for himself. From his humble days in Oregon and Washington Territories, Joseph Gale's ambitions and will to succeed had made him a man with whom to be reckoned. By 1901 he had served on the oyster board in Mason County, been a justice of the peace for three terms, served as deputy state fish commissioner for eight years, was currently a director of the Oyster Bay School in Kamilche, and had helped found the *Mason County Journal*. In the *Journal*'s 1901 special supplement he is called "enterprising." His home, including a ranch of "214 acres" and a "quarter of a mile of waterfront," is described as "one of the most pleasant and delightful" in the county. He even had a telephone in his new abode.[1] In a photograph of his "show place" home accompanying the 1901 article it is just possible to make out the figures of a man and woman seated on the covered porch and, down the slope in front of the house, two horses. During the previous season, the newspaper reports, Joseph had shipped "2,500 sacks of oysters, and during the busy season employs twelve men." Quite a reversal of fortune.

In the courts just three years earlier he had presented himself as nearly penurious. The records show that he had a habit of hiding his money, hoarding his assets, and complaining publicly that he was a poor and victimized man. It was, however, hard to continue to seem hard up with the demands that Lillian placed on him. She had not agreed to live like a pauper when she married him. He could not continue his charade as a penniless man easily while being seen with his new wife in public and continuing to occupy a place of distinction in the state and local political scene.

A tall man, he was well-dressed these days, though still rough around the edges. His hands were the hands of a man older than fifty-three. His long, dark beard and his hair were both showing considerable white. His face was deeply lined from the years he worked on the bay, and his splotchy skin showed the years of heavy drinking.

That night at the party he had seemed, many noticed, not only a well-to-do but a healthy man as he whirled Lillian around the floor for one dance after another. No one present that night could doubt his affluence, with that big new house built so soon after he had claimed himself to be virtually destitute. His apparent recovery of strength and money was remarked upon in whispered side conversations among his neighbors. Were those laments of his a ruse to avoid helping Katie? It had been suspected all along.

As much as the partygoers marveled at Joseph's miraculous recovery, even more did they privately resent his treatment of his deceased spouse, Katie. The swift marriage to his Seattle mistress was deemed unseemly, even in this sometimes reckless frontier community. They likely didn't know he'd had yet another spouse, Calista, left long ago in Olympia.

When Joseph entered the barn to get the carriage ready for the homeward journey, he found the harness hanging on a peg where he'd left it. Then, in the dark, he heard what he thought was a soft footfall behind him. As he turned, something struck him hard on the temple. It was a blow that nearly split his head open, rapid and sure. He cried out, then slumped to the floor. His horse shied and jumped away, though not far because it was tethered. Still, the horse sought to avoid the man and the danger it sensed. His son Ray's young friend Adolph Johnson was standing outside with the other boys, near Gale's buggy waiting to help hitch the horse to it. A few other men were standing in the open near Adolph, smoking and recalling stories from the party. At the odd cry, they all ran into the barn and found Joseph lying near the horse's feet, his head bleeding from the deep gash at the temple. They all assumed he had been kicked.

The cut was over the left ear, about six inches in length, his skull exposed. The first newspaper report quoted doctors as saying that Joseph might survive, for the horse that struck him was, fortunately, unshod. Several men loaded Joseph into a carriage. He was confused, drowsy, hardly able to keep his eyes open. Blood seeped down his head, over his ear, into his hair and beard. The men directed the carriage to the general store in Old Kamilche. Two of them carried him inside and stretched him out on the counter to wait for the doctors. He was barely conscious, yet still alive. Someone found a gauze bandage among the goods in the store. Another unwrapped it and held it tight against the wound. One of the men went for water and held a full cup to Joseph's lips. Joseph could not accept it. Yet another man found a bottle of smelling salts on one of the store shelves and waved the bottle under Joseph's nose. All of this happened within a very few moments. The men talked among themselves and to Joseph, who was not responsive. He was breathing hard and muttering something. No one could make out what he was saying. One man put his ear close to Joseph's mouth but still could not make out his words.

The women, alerted now by the men who had run inside to report the accident to the others still in the hall, came to the store in a wagon. Several held Lillian, their arms around her shoulders. They entered the store together. The women kept Lillian away from the counter where Joseph was stretched out. She looked at his unmoving form and sensed the gravity of his condition. She stood with resignation, grim and pale, and watched the men attending to him.

Someone had telephoned Dr. Hamilton and he was the first to arrive. Still, it was a good fifteen miles from Olympia to Kamilche, and even pushing his horse at a fair clip he was forty-five minutes away. Doctors Beach, Redpath, and Ingham, all of Olympia, arrived as the first dawn light was breaking, a little before 7:00 a.m.

After the medical examinations, Lillian was allowed to come forward and kiss her husband's cheek. His eyes were closed. He seemed unaware of her, or anyone or anything else for that matter. His breathing was irregular now and there were occasional tremors in his arms and hands. She whispered words of encouragement to him.

The doctors decided to bundle Joseph tightly and take him to the hospital in Olympia. It was now fully light. Lillian rode with him and with two of the doctors in the back of a flatbed wagon drawn by two horses. She remained by his side during the next hours of his waning life. Joseph died without regaining any apparent awareness of his surroundings on Monday night, the twenty-third of September. Lillian was by his bedside, now a well-to-do widow.

No one knew with certainty what had happened, though the night and Joseph's death were a subject for speculation for years to come. My account is based on newspaper articles and recollections and suppositions long after the event. It is not an "official version" of events. But it is not entirely fanciful.

The boy Adolph, who was right outside the barn when Joseph was struck, suspected his whole life that Joseph's death was the result of foul play. He "got to thinking it over," he said. He didn't think "Joe" was kicked by a horse at all. By Thursday, September 26, Adolph wasn't the only one who suspected foul play. "Sensational Rumors" were circulating, declared headlines in local papers. Some friends of Joseph insisted that the wound on his head was made by a knife. The doctors dismissed this possibility. They even changed their opinion about the horse. The horse, they now reported, was shod and the injury was caused by the hoof of a "vicious horse." It wasn't likely the Gales had a "vicious horse" in their stable. Nevertheless, this revised account went forward almost unchallenged.

Some members of the Fraternal Order of Eagles were suspicious. They called for an investigation. After all, Joseph had been "threatened" by people in his neighborhood. "Four years ago," an article in the *Morning Olympian* reported, Joseph's cattle "had their tongues cut out during the night." Who could have hated Joseph so much, to have taken such measures? In another incident, Joseph had nearly been cut up by a "chinaman," as the paper reported it, on Oyster Bay in 1897. These events and Joseph's treatment of Katie were recalled by his friends as Joseph lay dying.

The inquiry was aborted and all calls for further study dropped when attending doctors again insisted that their examination of the wound showed without doubt that it was caused by the hoof of a shod horse. Many were uneasy about this verdict, but there was no further probe into the matter by the "brothers," "out of respect for Mrs. Gale." "Just how the accident occurred will never be known," the *Mason County Journal* reported at the time of Joseph's death. That's how matters were left.

Adolph Johnson wrote, years later, "He got his just desserts [*sic*] for the way he treated his Indian family." Adolph's views no doubt reflected those of many in the Oyster Bay community.

It was on a late September day in 1901 that Joseph Gale was laid to rest in a Shelton, Washington, cemetery.

His fraternal brothers arranged for an elaborate memorial and funeral service. It was held in Shelton's Ancient Order of United Workmen Hall.[2] Joseph was a prominent man, prominent and respected enough that the Thurston County–based Olympia Eagles Lodge chartered the steamer Northern Light so that they could come to Shelton for the day to honor their deceased brother. The Order of the Red Men, to which Joseph belonged, joined with the Eagles to lead the large procession from the hall up the long hill to the cemetery on the edge of town, a patch of ground not much more than a groomed bit of prairie.

Men from the Society or Order of Red Men fraternity officiated. Founded in 1765, the society was originally called the "sons of liberty." It was modeled, its history notes, in some ways after the organization of the League of Iroquois. Only "free white males of good moral character" who believed in "the existence of a Great Spirit, the Creator and Preserver of the Universe" were eligible for membership.[3]

Whatever various functions the brotherhood may have served in the lives of these Thurston and Mason County men, it is hard not to see the ironies in Joseph's membership in the Red Men. Indeed, even those fraternal orders not patterned after a romanticized version of Indian society enjoyed elaborate and secret rituals. In a period when many white men were suppressing and belittling the religions of actual Indians in their "neighborhoods," their own arcane organizations abounded with arguably peculiar ceremonials and rites kept secret from those outside their fellowship. As a party to these secret societies, Joseph enjoyed the fellowship of his brothers and was sent to his grave with all the pageantry and ostentation befitting his stature among them.

When he died he had $444.93 cash in the bank, household furniture valued at $250, nine head of cattle, two head of horses, and two float houses. He held a $1,000 insurance policy with the Brotherhood of Yeomen and real estate valued at about $50,000, over $1 million in current dollars. The Seattle and Oyster Bay enterprises had treated him well.

The mystery of Joseph's death will not be solved. But as Nathaniel Hawthorne wrote so many years ago in *The House of the Seven Gables*, "it were folly to lay any stress" on stories of the kind that circulated years after his passing. He was a controversial man in his time, not well liked by some and perhaps hated by others. Given that his fatal blow went unwitnessed, stories "were sure to spring up," and in Joseph's death as well as in that untimely demise of a similarly difficult man in Hawthorne's novel, these stories "sometimes prolong themselves for ages afterwards, like the toadstools that indicate where the fallen and buried trunk of a tree has long since mouldered into the earth."

There are no toadstools around Joseph's tombstone. It stands there now, forlorn, with no kin or spouse buried around or near him. The land around the stone is scorched, dry, and barren. It seems, in contrast, that the fecund blackberry vines, the lush salal, the abundant ferns, and the bigleaf maples around Katie Gale's tombstone in the woods above her old home tell the tale of the vast difference between these two, even in death.

23 *The End of an Era*

A SHORT, sad notice appeared in the April 25, 1905, *Morning Olympian.*

> MRS. FANCHIER DEAD
>
> Mrs. Maud Fanchier, wife of Burt Fanchier, of 216 Plum street, died Wednesday night of cancer of the stomach. She will be buried at 2 o'clock on Saturday at the Masonic cemetery. The funeral will be from the Fanchier residence and the Rev. S. Crockett of Christian church will hold the services. Mrs. Fanchier was formerly Maud Gale, the daughter of the prominent oyster man. She inherited property to the amount of about $30,000 in oyster lands which passes on to her eleven-months-old baby girl. Mrs. Fanchier was only 19 years of age at the time of her death.[1]

The value of Maud's bequest to her daughter was nearly $800,000 in today's currency. Her will was filed on May 5. In it she wrote,

> I give, bequeath and devise unto my beloved daughter, Inez Maud Fanshier, all the property both real and personal of every kind and nature whatsoever owned by me at the time of my death save and except and subject to the estate in a portion of my real property hereinafter bequeathed and devised to my beloved husband, T. B. Fanshier. Second I give, bequeath and devise unto my said beloved husband, T. B. Fanschier, the rents and income from my real estate

> until my beloved daughter shall have attained the age of 18 years, at which time everything shall revert to her.

Within just a few years of Katie's death, then, another will was read and oyster lands passed on again.

Maud had married Herbert (also known as Bert, Burt, T.B., and Thomas Bertram) Fanshier in Shelton in September 1903. The article in the *Morning Olympian* reports that "the event was quite a surprise to their friends, who were kept in ignorance of the coming nuptials." They both lived in Olympia and returned there the day after the September 16 evening wedding. The sudden marriage may have been a necessity. Inez was born within the next nine months.

The son of E. G. and Mary Fanshier, formerly of Illinois and Indiana, Bertram was born in Fall River, in the southeastern section of Kansas, in 1878. Bertram and E.G. were bottlers at Olympia Brewery, though after Maud's death Bertram became a brakeman for the railroad.

Upon his death, Joseph's estate had been divided equally between Lillian Gale and the two children. Lillian left Oyster Bay and moved to Olympia within the month. The children were to go back to their studies after the funeral. However, Maud and Ray apparently stayed in Lillian's care when they were not in school. J. W. Ludgate, who eventually bought the Gale property, was appointed guardian of the children by the court and administrator of Joseph's will. He apparently managed well. The children received regular stipends from the proceeds of the oyster beds.

Curiously, the records of St. Amable Academy do not show Maud in attendance after October 1901. Perhaps Ludgate allowed the children to attend another school in each other's company.

After Maud's death in 1905, Ray lived with the Fanshiers in the 400 block of Fifth Avenue in Olympia and attended People's University. People's was a progressive institution established by John R. Chaplain, a Congregational minister, who had dreams of establishing a university in southern Puget Sound and was able to attract like-minded people to settle in Olympia and join his enterprise.[2]

People's University was, Chaplain said, "unfettered by denominational boundaries, by fixed theological creeds, by the dangerous demands of either accumulated wealth or combined numbers, by the unrighteous requirements of social 'castes,' by the unnecessary burden of foolish and expensive styles and fashions, or by the disastrous influences of political dominations, its aim is to meet all the people on the broad and fraternal plane of co-partnership, seeking the best and highest in human character."[3]

The university was a stock company and boasted shareholders from "every state in the union." In 1903 it had already acquired four thousand acres of land in and around Olympia and secured a faculty. Travel was to be part of the four-year course of study. The school declared it would provide "guides, chaperons, and instructors" for the students' forays abroad.

Ray Gale graduated from People's commercial department on June 1, 1905. The graduation itself was spread over several days and featured a baccalaureate sermon, piano and vocal solos, and a class paper titled "History and Prophecy" delivered by Fred Tinkham, the local son of a Massachusetts-born meat dealer.

In 1906 Ray, in the court papers called a "consumptive," petitioned the court to sell his real estate on Oyster Bay. This included a one-half interest in the estate of Katie Gale and a one-third interest in the estate of Joseph Gale. He wanted, he said, to be "removed to a different climate" for his health. Among other properties, he held interest in a float house, two top floats, one sink float, two horses, and a buggy. He invested the proceeds of the sale in Yakima real estate.

He apparently did not leave Olympia immediately. The fact that he was "consumptive," presumably meaning that he had tuberculosis, didn't seem to slow him down. He was the captain of the Olympic Athletic Club boys' basketball team during the 1907–8 season and a news account in December 1907 said the team had been practicing hard for several weeks. In July of the same year he traveled with friends to a Baptist Sunday school convention at Burton on Vashon Island, Washington.

Ray Gale, age twenty-one, was living in a boardinghouse in Olympia and working as a bottler at a local brewery when the 1910 Federal Census was taken. By 1915 he had moved to Los Angeles and was living on Judson Street. The last record I have found of Ray, still a brewer, is his Los Angeles, California, World War I draft registration. It was filed on June 5, 1917. I have found no record to suggest that Ray was actually inducted into the army. At the time he registered for the draft, Ray was married and working for the Maier Brewing Company. He had moved to South Broadway, the street that was then known as the commercial center of Los Angeles. The entries on the draft card indicate that he was tall and slender with brown eyes and dark hair. The draft card also notes that Ray "claims to be tubercular." The brewery where Ray worked was shut down in 1920 during national Prohibition. Where Ray went and what he did after that remain open questions.

Inez Maud Fanshier, the baby daughter Maud left behind, remained in the household with her father, Bertram, who remarried and had three sons with his new wife, Fannie.

Her father managed her estate. The tidelands where Joseph and Katie's fortune was made were farmed by the Olympia Oyster Company. In or around 1920 Inez married a bookkeeper named George Hutchings; she died in Tacoma at age twenty-six in June 1930. She had no children.

By the time Katie and then Joseph died, James and Louisa Kettle Tobin had long since moved to their land on the west side of Eld Inlet, near Mud Bay. Their land patent had been granted in 1890. Their descendants are among the celebrated heroes in the Northwest Native peoples' struggle for justice. For example, Louisa and James were Maiselle Bridges's grandparents. Maiselle Bridges is known for her prominent role in the Puget Sound "fish wars" that led to the 1974 Boldt Decision in *United States v. Washington*. This landmark case is a tribute to

Maiselle Bridges's and her family's enduring lives at Frank's Landing on the Nisqually River, the legacy of Kettle Labatum, and the will of people like Louisa and James Tobin and their relatives in those early post-treaty years.

Grandma Sallie, Maiselle Bridges's name for the woman who was the wife and then widow of Harry Weatherall, lived in a float house near the Tobin ranch even before her husband's death in 1907. Maiselle's mother, when she was a child living at home with the Tobins, was sent to the float house sometimes to borrow flour or sugar. Sallie, even as she slept through these visits, always knew when "Angie," Maiselle's mother, had been there because her "little dog told her."

Louisa Kettle Tobin made baskets and sold them in downtown Olympia into the 1930s, along with mittens she made from wool she had carded. Maiselle Bridges, who accompanied her, remembers that she always bought a piece of carnival glass at Miller's Department Store at the end of a day in town.

The Tobins put in an orchard and dug a well. At first they had a log house. And there, near that house, up in the wooded part of the property, they carefully tended a family cemetery.

A 1907 *Daily Ledger* article depicts James Tobin as a "leader among" the Indians on Mud Bay, "highly respected among the whites as a well educated Christian citizen, who exerts a power for the good." The Tobins' fortunes changed afterward and they sold oyster tidelands and ultimately lost other property in tax sales. A family story says that James Tobin had backed Sallie Weatherall in her court case and that the money spent for that case ultimately led to the loss of the Tobin properties.[4]

In the late 1920s and 1930s, during the time Maiselle Bridges lived with her grandmother and, she said, "when the dogwood was in bloom, and the flounder was the fattest," the Yakama relatives came from over the mountains. Horse clams, butter clams, and steamer clams were gathered in huge cedar baskets and set in water in the stream below the property to clean out overnight. Many were dried and taken back to their Yakama homes at the end of the summer.

The Tobins continued to be active Shakers. Conventions lasted for up to two weeks. Louisa Tobin was one of the main cooks, and she canned fruit and deer meat to prepare for these big meetings.

Their eldest child was Kate, or Catherine, born while the family was still on Oyster Bay. Perhaps she was named for Katie Gale.

Chief Kettle, Louisa Tobin's father, died in 1903. He had "contracted" what has been described as a cold. Apparently it was not thought to be a serious illness at first. The old man took to his bed and succumbed.

Louisa was his only surviving child. According to newspaper accounts, the family ordered "a most beautiful white" casket, "decked with silks and handsome robes." A large ceremony with Indians and whites in attendance was held to grieve and honor him.

Big Frank, living on the Skokomish Reservation, died of consumption in 1897. Adam Korter died in 1888 shortly after the death of one of his children. The Kennedys were both dead by 1900. Franklin had become a judge and died at age seventy-seven in 1888 and Anne in 1898.

Some Indians, at least the Mud Bay Indians, those who had long since settled their homesteads and retained their tideland claims, stayed in the oyster business as independent growers and dealers for some time to come. A 1907 *Ledger* article notes that many of them were "wealthy" and had "large, commodious houses."

Doctor Jim's death in 1905 was reported in the local newspapers. The Shelton paper offered a somewhat benign account of Doctor Jim's ordeal: "The body of Dr. Jim, the aged Indian who had been missing for a week from Mud Bay, was found near Geo. Barron's new camp on Oyster Bay Wednesday. Deputy Coroner Alden viewed the remains and decided an inquest unnecessary as the man came to his death through falling overboard from his canoe. Dr. Jim, one of the oldest Indians in this section, claims to have seen the first white man come to Fort Steilacoom," which would have been about 1825. Doctor Jim may have been alive when Fort Steilacoom was first occupied, but he would have been only a baby. According to various census records, Doctor Jim was probably near eighty when he died.

The *Olympian* was more specific, and the story more horrifying in its detail. Dr. Jim had been heard calling for help by the crew of the *Tarrynot*, an 1878 steamer that had been rebuilt in 1898:

> While the captain of the *Tarrynot* played cards in a Kamilche cabin, Dr. Jim, the pioneer Indian, screamed for help from 10 o'clock at night until 1 in the morning and finally drowned a few yards away from the unheeding players. With the cries of the despairing, dying old Indian ringing in their ears, they shuffled and dealt and lost and won. Thinking the screams were those of oystermen calling back and forth to each other, the young men sat around the table with no thought of the old man outside, who clung to his canoe and called and who at last, worn out, slipped back into the water.

As a last insult, his body, found floating near Squaxin Island (in this account), was wired to a piling until someone came to claim the remains.

If he had been making the journey from Squaxin Island to New Kamilche or Oyster Bay in the evening he would have faced some challenges depending on the tides and currents. He was alone, and probably in a small, shovel-nosed canoe, nine or ten feet long. These canoes rode only an inch or so above the water.

Doctor Jim was among the many who died from drowning during this era. Squaxin George, over eighty himself, though an expert navigator, drowned off "the boom at Potlatch," on Hood Canal. His craft had been upset by the choppy water. Jennie Frank, the wife of Charles Frank and daughter-in-law of Big Frank, drowned in the Skokomish River in 1907. She was canoeing with three other women when their canoe capsized. Her body was found the next afternoon under a root on the river bed. Mrs. Frank was only thirty-two years old and left behind "two young children."

Sandy Wohaut, often referred to in newspapers as "Old Man Sandy," died in 1909 at age eighty. In her memoir, Cora Chase, the daughter of Frank Gingrich, comments that she heard "weird music and drums" played for Sandy Wohaut by his Oyster Bay kin during his last days.

He "died several times, but came back to life." He was born in about 1829 and married Chitsa, the sister of Doctor Jim. Chitsa died in 1911. The couple left no surviving children. They were, the record says, "long dead." Chitsa Sandy left her property to Mud Bay Sam, who cared for her in her old age.

Olympia Jim died in 1910 with no living children. The children from his first wife, Sally, were all dead. Sally herself died in 1899. Jim married again in 1900. The children from that marriage all died around the same time as he did. Edna died at age three, Mitchell at age two months, and Amelia at age four.

Kowitzkaka, or Mud Bay Sam, died in 1911; he was between sixty-five and sixty-nine years of age. His death was reported widely and he was sorely mourned by his extensive community of Shakers, kin, and friends. His death was said to be "sudden," following the consumption of a "hearty supper," after which he "fell to the floor and doubled up in convulsions." He was thought of locally as a wealthy man and had been, since 1906, the titular head of the Shaker Church. The *Olympian* described him as a man seen often in the streets of town. He wore a "straw hat with a wide rim and around this rim was seen a ribbon of either yellow or red." His entourage included, apparently, several Shaker Church fellows. He had divorced his first wife, Emily, in 1907, complaining in court of her "nagging." He married Ellen Sam "ceremonially." Ellen was the widow of Mud Bay Sam's elder brother, Mud Bay Louie, or Louis Yowaluch. She died in 1913. The records show that she had no children or grandchildren. Two daughters, the children of Mud Bay Sam and Emily, survived him. Two children born to them died in infancy. A son, Thomas, had died in 1906. Sam held a "potlatch" in November 1907 to honor the passing of his brother and son and to facilitate the election of a new head of the Shaker religion. Louie had held the position after the death of John Slocum. The potlatch was attended by Quinaults, Puyallups, Yakamas, and Nisquallies, among many others from out of the Oyster Bay and Mud Bay area.

Dick Jackson lived to the age of eighty-eight. He died January 7,

1929. He had raised a second family. His elder daughter, Mary, took over the Oyster Bay homestead. Dick lived long enough to be a valuable contributor to the T. T. Waterman and Ruth Greiner maps of the area.[5] He also provided testimony in the important Court of Claims cases in 1927. In that testimony, when asked if he ever received any annuity goods, he answered, "Two fishhooks and one knife." He affirmed that "Shelton, Doftmeier, Sylvester, Simmons, Crosby, Barnes, and Bush" took the local Indians' land away before the treaty. At the end of his testimony, he said,

> When the treaty was made the Indians reserved their right for their fishing and hunting. They promised them that even if the creek was running through a white man's field, if there was any fish in there, they have a right to hook that fish out, or if there is any wild berries inside of white man's ranch, they have a right to go pick inside of that fence and get their own food. That is the promise that they received. . . . They reserved everything in the salt water and in the creeks and in the rivers and up on the hills, and that is what made the Indians agree to this treaty that was made, because they reserved all of this; they thought they were going to have it all to themselves.[6]

Dick Jackson died after an honorable life as an oysterman, a spiritual leader, and consultant to anthropologists. The contributions Dick Jackson and Louisa Tobin made to the anthropological record have proven to be incomparable aids in reconstructing the pre-treaty landscapes of Squaxin Island, Mud Bay, and Oyster Bay.

By 1902–3 John Leslie had his engineering license and was engineer on the steamer *City of Shelton*. He was living in a boardinghouse in Shelton in 1910. John Leslie died in 1956 at the age of eighty-two. He was apparently unmarried and without children. He was buried in Shelton Memorial Park, though he had lived most of his life on Squaxin Island.

Others survived and even defied the capitalist overtake of the local economy, continuing to support themselves in productive ways that predated the hot-and-heavy wheeling and dealing of the 1880s and

1890s. "Auntie" Slocum, as white Sheltonites referred to her, was the surviving spouse of Chief Slocum, the father of John Slocum. She lived with her blind spouse on a float house anchored in Oakland Bay. She paddled from the float house to oyster beds where she reportedly harvested shellfish to sell in town into the early part of the twentieth century.[7]

"Auntie Slocum" died in 1903. Her passing was noted in an article in the Olympia newspaper. She died at home on Big Skookum and was buried in Oakland cemetery. In the column next to the "Auntie Slocum" obituary, the paper carried the story of Chief Kettle's death.

What we know about Harry Weatherall's life is based largely on his obituary and comments of friends, neighbors, and Sallie Weatherall made during the suit Sallie brought against his estate after his death.

Harry Weatherall as a young man had left England to "sail before the mast" and, after a wound sustained in a "sailor's riot" in Buenos Aires, made his way to Puget Sound in 1872. He was only twenty-three years old but managed to amass a small fortune in the oyster trade, at least partially, if not wholly, on the back of his spouse, Sallie Weatherall. He died a miserable death in June 1907. He was drinking heavily. He regularly came home, one witness said, with a gallon jug of liquor, and that would last him only four days. He drank "beer and whiskey and alcohol and Chinese whiskey. That pretty near drove him crazy at one time." "He would just lay around and after Sallie left the bay he stayed in the float house most of the time. He would buy goods and bring them in, canned goods and he would live on them most of the time and then with the booze he had there he just laid around stupid." He was, apparently, always a heavy drinker. Even in the woods, he'd have his jug or his bottle. He'd bring his bills to Bush Hoy to make out for him, while he was still shipping oysters.

He was buried in a local Odd Fellows Memorial Park. He left behind:

1 A float house on shore used as residence
4 lengths of walk to the boat house

1 boat house
1 launch and equipment
1 small round bottom row boat
1 Chinaman's Float house, tools, paraphernalia and belongings generally
3 Top Oyster Floats
3 Oyster sinks
2 Skiffs
2 Guns
Stock in Capital City Oyster Co.
and one gold watch and chain.

He also held "some of the largest beds in the Northwest." Sallie is not mentioned in his obituary.

Sallie Hall Weatherall lived a few years more but suffered greatly from her years of working on the oyster beds. She "took sick" a number of times but ultimately "couldn't hardly do anything." She had "the rheumatism" and left Oyster Bay to be cared for by her relatives the Tobins on Mud Bay. Harry visited her occasionally, often walking across Schneider's Prairie from Oyster Bay to the Tobin ranch.

Sallie was left with nothing after Harry's death but was cared for by the Tobins until her own death at age eighty in June 1913. Harry and Sallie, like so many of their generation on Oyster Bay and Mud Bay, left no children behind.

Post-1900 Oyster Bay saw other changes. Though there were few Chinese on Oyster Bay during Katie Gale's time, Chinese men who were there had slowly gained a reputation as good workers. Their only competitors for jobs were Indians, and thus the whites did not see them as threats and were, apparently, happy to employ them in occupations they didn't care to take on themselves. After 1900 they worked in greater numbers on Oyster Bay as foremen and clerks as well as laborers.

Japanese workers came to Oyster Bay in numbers in the early

twentieth century. In 1900 there were at least three Japanese laborers on Oyster Bay. They were, at first, primarily single men, late twenties to midthirties, working side by side with a dozen or more Chinese in a community of English, Irish, Canadians, Germans, Swedes, and Americans. By that time few Indians worked in the tidelands on Oyster Bay. The Slocum and Simmons families were still in the business. The Tobins, who had beds in Oyster Bay, had long since been working their properties on Eld Inlet.

Census records from 1910 Oyster Bay list nearly twenty individuals "working at oystering" who were born in Japan. They had immigrated between 1900 and 1907. By 1910, some women had immigrated. Several of the Japanese were members of small families in which both spouses and other relatives were working. In Shelton, two young Japanese men were servants and oyster openers at the "oyster house" in the downtown district.

Some of the Japanese oyster workers in the early 1900s were part-timers or worked seasonally. E. N. Steele notes, "Two young Japanese men, by name of J. Emy Tsukimato and Joe Miyagi," graduated from public schools in Olympia and earned their way by acting as "house boys," opening oysters for J. J. Brenner, or working on the oyster beds during summer vacations.[8]

There is very little in the published or unpublished histories of the oyster industry about these essential Japanese laborers and their contributions.

All through the early twentieth century, oyster growers established families in float houses, perhaps acquired from earlier Indian occupants. These were moored to "good producing beds." The families were "usually Japanese" and the float houses were linked to a "top float and a sink float." Practices hadn't changed much from earlier periods.

The high-sided sink float was still used to hold harvested oysters below water level when the tide came in. A float house itself "had a flat bottom so when the tide was out it settled on the tide-flat." It was "fitted up with sleeping quarters, food and cooking utilities." The cabin-like living quarters were built on "six logs with a diameter of six or seven feet" bound together. This was "chained to . . . pillars sunk" into the mud flats.[9]

Through the late 1910s and 1920s, according to Kazuo Ito's story, there were "six Japanese families on Mud Bay and thirteen or fourteen at Oyster Bay." Japanese and Japanese American families continued to work and live on Oyster Bay through the 1930s.[10]

Many of these families were incarcerated, most at Tule Lake, during World War II. Oyster beds suffered from the loss of this labor force. They were welcomed back after the war and descendants of these laborers are still in the area.

The transition from mostly Indian laborers and some Indian growers to Japanese labor and white ownership of the commercial enterprise of oystering was somewhat gradual. The older Indians were dying and what children survived were being assimilated into white society or moving on to other occupations. More Japanese came to work on the bay when their labor was needed to build dikes. Growing methods and technologies were changing, and Japanese oysters were imported to replace the Olympia oyster. The development of the still-booming oyster business on the bay was consolidated into the hands of fewer and fewer men, who developed business relationships with Japanese entrepreneurs in Japan during this period.

Today, about seven hundred acres of the Oyster Bay tidelands, a muddy equivalent of a Kansas cornfield, are farmed by the Olympia Oyster Company. The offices are located on the site of the Gale property, just above the old Big Frank/Bettman oyster beds. The company is said to have an annual revenue of $1.5 million. The huge, now global, Taylor Shellfish Farms, founded in the 1880s, also cultivates beds in Oyster Bay. In 2009 Taylor Shellfish was reported to have annual worldwide sales of $50 million and to own or lease twelve thousand acres of Washington tidelands. Work plat maps of oyster beds in Oyster Bay still bear the names Tobin, Slocum, and others who first filed for and claimed those beds nearly 130 years ago.

About two and a half miles west of the head of Oyster Bay is the Little Creek Casino Resort complex, and overlooking it, on the rolling hills behind, is the tribe's world-class PGA golf course and a huge performance center that attracts big-name entertainers and sellout audiences. The Squaxin enterprises are, as of this writing, one of the largest employers in Mason County. Over three-quarters of their six hundred–plus employees are nontribal. The casino and golf course, with a beautiful hotel and restaurants, are only the most visible of several Squaxin Island Tribe businesses. The others include the Kamilche Trading Post, the Skookum Creek Tobacco Company, and a beautifully designed museum complex. Not bad for a tribe that the *Mason County Journal* reported in 1897, at the death of John Slocum, to be "almost extinct." This success, of course, belies 150 years of struggle. Nevertheless, it is satisfying to see these flourishing businesses.

Most satisfying, from the point of view of Katie Gale's story and the long history of the many Squaxin predecessor peoples' involvement with the oyster industry, is Squaxin Island Tribe's Hartstine Oyster Company. The tribe grows oysters on more than forty-one acres of tidelands around Squaxin Island and Hartstine Island and sells and ships oysters, shucked and in the shell, all over the world.[11]

Across the road from the Squaxin Island Tribe casino, near an espresso stand, there in the woods and almost impossibly hidden by a tangle of trees and brush, is the small Kamilche cemetery, where the stones of Franklin Kennedy of Kentucky and Anne Kennedy of North Carolina, European American settlers who came to the bay in 1857, still stand. In that sanctified ground, somewhere under ivy and blackberry vines, lie the remains of Nellie McClure and Adam Korter. This obscure graveyard is a reminder of that remote time on Oyster Bay when another woman, who lies nearby in an even more humble graveyard, lived a brave life.

24 *Winter Sister*

KATIE GALE kept me company all through one winter.[1] She has not been far from my mind over the past several years, as I've spent many hours studying archived materials and photographs. I've watched world events unfold with her by my side; she's witnessed, with me, Arab spring and economic collapse. We've worked through earthquakes and tsunamis together. We've weathered ice storms and power outages.

The first winter, however, was the toughest. I noticed that I was mostly quite grim then. Something in me turned sour; too often there was a sadness I couldn't sing away. I wanted Maud to live a full, rich life. But she didn't. Then I discovered that her own daughter died with no children.

I haven't found out what happened to Ray. Stan Graham and I talk about him often. We try new searches and make fresh calls when one of us has an idea. We haven't given up the hope that he had a child and that somewhere Katie Gale has living relatives. They might never have heard of her.

In my imagination, Ray, the athletic though tubercular graduate of People's University, managed to live through World War I or didn't get called up at all. I like to think he continued to work at the brewery in Los Angeles until Prohibition. I like to believe that he raised a family and retired, healthy, to a sunny Yakima farm where great-grandchildren visited for pony rides and stories about Granddad's youth on Oyster

Bay. There is no evidence of this or of him after the draft registration document.

The bay I look out on is the same one Katie watched but, like all things, it changes with each passing moment. Sometimes it is dark and frothy on a high tide or when a storm is moving in from the coast or down from the Black Hills. Sometimes, in a late-afternoon pink sky, just moments before the sun sets, the mud at low tide shimmers gold and copper. In a certain light, serpentine shapes, etched onto its surface by the action of the underground streams that seep from the banks, glisten like fork marks in fresh icing on a fudge cake. Often the wind changes suddenly and brings heavy, stinging rain or bright nuggets of hail that assault the earth for an exciting few minutes. My old springer spaniel, dead now almost two years, used to laugh and chase the little balls, scooping up a mouthful even as they melted. The cat still runs for cover as they pelt the deck. I am glad, then, that I am not out there, bouncing over the whitecaps, in a boat or canoe like the one Doctor Jim had.

Sometimes, on those winter days when I was first tackling Katie Gale's story, the southern sky opened and the sun I had nearly forgotten in the previous week of fog and mist and low, sad clouds pierced me. The dog would find a warm spot on the porch, flatten out his body, stretch his legs before him, and dream of spring. I must have another spring, he said. And we did have one more.

When I walk on the road above my house, I wonder if Katie trudged this same route when it was just a footpath or a buggy track. It is the road from Old Kamilche and Schley, the route Joseph's horses would have followed had he not met with his demise that early September morning. When I go to the beach, I look down the bay to where she lived and think I see her when an unexpected shadow moves against the trunk of a budding broad-leafed maple. I wonder if someday she will overcome me. Or if I will overcome her.

It isn't hard to imagine her into my life. Sometimes I can almost hear fiddle music coming from the long-gone Gingrich float house.

Sometimes I believe I am hearing the sound of the little steamers moving in and out of the bay with dry goods and mail or stacked with burlap bags of oysters. Sometimes I think I can hear the laughter of children or the voices of Chinese and Japanese workers calling to each other across the mud flats and the mounds of bleached shell.

My home, my life, the part of the earth I call mine, is populated with ancient souls not unlike my own, souls who have known triumphs and sorrows, lived and died here, and who buried their babies and each other beneath my feet.

I have come to know this place as thoroughly as I hoped when I first heard another anthropologist and writer who spent many years in the Pacific Northwest, the poet Gary Snyder, exhort me to "dig in" and take responsibility for my little spot on the planet. I took his words to heart.

Every day I choose to participate in the moral, legal, and social structures that constrain and define who I am in this society. It is these same structures that decide who will be the "other," the savage or the uncivilized, at any particular historic moment. Every day I choose to recognize or not recognize how what I have and call my own has been won over generations at the expense of others and that I, for this moment in time, am triumphant because I am one of those who have inherited the right to define. And yet one day I will be no more, my own memories and dreams will no longer exist. What is the nature, then, of my own victories? Surely my life is as insubstantial, as ephemeral, as was Katie Gale's. I will become like her, another mostly anonymous wraith, a specter who will walk the shores with all the others.

I have learned in writing this book that cruelty is not the domain of any nation or people. Domination and power over others is not a one-time thing; it is nothing as obvious as an invasion or a rapid takeover. It is, I understand better now, a system of beliefs about the superiority of oneself and one's culture and the exercise of tactics, strategies, and maneuvers that accompany those beliefs. These beliefs are present in every transaction. This means that, as Michel Foucault, a French philosopher, wrote, "these relations [of power] go right down into the depths of society, that they are not localized in the relations between state and its citizens or on the frontier between classes."[2] They are everywhere. I am as much susceptible to engaging in these relationships as were Katie and Joseph Gale.

We'll never know much more about the people I've written about than what is between the covers of this book. They lived and died doing the best they could and left faint footprints in their passing. There were others, all of whom lived lives that counted, and there is so much more to tell. To paraphrase W. H. Auden, there is always another story. And as my work has shown, there is much more than meets the eye.[3]

Katie Gale, only one among the many who have passed this way, resilient in death as in life, called out unambiguously to have more said of her. For this we, those who have come lately to this place called Oyster Bay, can be grateful.

Postscript

HISTORY, BERNARD BAILYN tells us, is an imaginative construction. However, historical imagination cannot run willy-nilly. It is something to be cultivated and paid attention to because imagination and one's intuitive impulses generate and guide good research questions. Still, the answers divined from imaginative queries must be bound by documentation and limited, to a great extent, by the evidence that has survived. That is, facts must be allowed to act as a confining straightjacket.

As a historian, you may have some bare-boned facts to begin with, but you've got to make something of them if you are to tell a story. You've got to use your wit and struggle to make sense of it all, even with your arms pinned behind your back by that jacket of real evidence. After all, your brain is still free. Your heart is still beating. And like the Scottish judges during the Enlightenment, you are free to ask, "What really happened here?" and not be bound by past interpretations.

Nevertheless, the writing of history must be somewhat limited by the obligation to be at least consistent with what has been previously established by careful work. That is, new accounts must somehow "fit" with what is already known. Or present a good rationale for why they do not.

I try always to remain cognizant of Bailyn's guiding words and caveats. Construction done with the kind of evidence I have requires some leaps of faith. I believe those leaps are well considered and informed, and reasonable given what I've found in the record. I'm not taking big jumps, as do the revolutionaries in science, the fellows who decide that continents drift. Mine are tiny steps taken in order to make some sense of a lot of information and emerge with a good story. I've followed lots of trails in order to verify information. I've followed every lead in order to ground my work. Still, I'm making many leaps.

Small facts can be made to speak to larger issues. Apart from recounting Katie's life, a life that seemed to call out for attention, a look at Oyster Bay in the late 1800s may add to or even correct history's depiction of the lives of post-treaty Indian peoples of Western Washington and the choices they were making about how to live their lives in a period of enormous change.

Beyond that, I write Katie's story for the descendants of those who lived on Oyster Bay long ago. I write for the young women and girls who are the descendants of Jennie Krise and David Whitener and the T'Peeksin people particularly.

Much of my book is based on primary source documents. I footnote many of the documents I consulted, but this book is part memoir and written for the general public, not an academic audience. Therefore it is not as consistently sourced as it would be if produced specifically for other scholars. I consulted and re-read many published and unpublished works, many of which I had read throughout my more than fifteen years working as a consultant for the Puyallup Tribe of Indians. For those who wish for more, there are several excellent, well-researched volumes by scholars on this period and region in print and generally available. These are texts that problematize and examine the history of the Northwest and the relationships between Indians and non-Indians. Richard White's work influenced my thinking on Puget Sound history. His *"It's Your Misfortune and None of My Own": A New History of the American West* is a brilliant reframing of the European American settlement of the American West. *Beyond the Reservation: Indians, Settlers, and the Law in Washington Territory, 1853–1889*, by Brad Asher, covers the time period in which I'm most interested and addresses many of the legal issues that had impact on the players in my drama. Brad Asher is also author of "A Shaman Killing Case on Puget Sound, 1873–1874," published in the *Pacific Northwest Quarterly*. Jay Miller's *Lushootseed Culture and the Shamanic Odyssey: An Anchored Radiance* presents a beautifully written and respectful exegesis of Lushootseed Coast Salish culture. That volume is an additive to his earlier volume, *Shamanic Odyssey: The Lushootseed Salish Journey to the Land of the Dead*. Paige Raibmon's *Authentic Indians: Episodes of Encounter from the Late-Nineteenth-Century Northwest Coast* takes a unique look at Indian resistance to assimilation and the colonial imagination. *Oregon and the Collapse of Illahee: U.S. Empire and the Transformation of an Indigenous World, 1792–1859*, by Gray H. Whaley, is an excellent recent study that gives a well-researched depiction of the time leading up to my focus. *American Indian Policy in Crisis: Christian Reformers and the Indian, 1865–1900*, by Francis Paul Prucha, describes in detail the incidents and conversations that inspired the development of Grant's Peace Policy. *Be of Good Mind: Essays on the Coast Salish*, edited by Bruce Granville Miller, is a fine addition to the growing field called "indigenous historiography." Coll-Peter Thrush's *Native Seattle: Histories from the Crossing-Over Place* gives critical attention to the biracial, biethnic origins of Seattle. The years covered by *Native Seattle* overlap with years covered by the Katie Gale story. *Shadow Tribe: The Making of Columbia River Indian Identity* is a very good, inclusive history of Columbia River Indians by Andrew Fisher. Stephen Dow Beckham produced a classic account of the Rogue River wars in *Requiem for a People: The Rogue Indians and the Frontiersmen*. Alexandra Harmon's *Indians in the Making: Ethnic Relations and Indian Identities around Puget Sound* and other essays by her have contributed immeasurably to the discussion of identity and assimilation in the Northwest.

"'I See What I Have Done': The Life and Murder Trial of Xwelas, a S'Klallam Woman," by Coll-Peter Thrush and Robert H. Keller Jr., and *Many Tender Ties: Women in Fur-Trade Society*, by Sylvia Van Kirk, are two works that focus on Indian–European American marriages.

See also Peyton Kane, "The Whatcom County Nine: Legal and Political Ramifications of Metis Family Life in Washington Territory." A more general book on Indian and European American relationships is *Shadows of Our Ancestors: Readings in the History of Klallam-White Relations*, edited by Jerry Gorsline. It includes essays on the Isaac Stevens treaties, the Shaker Church, and smallpox as well as the story of the Klallam woman Seam-Itza and her marriage to a European man named Alexander Vincent. Other works on marriage generally include "'Why She Didn't Marry Him': Love, Power, and Marital Choice on the Far Western Frontier" by Cynthia Culver Prescott. Peggy Pascoe has written about gender issues in Western history as well as intermarriage and miscegenation laws. Her books include *Relations of Rescue: The Search for Female Moral Authority in the American West, 1874–1939* and *What Comes Naturally: Miscegenation Law and the Making of Race in America*. In my text I mention Helga Estby's walk. That story is chronicled in a fine book by Linda Hunt called *Bold Spirit: Helga Estby's Forgotten Walk across Victorian America*.

For more detail on disease, *American Indian Holocaust and Survival: A Population History since 1492*, by Russell Thornton, provides a general overview of disease and demographics in the Americas. More often referenced is Robert Boyd's *The Coming of the Spirit of Pestilence: Introduced Infectious Diseases and Population Decline among Northwest Coast Indians, 1774–1874*.

General ethnographies of the indigenous people of southern Puget Sound are few. The classics are Marian W. Smith's *The Puyallup-Nisqually* and Herman Haeberlin and Erna Gunther's *The Indians of Puget Sound*. William Sturtevant, ed., *Handbook of North American Indians*, volume 7, *Northwest Coast*, is an oft-noted and quoted source. I won't take the space here to note the limitations of this and previous volumes in the series. It is a general reference to be used and read critically. Smith's book is of great value specifically because it is based on interviews with people whose experience and memories dated to the early post-treaty period. She also relied on notes supplied by Arthur C. Ballard, who collected myths, kinship terms, calendric terms, and information about fishing weirs and other details of Native life from Indian friends and neighbors in the Auburn area. His unpublished work includes a lengthy deposition given in a 1952 court proceeding.[1]

The story of Katie Gale, more personally told than some of these, adds dimensionality to the history of women generally and Indian women in particular in the post-treaty, early statehood days of Washington. Reading this account of Katie's life, I believe, opens a window for the reader to the challenges posed to and strategies employed by Indian women who chose not to live on a reservation. This narrative provides an example of ways in which Indian people, and women particularly, related to land and the capitalist economy in this era. Katie's decisions and struggles provide a glimpse of the dynamics that held sway in Indian-white marital relations. The account of her actions during the 1890s also serves as a case study of ways in which Indian people mobilized the law to serve their interests.

There are many less central but compelling issues raised by Katie's life and the story of the late 1800s on Oyster Bay. The scarcity of multigenerational families among both Indians and whites on the bay, for example, raises questions about leadership and eldering in this transitional world. Who was there to provide a foothold? To establish rules? To reinforce an ethic? The multiplicity of white-Indian marriages, even those born purely of self-interest, and the relatively friendly, cooperative relations between whites and Indians, particularly before the consolidation of the oyster industry and statehood, speak to a world of possible futures while people were still on somewhat equal footing. Yet, in a relatively short period, ideologies of class, race, and gender, the hegemony of American capitalism and the values that are integral to it, and, to some degree, illness and death, first relegated Indian people to the position of laborers and ultimately obscured or even eliminated altogether their participation in the oyster business until the late twentieth century.

Conventional wisdom repeats stories that Indian women were

married "Indian style" to white men to justify the men's claims to women's tidelands or qualify them for larger homesteads. These men then presumably nudged the women out of the picture. One memoir claims that Indian men were cheated out of lands during gambling games. My work leads me to suspect that these stories perpetuate a prejudice, one that suggests that Indians, particularly women, were not clever enough to know what was up and were easily one-upped by stereotypical conniving whites. A close look at the data does not seem to support these colorful, European American–centered perceptions of the period. Though the immediate result of these alliances may have been to reduce the number of Indian people involved in the oyster business, a close look at the records reveals that many Indians in fact knew the law and pursued the legal avenues available to them to retain their livelihoods and succeed in the new economic milieu, at least for a short time.

Indeed, the at least short-term successes of some Indian oyster growers survive in the record. The names of Slocum and Tobin, among others, remain on current Oyster Bay oyster bed charts, though these resource areas have long belonged to others. Nevertheless, they filed homestead claims, took action to secure oyster beds when the Callow and Bush Acts were passed, and knew what their rights were as citizens after they took homesteads. However, most of the other names, the names of the many Indian people who were actors and subjects in the economic reality of the late nineteenth century, are harder to document.

There are other accounts of this period that speak specifically to the early foundation of the oyster industry. Those I have examined tend to repeat half truths or unsubstantiated stories of the era. E. N. Steele's *The Rise and Decline of the Olympia Oyster* contains some significant inaccuracies. He lists Joseph Gale among the names of Indians who were oyster growers, for example. Humphrey Nelson's *The Little Man and the Little Oyster*, like Cora Chase's book, is a lively memoir, but his comments on Indians in the industry are limited and apparently hearsay. Kriste Johnson's thesis, "Bridging the Gastronomic Gap: A Method for Preserving the Olympia Oyster as Foodstuff," though fascinating, relies heavily on Steele and Nelson for historical material and thus repeats misrepresentations. Curiously, one can find many accounts that claim an ancestor was "the first" to ship oysters or grow oysters commercially. These accounts don't jibe with early histories of Oyster Bay that I've been able to document here.

Katie Gale became almost an obsession years ago when someone loaned me a copy of Cora Chase's *The Oyster Was Our World*. Cora herself was an icon, a writer and the wife of W. Corwin Chase, a woodblock artist and frequenter of the ebullient colony of artists and performers who orbited around the person of Orre Nobles and his elegant home on Hood Canal in the 1920s. Stories circulate about Cora, too. She was known, apparently, as a fierce vegetarian whose evangelical approach to the simple act of eating still provokes comment from elders in the area if her name happens to come up in conversation. Cora's early days were spent on Oyster Bay, Totten Inlet, southern Puget Sound, where she lived on a float house with her oyster-culling parents and grandparents. In her manuscript she mentions, almost in passing, that her parents worked during the winter of 1897 for an Indian woman named "Kitty Gail," who owned "a large bed up the bay from New Kamilche."[2] Accompanying the anecdote is a picture of Katie's culling house. Cora relates a brief story of Katie's relationship with her white husband: In 1893 "Kitty put up a fight for her rights, and managed to retain half the oyster land, and an old shack on the property, while Joe built a fine new home for his white bride." The bride's name, I learned later, was Lillian. She was a woman with whom his friends said Joseph had been spending time for several years after 1893, abandoning the everyday operation of his oyster business to his Chinese-Umatilla supervisor, Tom Kee. But Joseph didn't marry Lillian until after Katie died in 1899. Before then, the children and Katie were on their own. Cora's version of the story continues, "On one occasion, during the controversy, when Joe was threatening Kitty, hoping to get her to relinquish all rights, they were near two trees standing close together — the trees that is — and Kitty reached between the trees and got Joe's long beard in her hands, and twisted it around the tree until he gave in to her demands."

The story of Katie's "handling" of Joseph, told with great relish and mixed with admiration of Katie's decision to stand her ground, became mythologized, condensed, conflated, and confused over the years. Adolph Johnson, who moved to Oyster Bay with his parents in 1893, had heard a version. "Joe got drunk and Kitty drug him near a small tree. He had long whiskers, and Kitty tied them firmly to this tree and made Joe holler, 'Uncle.'" Both Adolph and Cora report that Joseph and Katie had married "Indian style." That they were not legally married is a story that still circulates. In one more recent document, Katie is called a "common law wife" and her marriage to Joseph characterized as one that took place in an "Indian ceremony."

The colorful story of Katie and Joseph's fight was passed along to Cora Chase, and probably many others, from Florence Waldrip Taylor. The tale has been picked up from Chase and still circulates. Because Katie is depicted as plucky and strong, some who have heard of Katie, even today, say that "she was a woman ahead of her time."

Why did the stories of Katie continue to circulate? Why was she characterized as a "common law wife"? Was she a "woman ahead of her time"? And what does that mean? Did she break out of some carefully manufactured social and cultural mold for late nineteenth-century women? Did she act out against all expectations for even these denizens of the rural Northwest, many of them, surely, themselves oddballs and eccentrics?

When I first read Cora Chase's book, I thought I could read between the lines that stories of Katie Gale had made an impression on the young Cora. I later discovered that the period when Cora's family had worked for Katie was during the time of her second divorce proceeding and that Cora's father had helped see Katie through a difficult time of her life. Indeed, he had championed her in the courtroom.

Frank Gingrich, Cora's father, was a populist and printer, a fellow well liked on the bay, a "kloshe tillicum."[3] His mother and siblings had died in the diphtheria epidemic that swept the bay in 1883. He was also a progressive humanist. He came to Katie Gale's defense in that 1898 divorce proceeding. He had known her for ten years by that time and wrote in his deposition that she was a "good and faithful wife" to the plaintiff, her husband, Joseph, and of "virtuous character."[4] He said that though her husband was making around $125 a week from the oysters shipped from his beds (nearly $4,000 in today's currency), Katie was maintaining and supporting her children through her own efforts.

I had other work to do in the archives during the period when I first read Cora Chase's account, long before I found Katie's tombstone, so I took the time, out of curiosity, to look in the early state tideland records. I found Katie Gale's applications for oyster land, as well as names of other Indian claimants. I filed these notes away for future reference.

Katie Gale's name came up again for me when, a number of years ago, still before the tombstone was found and I had begun work on this story, the road on which I lived was to be named. I tried to persuade my neighbors to pick the name "Katie Gale Lane," but based on the scant information I had about this woman at the time, I was not successful in convincing the others that she was important enough. In those days I didn't even know where on the bay she had worked and lived. We settled for the distinctly nonspecific "Oyster Beach Road," forever confused by first-time visitors with nearby "Oyster Bay Road," as "Katie Gale Lane" never would have been.

Katie Gale went back into my files, a curiosity. I did not expect I'd ever know much more about her than I did then.

Acknowledgments

ON MAY 31, 2011, I paid a visit to David Whitener, a man who filled many leadership roles with the Squaxin Island Tribe during his lifetime. David was a colleague of mine at the Evergreen State College. And David is a direct descendant of people who are part of the Katie Gale story. Notably, he is a descendant of William and Jennie Krise.

Many summers ago, David invited several of us who were taking part in an Evergreen State College faculty summer institute to come with him to Squaxin Island. There, with David as our host, we camped, made drawings, cooked and ate together, and listened to his stories about the island. It was a gift.

When I first approached David about writing the Katie Gale story, seeking his blessing, it was November 2004. We had a few conversations about her. Yes, he had heard of her. His family called her Kitty Gale. He told me what little he remembered hearing about her. I discussed my hopes for the book and the project and I was honored and pleased that he was interested in the work.

During that May 2011 visit I placed the almost-finished book in his hands. I told him about the dedication to him. This full circle meant a lot to me and I'm certain it did to him. He had a report prepared for the Squaxin Island Tribe on a night table beside him. He picked it up and passed it to me. "You're quoted in here," he said. It was a brief history of the Tobin family cemetery. Indeed, I was mentioned in the text. This exchange reminded me once again of the friendship and collegiality I'd always felt with David.

Then he quoted Mary Hillaire, a member of the Lummi Tribe and another of our Evergreen colleagues. Though long gone, her words and guidance still mean a lot to many of us. David looked at me and said, "What did you do? How did you do it? What did you learn? What difference did it make?" I took that as a challenge. Now that the project is completed and the book is nearing publication, it is time to do a "self-evaluation," something we at Evergreen always did at the end of a program of study. I realized that the book would not be complete, nor would the work be finished, until I'd taken this final, self-reflective step. Thanks to David, that is what I'm doing in my life now. David passed away in November 2012.

I can't know for certain how much Mary Hillaire's perspective on learning about culture guided my project. Reminded by David of some of her other words, I thought about how I'd approached the work of this book: "If you are going to learn about people, you must look at their relationship to land and water, their relationship to each other, their relationship to work, and their relationship to each other," she'd said. If I didn't follow her formula explicitly, I certainly owe an enormous debt to her for the words and wisdom she shared with many of us during the early years of the Evergreen State College.

Likewise, Bruce Subiyay Miller, a member of the Skokomish Tribe and a friend and colleague from the late 1960s until his death, has been a tremendous influence on my perspective and values. Bruce's work in the region as educator, weaver, and ceremonial and spiritual leader was acknowledged in many ways. He was, among other things, the recipient of a National Endowment for the Arts Folk Arts Fellowship in 2006. His much too early passing left a hole in many hearts, including mine.

I can't begin to measure the many ways in which working with Yvonne Peterson, a member of the Chehalis Tribe, has informed the sensibilities I brought to this project. We were colleagues at the Evergreen State College and worked together on several public school curriculum projects. Before and after that, I valued her friendship, perspective, and challenges.

Maiselle Bridges, renowned Frank's Landing elder and activist in the Puget Sound "fish wars" of the 1970s, revisited stories she had told me earlier about her grandfather and grandmother, James and Louisa Kettle Tobin, who were resident on Oyster Bay during the time Katie was there.

I wouldn't have met Maiselle Bridges had Rhonda Foster, director of cultural resources for the Squaxin Island Tribe, not enlisted my help in a project to document and protect the Tobin family cemetery on the Tobin ranch site. Carol Burns, videographer and director of the film *As Long as the Rivers Run*, facilitated the meeting with Maiselle Bridges. *As Long as the Rivers Run* documents the demand that the right to fish be respected. Her friendship with Maiselle Bridges stems from the 1968–71 struggle depicted in the documentary. Rhonda herself has deep family ties with the Krises, who are mentioned and acknowledged a number of times in this book.

Hank Adams, an activist, scholar, and strategist who has worked tirelessly for Native American rights for more than forty years, introduced me to Grant's Peace Policy many years ago, when we were both at the Evergreen State College. I remember walking into his house and marveling at the dozens of cardboard boxes full of documents he had. They were everywhere: on the floor, on tables, on the stairs. I couldn't have imagined that someday my own place would look just like that. He was truly an early inspiration for my scholarship, my dedication to telling the stories I try to tell, and for helping me, a white anthropologist, define my role in the work.

I want to thank those who encouraged me to write this book when it was in its early stages and I was unsure of myself. Particular thanks go to the wonderful writer Luis Urrea and my writing group at Summer Fishtrap in 2008. I received encouragement and support to finish this project there in the embrace of friends and in the beautiful Wallowa Valley. I was not unaware of the history of Wallowa and Chief Joseph's band as I set out on my own journey with Katie Gale's story.

It's a good story, my Fishtrap friends said, though I'd read just a chapter to them. Special thanks to Luis for the phrase "a literature of witness and respect." When he said it I knew that's what I would try to produce. I'm grateful for Cindy Urrea's words of advice. My hesitation to improvise and imagine big chunks of this story to make it work were overcome with her help. After Fishtrap, I knew I could continue to make the book personal while grounding it in research.

Many thanks to the freelance Seattle-based editor Anne Kellor. Anne read through two early drafts of the book. She gave me more ideas than I can ever thank her for. She asked more questions than I thought I could answer. My prose was much improved by her suggestions.

It is not an exaggeration to say that this book wouldn't have the rich detail it has were it not for Stan Graham and Shirley Erhart, both with the Mason County Historical Society Museum. Stan's enthusiasm for this project matched my own. He was in every way a collaborator. I have relied on his tenacity. Shirley Erhart dug in, found leads, and shared in the excitement of discovery. She peppered me with clippings, reprints, and copies of *Mason County Journal* articles and generally kept my interest alive with details. Billie Howard, the Mason County Historical Society's museum director, put up with our cries of delight when some new connection was made. She was always generous with her time. The resources of the Mason County Historical Society Museum, generally, were invaluable.

I have always valued conversations with Charlene Krise, director of the Squaxin Island Museum. She shared her enthusiasm for this project when I first mentioned it to her. She also shares my passion for research. I have appreciated her continuing interest and support and hope she finds the book useful.

In October 2011 I visited Jim Tobin, the grandson of James and Louisa Tobin, in his café in Amanda Park. Jim Tobin is enrolled at the Quinault Reservation. I presented him with a copy of the photograph I had found of his great-grandfather, Chief Kettle. We talked at length about stories he'd heard as a child about his grandparents and other ancestors. He generously gave me permission to use photographs of his grandparents from his collection. I thank him so much and hope he'll find this book of interest.

It was Tallis King George, a colleague and research enthusiast, who lead me to the treasure trove of Mud Bay photographs at the Alaska State Library. I thank her for remembering my interests and for our continuing correspondence.

Elaine V. R. Taylor, a genealogist, did some important tracking for the project, especially as we were in pursuit of Inez Fanchier's family. She also modeled a good way to organize and handle the data I had collected. I owe a lot to Pete Bloomfield for coming forth with his recollection of the little cemetery he'd seen while logging in the late 1950s.

Candace Wellman, a historian of the Bellingham, Washington, area, posed provocative questions and shared information on several cases involving Indian women and European American spouses. In the past year we've had occasion to talk and exchange even more finds. Especially valuable were some of the leads to information on the Collins family of Arcadia Point. Shanna Stevenson, still with the Thurston County Historic Commission when I talked with her about the project, offered good leads as I looked for information on Olympia and its docks in the late 1800s.

I am particularly grateful to Bev Smith, a freelance writer and horse person extraordinaire. She helped me to visualize the details of a possible attack in a horse barn that may have led to Joseph Gale's death.

Tim McMillan, current manager of the Olympia Oyster Company, found photographs in the company's collection, shared stories, and reviewed and interpreted historical oyster industry photographs for my benefit. His explanation of early techniques in oyster cultivation helped to further my understanding of what I was seeing and reading in the nineteenth-century documents. He shared stories he had heard about Abner Smith, Joseph Gale's friend, and other early oyster growers.

Justin Taylor was descended from Taylors and Waldrips. He was generous with his time, and I cherish the gift of his stories about visiting the Joseph Gale house as a boy during the period when his Waldrip relatives lived in it. The house still stood on the property that was and is now owned by Olympia Oyster Company into the 1990s. It was occupied by various managers and workers, the last, perhaps, the Nagai family, who worked for Olympia Oyster Company. Taylor described the inside of the house and how the trail came down from what is now called Bloomfield Road to the property. His mother knew Katie Gale, a thrilling fact that made me feel so much closer to her. Justin Taylor passed away in the winter of 2011. I am honored to have known him.

Dee Depoe, a librarian at Timberland Regional Library, allowed me to read and copy the ledgers from the McDonald store at Arcadia. These valuable ledgers were passed down through her family and are in her possession.

Stephanie Johnson and Jim Simard at the Alaska State Library helped me with access to James Wickersham's photographs of Mud Bay in 1892 and suggested avenues for notes that might help in interpretation. Jim also directed me to the very helpful Sean Lanksbury at the Washington State Library. There is more to be done and I know Sean, Jim, and Stephanie will do what they can.

Nancy Brewer, Duane Fagergren, and Charlie Stephens have all been around shellfish and Oyster Bay for a long time and each has helped me. Duane gave me a photograph of a float house that may be the last one seen in the area. Nancy Brewer gave me firsthand experience with the culling and opening process. We looked at sink floats together. We stood in a culling house and talked about what it was like to be out there, rocking with the waves, cold and wet. Charlie introduced me to Justin Taylor and offered kind and supportive words throughout the research period.

Steve Lundin lives just below the site of the Tobin ranch on Eld Inlet. His personal research on the Tobins helped me immensely. It was he who led me to Sallie Weatherall's court case. It is from that case that we have the best descriptions of Chief Kettle and of the point of view of the Indian community. Steve and I share an enthusiasm for documenting the history of the Tobins and the late 1800s–early 1900s life on the Eld Inlet and Mud Bay. Steve's abiding dedication to finding details to add to that story is truly admirable. I thank him for his help on this project as well as his friendship.

Staff at the Washington State Archives and their Southwest Regional Archives were always helpful. Lannie Weaver was especially generous with her time and interest in this project. Others have put up with my dozens of requests for help over the past few of years. Thanks so much.

Various other archivists helped. These include Joy Werlink, research librarian, and Lynette Miller, head of collections, both at the research center of the Washington State Historical Society; J. Norman Dizon at the Providence Archives; and Karl House of the Puget Sound Maritime Historical Society, an affiliate of the Seattle Museum of History and Industry.

Special thanks to Kathleen Knies at the Puget Sound Maritime Historical Society for finding a picture of the steamer *Willie* that I requested, even though she and her staff were in the middle of the Seattle Museum of History and Industry's move to a new home.

Cheryl Roffe, collections manager for the Lane County Historical Society and Museum, helped me track down invaluable information on the Gale family and the "Lost Wagon Train." Her help allowed me to add depth to the Joseph Gale story.

Drew Crooks, a historian of Olympia, helped me with a few sticky questions, especially in my quest to learn more about Katie Gale's attorneys.

Though she was not directly involved in this project, I thank Judy Wright, historian and archivist to the Puyallup Tribe, with whom I worked in the early 1990s. Judy mentored me, especially in understanding the treaty and early post-treaty history of the first people of Western Washington.

The first draft of the Katie Gale story was for an article subsequently published in *Columbia*, the magazine of the Washington State Historical

Society. Jo Ann Ridley provided specific editorial advice on that article. The conversations with her at her home on Totten Inlet, not far from my own and the setting of the story, were most valuable. Her lifetime of work and stories about it helped to illuminate my own particular struggles and gave me courage. Her ideas for enhancing the work were always useful. I cannot thank her enough for taking time for a friendship and offering her assistance. I miss her very much. Joanne Miller read a draft of the same article. My prose was enhanced by her suggestions. Other early readers included Susan Christian, who always asks the hard questions and catches my not-so-subtle drifts into rants. She was quick to answer my questions about usage.

Fritz Wolff, the author of *A Room for the Summer: Adventure, Misadventure, and Seduction in the Mines of the Coeur D'Alene*, read a much later draft. We had an accidental meeting that led to a conversation about writing. His comments after he read my manuscript gave me renewed confidence.

Trova Heffernan is the director of the Legacy Project and creative director of the Heritage Center, both projects out of the office of the Washington Secretary of State. We exchanged some important details regarding the Kettles and Tobins. It was good to have a person as excited about research as I. I'm looking forward to reading her work and finding excuses to talk in the future.

I presented early versions of Katie Gale's story "in progress" to a history of women in the West class at the Evergreen State College, the Henderson House Museum in Tumwater, the Pacific Northwest Historians Guild conference in Seattle in March 2005, and the Mason County Historical Society in September 2005. All of these audiences asked good questions and helped me to focus my telling of Katie's story. Carla Wulfberg, the director of the Henderson House Museum, has been unflagging in her support for my work. I thank her for that.

Versions of the story have appeared in the *Oregon Historical Quarterly* and *Columbia* magazine. Thanks to Marianne Keddington-Lang, then at the Oregon Historical Society Press, and Eliza Jones and Aaron

Lisle, who worked on the *Oregon Historical Quarterly* article. Thanks to Christina DuBois at *Columbia*, a publication of the Washington State History Society, who edited and prepared "Tideland Tales" for publication in that wonderful magazine.

Dear friends listened patiently as Katie Gale became my primary topic of conversation over several years. One, Marilyn Frasca, read the whole book in its next-to-last-draft version and made helpful comments. Sally Cloninger was ready to advise and support. They both made certain I was fed well, particularly during the last few months of my journey. Northwest photographer Mary Randlett's friendship has helped me to "see" better. Her enthusiasm for my work generally has meant a great deal to me. She said, "You've got to get this published." So did Karen James, an old friend from graduate days at the University of Washington, where we were both students in the anthropology department. She shared some important sources with me and gave me pep talks regularly. It helped to have her rooting for me. Another anthropologist and friend from my university days, Elizabeth Diffendal, helped me enormously as I set about the task of revising. My walking group members helped me to keep balance and occasionally asked probing questions that caused me to rethink elements of the story. Joy Gold gave me an important clue that helped me with research on mid-nineteenth-century funerary practices.

Dr. Erika Bourguignon was my guiding light and inspiration when I was an undergraduate at Ohio State University. Though I had many mentors after, including the memorable Melville Jacobs at the University of Washington, it was Dr. B. who set the bar for me. I am deeply grateful for what has been a wonderful career because of her.

The editors and reviewers at the University of Nebraska Press have truly shaped this book and nudged me in important directions I would not have thought to go on my own. I am deeply grateful to Matthew Bokovoy, senior acquisitions editor, for reading my manuscript and seeing its potential. The anonymous reviewers prodded me and caused me to rethink many of my initial points. Heather Stauffer, editorial assistant, steered me through the long process of rewrites and preparing the manuscript for final editing, and Sara Springsteen, associate project editor, guided me through the copyediting process. Joy Margheim's much-appreciated copyediting forced me to relook at many of my own words and ideas. Her contribution to the final book is immeasurable. I thank them all.

Last and first, I thank Katie Gale. Katie Gale bid me do this work. I am certain of that. I hope I've done her story justice.

Many others have contributed to this work. I apologize to those whose names I have not remembered to acknowledge.

Responsibility for this book is mine alone. I have interpreted what I've learned and molded a story that I believe is sensible and consistent with the facts. Any errors are mine. I would be delighted to know where I seem to have gone wrong or where I clearly haven't got it right.

Chronology

+/-1000 BP–1850s
T'Peeksin and predecessor T'Peeksin peoples occupy Oyster Bay, establish camps and village sites, live a maritime and hunting life.

1818
Chief Kettle, aka Labatum Kettle and Old Man Kettle, Louisa Tobin's father, born, arguably on Case Inlet or Satsop River area.

1822
William Krise born in Warren County, Ohio.

1847–48
Joseph Gale born.

1850
Donation Land Claim Act.

1853
Joseph Gale leaves Illinois with family to travel to Lane County, Oregon Territory.

Smallpox in Western Washington.

Washington Territory formed from Oregon Territory.

1854
Treaty of Medicine Creek is signed at She-Nah-Num with representatives of T'Peeksin present.

1855
Chief Kettle, Louisa Tobin's father, comes from Case Inlet to Squaxin Island, designated a reservation but used during the war to confine area Indians, including potential combatants. Her father gives up his guns to the Sherwood brothers, according to Tobin's notes to Ruth Greiner.

1855–56
War between Indians in Washington Territory and the U.S. Army and armed militia and volunteers. Ended in the controversial hanging of Leschi, exonerated in 2004. Impetus for the war was the Medicine Creek Treaty. Many Indians in Puget Sound incarcerated for the duration.

1856
Presumed year of Katie Gale's birth.

James Tobin born.

1860–61?
Louisa Kettle Tobin born.

1862
Homestead Act.

1863
A territorial act "to encourage the cultivation of oysters" is passed January 1863. It is amended several times between 1863 and 1879.

1868
Katie is twelve and in the Oyster Bay area.

1870
Joseph Gale in Cottage Grove, Oregon, working in a sawmill.

1871
Lillian McDonald, Joseph Gale's third spouse, born in Scio, Oregon.

Dustin Sands Jr., son of Dustin Sands and Calista, Joseph Gale's first spouse, is born.

1874
Cesalle (aka Seesall or Cesall) working for farmer John Campbell on Big Skookum Inlet.

1875
Indian Homestead Act.

Joseph Gale in Olympia.

1877
Hattie, Katie's eldest daughter, born (according to census age from 1892; according to her tombstone age, she was born in 1879).

Joseph Gale marries first wife, Calista.

1878
Henry, Katie's eldest son, born, according to tombstone age.

Joseph Gale moves to Mason County and establishes himself in the oyster business with J. A. Smith and Dick Helser. Taylor and Burr run the *Old Settler* in the bay to take oysters to market. Runs from head of Oyster Bay to Olympia.

1879

Hattie, Katie's eldest daughter, born, according to tombstone age.

1880

Chief Kettle is listed in census as "oysterman."

Joseph Gale and Abner Smith are cited in oyster violation. Witnesses brought forth are the Tobins, Skookum George and his spouse, Sally, and others.

1881

John Slocum's death, rebirth, and vision establish the Shaker Church and religion.

Puget Sound Oystermen's Association is formed with Gale, Helser, and Smith.

Joseph Gale divorces Calista.

1882

Chinese Exclusionary Act restricts Chinese immigration to the United States and denies naturalization.

1883

Transcontinental railroad/ Northern Pacific Railway links Chicago and Seattle.

A child is born to Joseph and Katie Gale. Likely named Elizabeth A. Gale.

Diphtheria epidemic on Oyster Bay, according to Cora Chase.

1885–86

Anti-Chinese riots in Tacoma and Seattle.

1886

December 19. Joseph Gale marries Kate Kettle. Witnesses are W. A. Parish and A. J. Smith. Abner Smith and Louisa Isaacs, daughter of Henry Isaacs, marry on the same day.

Maud Gale, daughter of Katie and Joseph Gale, is born.

Oyster beds freeze. Olympic oysters can be damaged at extreme low temperatures and whole reefs can be frozen in water and floated away from the beds.

1887

Dawes Act, or General Allotment Act, passed. This act allots reservation lands to individual Indian persons and opens land to purchase by non-Indians.

Joseph and Katie Gale purchase Bettman oyster beds, acquired by Bettman from Big Frank. Katie claims later that these beds were purchased wholly with her own, premarriage savings.

E. A. Gale, age four, living in Gale household. This is their daughter Elizabeth.

1888

April 28. Ray Gale, son of Joseph and Katie Gale, is born.

Franklin Kennedy, well-known Oyster Bay–area homesteader, dies.

Peter Stanup's last child dies. Stanup comes to Kamilche area to preach.

Two-year-old daughter of Adam and Harriet Korter, area residents, dies of whooping cough at Little Skookum; two other Oyster Bay infants also die.

Adam Korter dies. Harriet has lost a baby and her husband within a month.

Tom Slocum's mother dies at age seventy-five.

1889

Joseph Gale is listed on census living with Katie and five children: Hattie, fourteen; Henry, twelve; (illegible), six. The six-year-old, a female, no doubt Elizabeth, does not appear in further census records. "Mabel" (Maud) is three and Ray is one.

Washington becomes a state.

Louisa Smith is with Abner Smith. She is thirty-six. They are living with four children: Carl, fifteen; Archie, twelve; James, four; and Ida, one. Later the two older children contract tuberculosis and are sent to Yakima for their health. Louisa dies later of tuberculosis and Abner retires to Wapato, presumably to be near his adult children.

Old Man (Chief) Kettle is still on Oyster Bay.

1890
James Tobin granted a homestead of 160 acres on Mud Bay/Eld Inlet.

Various Indians apply for tidelands, including Mud Bay Charlie, Little Charlie, Olympia Jim, and Sally, Jack, and John Slocum.

Maud is injured by a fall and is apparently disabled.

Franz Boas visits the Puyallup Reservation and sees Peter Stanup preach.

1891
July 4. Potlatch with Chief Kettle on Mud Bay. Gold coins are given away. Kettle and others are in a buggy accident.

1892
More Indians file for tidelands, including Mud Bay Tom, Dick Jackson, Mud Bay Sam, Mud Bay Lewie "Youlouaut" (in tideland records), Olympia Jim, Sandy Wohaut. Shaker Church incorporated. Chief Kettle photographed at Mud Bay around July 4.

1893
February. Oyster beds freeze. Major damage to crop. Great Northern Railway links Seattle to St. Paul, Minnesota.

National economic panic.

Adolph Johnson's folks move to the head of Oyster Bay. He later recounts stories of Indian women working the oyster beds, including sorting and culling.

Peter Stanup, Puyallup, dies under mysterious circumstances.

July 21. Katie Gale files for "divorce and equitable distribution of their property on Oyster Bay."

Adolph Johnson reports in a later memoir that Sandy Wohaut was using a "dugout canoe" to load salmon gaffed in the fall on Kennedy Creek. He and Cora Chase mention the Indian women harvesting and culling oysters.

1894
Sandy Wohaut applies to tidelands board for appraisal of his holdings.

1895

Bush and Callow Acts passed in Washington State, allowing sale of tidelands to private citizens for purpose of shellfish farming.

Henry, Katie Gale's son, dies at age seventeen, according to his tombstone.

Joseph Gale is a Washington State fish commissioner.

1897

Big Frank, a signee for the Skokomish to the Point No Point Treaty and former Oyster Bay resident, dies. John Slocum dies.

Frank Gingrich is culling oysters for Katie Gale. This is the period described in Cora Chase's memoir, *The Oyster Was Our World*.

Joseph Gale is threatened by a "chinaman" with a knife. The "chinaman" is arrested, brought up before Justice Baldwin, and placed under a $300 bond.

Klondike Gold Rush and Seattle boom.

1898

Katie Gale executes a will.

Joseph Gale files for divorce from Katie. The 1893 divorce proceedings are not finalized. He calls off this suit when it is clear that Katie is dying.

Maud is in St. Amable's boarding school in Olympia.

The *Maine* is sunk and the Spanish-American War begins.

1899

August 6. Katie Gale dies. She is "separated" from Joseph. She leaves her considerable wealth to her two surviving children.

November 18. Joseph Gale marries Lillian McDonald of Scio, Oregon.

1900

Population of Chinese laborers on the bay has gone up. Japanese laborers also appear on census rolls.

Joseph and Lillian Gale are living in a new house on the property where Katie's house was. Maud and Ray are "at school" in Olympia.

1901
Joseph Gale has "40 acres of excellent oyster beds under a state of cultivation." He shipped 2,500 sacks of oysters the previous season and employs twelve men in the busy season. His "ranch" is 214 acres with a quarter mile of waterfront. Other oyster farmers on Oyster Bay are Taylor and Son, Waldrip, Helser, Hudson, Korter, Hurley, Jim Simmons, Harry Weatherall, John Flander, Dick Jackson, and H. M. Pierce. Sallie Hall Weatherall, who has been Harry's life partner in the oyster business, is not mentioned.

September 24. Joseph Gale dies of a "concussion of the brain." The funeral is "overflowing," with both band and choir performing.

J. W. Ludgate is appointed coguardian of Maud and Ray Gale.

1903
Maud marries; Chief Kettle dies, age given as eighty-five.

1904
Gasoline boats on Oyster Bay. The latest addition is the *Traveler*, owned by the Olympia Oyster Company. On its maiden trip, the *Traveler* carries forty-seven sacks of oysters.

Inez is born, Maud's first and only child.

1905
Maud signs a will and dies on April 26.

1906
Ray Gale graduates from People's University.

1907
Ray Gale is playing basketball for Olympic Athletic Club.

1908
Lillian Gale releases guardianship of Ray Gale (already living with Maud's husband's family).

Notes

1. MY LODESTONE

1. Henry and Hattie were Katie's children. A record of Henry's death lists his mother as Katie George and his father as Ryalia Johns. I found nothing more about Ryalia Johns or this marriage. Hattie is called Hattie Kittle in court documents. Joseph Gale mentions both Henry and Hattie in his depositions. A strong, though brief, picture of Hattie emerges in the court documents for Katie and Joseph's 1893 divorce filing.

2. I will use terms such as "Indian," "indigenous," or "Native" to refer to the descendants of First Nations peoples. Sometimes I will use one of these terms as the people I'm writing about use it. In some cases I'll be quoting a text directly. I understand that each of these terms has its limitations and can be misleading. See Harmon, "Lines in Sand."

2. FIRST SALMON

1. Miller, *Lushootseed Culture*, 15.

2. Miller, *Lushootseed Culture*, 19.

3. Waterman, "Geographical Names," 185.

4. Miller, *Lushootseed Culture*, 21.

5. Foster, Ross, and Henry, "Ethno-History of Mason County."

6. Miller, *Lushootseed Culture*, 26, 27.

7. Smith, *Puyallup-Nisqually*, 32.

8. Miller, *Lushootseed Culture*, 26.

9. Jerry Meeker biographical notes, Special Collections, University of Washington Libraries, Seattle.

3. WHERE YOU COME FROM

1. Smith, *Puyallup-Nisqually*, 14.

2. *United States v. Washington*, 384 F.Supp. 312 (W.D. Wash. 1974).

4. INDIAN POLICY DURING KATIE GALE'S TIME

1. See Beckham, *Requiem for a People*; and Prucha, *American Indian Policy in Crisis*.

2. Fritz, "Making of Grant's 'Peace Policy,'" 414.

3. See Mark, *Stranger in Her Native Land*; and Gay, *With the Nez Perces*.

4. Beck, *Seeking Recognition*.

5. Emerson and Smith, *Divided by Faith*.

6. In one of the interesting moments of Carlisle history, Geronimo and some other Indian leaders visited the school in 1905 on their way to Washington DC for Theodore Roosevelt's second inauguration. Geronimo was asked to speak to the students and is quoted as saying, "You are here to study, to learn the ways of whitemen, do it well. You have a father here and a mother also. Your father is here, do as he tells you. Obey him as you would your own father. Although he is not your father he is a father to you now. . . . Do as you are told all the time and you won't get hungry." Recorded in the *Carlisle Arrow*, March 9, 1905, and quoted in Landis, "Carlisle Indian Industrial School History."

5. SOMETIMES I SEE A CANOE

1. Howard, "Archaeological Site Survey of Southwestern Puget Sound."

2. See Center for Columbia River History, http://www.ccrh.org/comm/cottage/primary/claim.htm, for the full text of the Donation Land Claim Act. The status of so-called half-breeds was in flux during this period. In 1857 a bill was introduced into the Oregon Territorial Legislature that would give citizenship rights to the children of white fathers and Indian mothers. The text of this bill can be found at Oregon State Archives, http://arcweb.sos.state.or.us/echoes/link22.html. The bill failed.

6. OYSTER BAY

1. Morgan, *Peter Puget On Puget's Sound*, 4–14; and Bell, Walker, and Meany, *New Vancouver Journal*.

2. Journal entry for May 1792 in Meany, *Vancouver's Discovery of Puget Sound*, 107–8, quoted in McBride, "Viewpoints and Visions," 22–23.

3. Foster, Ross, and Henry, "Ethno-History of Mason County."

4. Genesis 1:28.

5. Richards, "Stevens Treaties."

6. The Northern Pacific Railroad link between Chicago and Seattle was not completed until 1883.

7. Territorial laws enacted between 1873 and 1879, for example, were meant to encourage the cultivation of oysters and laid out the means by which a citizen could stake, claim, and acquire up to twenty acres of tideland for cultivation. These laws were also meant to protect natural beds.

8. The legal status of Indians of Western Washington, particularly nonreservation Indians, was regularly debated during the 1860s and 1870s. Their rights to file for homesteads, become citizens, and vote were widely discussed by lawmakers and officials with the Department of Interior, especially after the Civil War and the passage of the Fourteenth Amendment to the Constitution. The Indian Homestead Act, passed March 3, 1875, extended the benefits of the Homestead Act of 1862, making it possible for Indians to legitimately file for homesteads, though with the provision that they adopt "civilized habits" and abandon tribal affiliation. In section 15 it provided that "every Indian born in the United States, who is the head of a family, or who has arrived at the age of twenty-one years, and who has abandoned or may hereafter abandon his tribal relation, shall, on making satisfactory proof of such abandonment, under rules to be prescribed by the Secretary of the interior, be entitled to the benefits of the Act entitled 'An Act to secure Homesteads to actual Settlers on the Public Domain.'" *U.S. Statutes at Large* 18 (1875): 420. See Asher, *Beyond the Reservation*, 76–80.

9. Howard, "Archaeological Site Survey of Southwestern Puget Sound."

10. Scalopine was around eighty years old when he testified before the Court of Claims in 1927 in the case known as *Duwamish et al. v. United States of America*. Scalopine provided evidence on behalf of the Squaxin Tribe.

11. T. T. Waterman writes it TEpi'lkwtsid, "caving down mouth." See Waterman, "Puget Sound Geography." Marian W. Smith says the term "derives from . . . the name of the inlet." *Puyallup-Nisqually*, 14.

12. See Jamison, "Plainfin Midshipman," for more on the habits of the midshipman.

7. THE DUTIES OF A WOMAN

1. Though the spelling "Kamilche" is used on modern maps, it was often spelled "Kamilchie" in earlier records and accounts. I will most often use the spelling "Kamilche."

2. Maud is spelled "Maude" in some documents, and in one census she is called Mabel. I'm choosing to use "Maud" in my text.

3. These costs are based on information contained in the McDonald store ledgers from the period, now at the Mason County Historical Society, Shelton, Washington, or in the possession of McDonald descendants.

4. Examples of all the baskets described as well as the berry rake and the cedar mat were collected on Oyster Bay in 1920 by T. T. Waterman and are stored as part of the cultural resource collection of the National Museum of the American Indian in Washington DC. The author has seen and studied each piece.

5. Women drying clams before open fires can be seen in photographs taken on Mud Bay in 1892 by James Wickersham. See the Wickersham Collection, Alaska State Library, Juneau.

6. *Weatherall v. Weatherall*, 56 Wash. 344 (1909), Washington State Archives, Olympia.

7. Chase, *The Oyster Was Our World.*

8. Excerpt from D. H. Lawrence's poem "We Are Transmitters."

9. Catherine and William Walter diary, Washington State Historical Society Research Center, Tacoma.

10. Commercial yeast had been available since 1876 or so. However, many rural householders still made their own, and many preferred it.

11. Joseph Gale and Joseph Kullrich were planning to open a wholesale oyster house in Tacoma when Joseph died.

12. See Waterman, "Puget Sound Geography." Vi Hilbert provides no translation for "Kamilche" in her comments on Waterman's maps in her edited version of Waterman's work.

13. Adolph Johnson remembers, "When the girls climbed fences and over logs, we could tell what brand of flour they used at home." Johnson, "White-Indian Marriages."

14. Many items on this list are from the variously dated McDonald store ledgers.

8. "PICKING GROUNDS"

1. Frank Mossman, "Early Days in Mason County," quoted in Jones, "Kamilche."

2. Jones, "Kamilche."

3. T. T. Waterman notes this posture in his notes describing a blueberry picking "comb" he acquired from Mrs. Annie Bob on Oyster Bay in 1920. T.

T. Waterman Catalogue, box 195, folder 5, National Museum of the American Indian, Washington DC. There is a good photograph of a woman bent in this way while digging clams among the photographs James Wickersham took in southern Puget Sound in 1892. See the Wickersham Collection.

4. A sluice fork has many tines, like a potato-digging tool, but "tines longer and closer together."

5. "Wind row" is a term used by dirt farmers. Tobin means that the oysters are raked into a row and allowed to sit while the workers rake elsewhere; they then go back and fork all the rows of oysters onto the float.

6. Couch and Hassler, "Olympia Oyster."

7. Whitener memoir, Squaxin Island Museum, Library, and Research Center, Shelton, Washington.

8. From notes prepared by Andria VanderWel, great-granddaughter of William and Jennie Krise, and Wesley Whitener, grandson of William and Jennie Krise, unpublished, Mason County Historical Society, Shelton, Washington.

9. THE PEOPLE IN HER WORLD

1. Winthrop's journal, quoted in Winthrop, *Canoe and the Saddle*, 321.

2. For example, many inlets and islands in the sound bear the names of English or American officers, those who served with Vancouver or Charles Wilkes. Among them: Puget Sound for Peter Puget; Hood Canal (originally Hood's Canal) for the British admiral Lord Samuel Hood; Bainbridge Island for William Bainbridge, an American naval officer; and Vashon Island for James Vashon of the Royal Navy. Seattle and Tacoma stand as notable exceptions.

3. Crooks, "Governor Isaac I. Stevens and the Medicine Creek Treaty."

4. See Leavitt, "Under the Shadow of Maternity."

5. Whitener memoir.

6. See *Puget Sound Courier* (Olympia), December 25, 1873; *Territory v. Henry Fisk*, Washington Territorial District Court Records, Washington State Archives, Olympia; Asher, "Shaman-Killing Case on Puget Sound"; and Asher, *Beyond the Reservation*, 187–88.

7. *Tyee* is Chinook Jargon for important person, or "master."

8. For more, see Asher, "Shaman-Killing Case on Puget Sound."

9. Miller, *Lushootseed Culture*, 48.

10. TRAVELS

1. Whitener memoir.

2. Accounts from Maude Burr Basse and Frank Mossman, quoted in Jones, "Kamilche."

3. Wright, *Lewis and Dryden's Marine History*, 268.

4. Wright, *Lewis and Dryden's Marine History*.

5. Whitener memoir.

6. Also see Stevenson, *Superior Shipping Service*.

7. Newell, *Ships of the Inland Sea*, 78–79.

8. Wright, *Lewis and Dryden's Marine History*, 295.

9. Wright, *Lewis and Dryden's Marine History*, 215.

10. Jones, "Kamilche."

11. Whitener memoir.

12. Wright, *Lewis and Dryden's Marine History*, 320.

13. Jones, "Kamilche," 24.

14. Whitener memoir.

15. See Swanson, "Bainbridge Island."

16. From "Simpson Investment Company History."

17. Isaac Van Dorsey Mossman quote from Mossman, "Crossing the Plains." See Phil and Vivian Williams's CD *Pioneer Dance Tunes of the Far West*. An essay based on their research accompanies the recording, in which they play the most popular tunes of the era.

18. Jones, "Kamilche."

19. For this and other details of early Olympia history, see City of Olympia, "Community Profile."

20. Beck, *Seeking Recognition*.

11. KATIE GALE'S EARLY LIFE

1. Mapes, "Winter Visit Pays for the Pipers."

2. However, the effects of industrialization on Puget Sound were already noted by the latter half of the nineteenth century. Washington State established its first fish hatchery in southwest Washington in 1895 to address issues of declining fish stocks.

3. See *United States v. State of Washington*, 873 F.Supp. 1422 (W.D. Wash. 1994), 1440.

4. "An Act to Amend an Act to Encourage the Cultivation of Oysters," approved November 14, 1879, in *Laws of the Washington Territory*, 118–20.

5. The Bush Act and the Callow Act are found in chapters 24 and 25 of *Session Laws of the State of Washington*, 36–41.

6. Washington State Department of Ecology, "DNR Bush Callow Act Handout."

7. Vowell, *Wordy Shipmates*, 77.

8. I'm following Marian Smith's classification (in *Puyallup-Nisqually*) here and, to an extent, Arthur Ballard's.

9. I've drawn principally on the published and unpublished work of Arthur Ballard, Marian W. Smith, and George Gibbs for these comments.

10. Rabbeson, "Report of Battle Connell's Prairie."

11. The story of Leschi's trial and his subsequent conviction and hanging and Captain Rabbeson's role in the trial is told in detail in Kluger, *Bitter Waters of Medicine Creek*.

12. Smith, *Puyallup-Nisqually*.

12. THE KETTLE CONNECTION

1. It was common practice for Indian people in Washington Territory to form relationships outside of their own territory and language or village group. Alexandra Harmon discusses Myron Eells's notes that "among 242 Twanas" he found "only 20 who did not identify at least one grandparent as Klallam, Squaxin, Chehalis, Samish, Nisqually, Snohomish, Port Madison, Puyallup, Chemakum, Duwamish, Skagit, Victoria, Klickitat, 'Skewhamish,' or Snoqualmie." This mixture of peoples and ancestry confounded government efforts to classify and compartmentalize Indian people. Harmon, *Indians in the Making*, 138.

2. Louisa Tobin's "real" name, according to her granddaughter Maiselle Bridges, was Tsa Tsa. Tsa is a termination of a number of women's names in the region. Maiselle Bridges, interview by author, Frank's Landing, Washington, August 1, 2000.

3. Ruth Greiner was a colleague of T. T. Waterman and was conducting interviews in the South Sound area for their project, Puget Sound Geography. Her notes are found in Waterman and Greiner, "Notes and Writings," frame 0164.

4. Ruth Greiner and some of the other early twentieth-century anthropologists cited in this book would have been using the Americanist phonetic notation when transcribing languages. It was developed by anthropologists for their own purposes. Greiner may have specifically been using the chart of phonetic symbols published by the *American Anthropologist* in 1916, "Phonetic Transcription of Indian Languages: Report of Committee of American Anthropological Association," produced by Franz Boas, Pliny E. Goddard, Edward Sapir, and Alfred Kroeber.

5. *Morning Olympian*, October 30, 1903.

6. Smith, *Puyallup-Nisqually*, 14.

7. Smith, *Puyallup-Nisqually*, 14.

8. Elmendorf, *Twana Narratives*, 3.

9. See page 272 in the Hilbert edition of Waterman, "Puget Sound Geography."

10. Winterhouse, "Report of an Archaeological Survey"; Howard, "Archaeological Site Survey of Southwestern Puget Sound."

11. Howard, "Archaeological Site Survey of Southwestern Puget Sound."

12. H. H. Johnson, Supt. Spl. Disb. Agent, Puyallup Consolidated Agency, Tacoma, Wash., to the Honorable Commissioner of Indian Affairs, Washington DC, April 20, 1910, Land Allotments 5329-1910, Allotments Quinault reservation, Duwamish Tribe Archives, Duwamish Tribe, Seattle, Washington, courtesy Trova Hefernan, director, The Legacy Project, and creative director, Washington State Heritage Center, Washington Secretary of State's Office, Olympia, Washington.

13. Smith, *Puyallup-Nisqually*, 14.

14. Kettle's wife was Sally until at least 1880 and then Mary or Mary Jack. Sally was apparently the mother of Louisa Tobin.

On the Fourth of July 1891 Kettle reportedly showered friends and kin with gold pieces in a Mud Bay giveaway. Two days later, on July 6, Kettle was injured in a runaway wagon accident. John Jackman was killed in the wagon accident after being "dragged some distance." Kettle recovered from his injuries. One of the uninjured in the accident was Big Frank, a signee of the Point No Point Treaty and at that time a resident on Oyster Bay and former owner of oyster tidelands that had been sold to Katie and Joseph Gale. Big Frank lived until 1897, when he died of consumption.

15. Kane, "Whatcom County Nine"; "Judicial Review of the Marriage Laws by Chief Justice R. S. Greene" (judicial opinion in *Territory v. Beale*), reproduced in *Bellingham Bay Mail*, June 14, 1879, 2; Asher, *Beyond the Reservation*, 71–72.

16. Katie Gale must have been with the Kettles on Oyster Bay from the earliest days in which they appear in the record. Katie, it is clear from affidavits, was known to William Krise from at least 1873, when Katie was seventeen, and C. C. Simmons, another prominent white settler, knew her from around 1868, when Katie was twelve.

17. This was not the Joseph Sherwood from Case Inlet. He is said to have died from a logging accident in 1873. This may have been a son or another Sherwood altogether.

13. NO CROPS OF ANY CONSEQUENCE

1. The statements from various teachers, doctors, and agents quoted in this chapter are from annual reports, letters, and notes prepared and sent to superintendents and other Indian agency administrators. They are available through the University of Washington digital archives, the National Archives at Seattle, and the National Archives and Records Administration in Washington DC.

2. Whaley, *Oregon and the Collapse of Illahee*, 43–45.

3. Collins, "Historical Sketch of Mason County." Also see Stannard, "Disease and Infertility"; Starna, "Biological Encounter"; Boyd, *Coming of the Spirit of Pestilence.*

4. The 1700s epidemic may account for some of the burials at Tse-whit-zen, the Klallam burial site inadvertently and tragically disturbed by a Washington Department of Transportation project. See Mapes, *Breaking Ground.*

5. Anderson, "Vancouver Expedition," 198. For more, see Morgan, *Peter Puget on Puget's Sound*; and Bell, Walker, and Meany, *New Vancouver Journal*, for journal passages.

6. This is only a partial list of diseases and epidemics that would have had devastating effects on the populations in the southern Puget Sound area. The best source for evidence accrued as of this writing is Boyd, *Coming of the Spirit of Pestilence.* Also see Robert Boyd, "Demographic History," in Sturtevant, *Handbook of North American Indians*, 7:135–48; and Thornton, *American Indian Holocaust and Survival.*

7. Catherine Collins was also a midwife and later, after her marriage to William Walter, she became foster mother to the well-known artist James "Jimmy" Tilton Pickett, son of Gen. George Pickett, a distinguished American Civil War veteran, and his Haida wife, sometimes referred to as Morning Mist or Sakis Tiigang, who died while James was young. The stories that surround her, her name, and James Pickett's life are, perhaps, romanticized and highly speculative. I defer to Candace Wellman (personal correspondence), who has been studying the Pickett story for many years. She has been a great help to me on this book.

8. A well-written and fascinating family history describes the early life of Sidney S. Ford Jr. in some context. See "Family History of Raymond & Corinne Blakeslee."

9. Kimball was presumably looking at census figures collected on reservations by agents. These numbers must be viewed skeptically, but they are the numbers with which Kimball was working.

10. Adam Wylie, Instructor, to Mr. Elder, United States Indian Agent, July 1, 1863, in *Squaxin Reservation.*

11. Harmon, *Indians in the Making*, 97–98.

14. RELATIONSHIPS

1. The Irish potato famine routed people from their homes during the years 1845–47. Of course, many of those impoverished and displaced by it left later. Though the Scottish "Highland Clearance" had taken place during the late eighteenth and early nineteenth centuries, the secondary consequences, that is, poor conditions for farming on the coast, high rents, and failure of the potato crops in 1846, fueled emigration to the colonies and America for some years to come.

2. See land entry files for Nellie M. Sutton, Adam Korter, Henry Isaac, and Dick Jackson, National Archives, Washington DC.

3. Howard, "Archaeological Site Survey of Southwestern Puget Sound."

4. Campbell's diary is in the John Campbell Papers, Special Collections, University of Washington Libraries, Seattle.

5. Collins, "Historical Sketch of Mason County."

6. Catherine and William Walter diary.

7. Information about the daily operations of the McDonald store comes from the McDonald store ledgers.

8. Whitener memoir.

9. I'm not suggesting that I believe the term "squaw" is appropriate in any context. However, in the late nineteenth century in Oyster Bay it was not always used by whites as a general term for Indian woman but rather was used to signify a particular relationship between Indian women and white men.

10. Robert Frost's comments on marriage are extracted from his testimony in *Weatherall v. Weatherall*, 63 Wash. 526 (1911), and *Weatherall v. Weatherall*, 56 Wash. 344 (1909), Washington State Archives, Olympia.

11. Personal communications with Nancy Brewer, former shucker, Kamilche, Washington, 2010.

12. See Alexandra Harmon's discussion of the consequences of intermarriage between Indians and Hudson's Bay Company personnel in *Indians in the Making*, 41.

13. See Harmon, "Lines in Sand."

15. JOSEPH GALE WAS AN ENTERPRISING MAN

1. *Mason County Journal*, Pan-American Exposition Supplement, 1910.

2. Kincaid, *James Newton Gale*.

3. Gale, "Notes concerning Joseph Marion Gale."

4. "Lost Wagon Train and Oregon Trail Cutoff Fever."

5. "Lost Wagon Train and Oregon Trail Cutoff Fever."

6. The Idaho State Historical Society Museum in Boise, Idaho, regularly screens a film depicting Ezra Meeker, Oregon Trail veteran, disassembling his wagon and floating it across the Loop Fork of the Platte River in his retracing of the trail in 1910.

7. Much of this information on the Lost Wagon Train is drawn from letters and journals in the collection of the Oregon Historical Society, Portland, or Lane County Historical Society, Eugene, Oregon.

8. The Campbellites were a Christian movement also known as the American Restoration Movement or the Stone-Campbell Movement.

9. Kincaid, *James Newton Gale*.

10. The *Transcript* was first issued on November 30, 1867. See Meany, "Newspapers of Washington Territory," 266.

11. The Oystermen's Association had at least annual meetings and held these at Hoy's store at Schley on Oyster Bay.

16. THE MARKS UPON HER BODY

1. See Foucault, *Discipline and Punish*; and Griffin, *Woman and Nature*.

2. For other examples of harsh treatment of an Indian wife by a white husband and other sources and stories of conflict in intercultural marriages, see Asher, *Beyond the Reservation*. These stories suggest that conflict in relationships seems to stem from vast differences in cultural expectations of the union. Asher, *Beyond the Reservation*, 65–66.

3. Katie Gale's petition relies on a number of precedents, including the territorial laws protecting the rights and property of wives, the fact that she was legally married to Gale in 1886, and laws that recognized the rights of Indian women legally married to white men. Because Katie had standing, Joseph apparently resorted to denigrating her "Indianness," complaining that it made her unfit to mother her own children. Katie, by turning to the law to resolve her dispute with Joseph, surely created an intellectual dilemma for him. She recognized the rule of law and was using her knowledge and standing to challenge him, though he would complain in 1893 and again in 1898 that she was an uneducated, superstitious woman. Her keenness and wit in dealing with him and enlisting very good representation to support her case presented a paradox he did not address.

4. On the Indian Homestead Act, see chapter 6, note 8.

5. Prescott, "Why She Didn't Marry Him," 25.

6. A territorial act passed in 1869 defined the rights of husband and wife to include "that all property, both real and personal, of the wife owned by her before marriage and acquired afterward by gift, bequest, devise or descent shall be her separate property and all property, both real and personal, owned by the husband before marriage, and that acquired by him . . . shall be his separate property." All property acquired after the marriage, except by gift, was to be considered common property. Women were to register an inventory of their separate property with the county auditor. "An act defining the rights of husband and wife," in *Statutes of the Territory of Washington*, 318.

7. The state's laws and activities regarding tidelands and shorelands are complicated. See Conte, "Disposition of Tidelands and Shorelands," for an overview.

8. The relevant section of the Medicine Creek Treaty, to which Squaxin predecessor bands were signees, is Article 3: "The right of taking fish, at all usual and accustomed grounds and stations, is further secured to said Indians in common with all citizens of the Territory and of erecting temporary houses for the purpose of curing, together with the privilege of hunting, gathering roots and berries, and pasturing their horses on open and unclaimed lands: Provided, however, that they shall not take shellfish from any beds staked or cultivated by citizens, and that they shall alter all stallions not intended for breeding-horses, and shall keep up and confine the latter."

9. Though some Indians were successful in filing claims, it was not necessarily an easy path, even for landed, "assimilated" Indian citizens. For example, Tom Sabudcup, a Squaxin, was charged by an attorney $25 an acre, or over $500, for help in making his 1895 application for oyster beds he occupied. The paradoxes abounded. The Indians who were allotted or who owned land were citizens and not eligible for special privileges. Yet under the treaty they should have had, at the minimum, the right to continue to take shellfish from usual and accustomed places.

10. The term "hegemony" denotes a cultural domination that is not questioned, indeed seems "natural." The values and structures of the dominant group are replicated and reinforced at all levels and have penetrated all processes in which members of the society engage.

11. There is considerable controversy regarding Chief Seattle's often-quoted December 1854 speech. It first appeared in print in the *Seattle Sunday Star* on October 29, 1887, in a version published by Dr. Henry Smith, who claimed to

have heard it delivered. A well-researched account of the popular speech and the mystery that surrounds it is found in Furtwangler, *Answering Chief Seattle*.

12. Joseph Gale would not have been called a "squaw man," given his actions toward Katie in the early years of their marriage. He was divorced before he married her. He was joined to her before witnesses in a legal, binding marriage. In 1886, after the birth of the girl Maud, Joseph and Katie stood before a justice of the peace in Mason County and said their vows. Abner Smith and his Indian wife, Louisa, were married on the same day, presumably in the same room, one couple after the other. In those days Joseph was clearly following an honorable path in his relations with Katie, perhaps one learned from his religious-minded, educated family during his boyhood days in Oregon. Whatever his faults as a husband, he had taken actions in these early days of their life together that made Katie Gale's success in the courts possible.

17. KATIE GALE GOES TO COURT

1. Prescott, "Why She Didn't Marry Him."

2. Frank Mossman was the son of Isaac Van Dorsey Mossman of Indiana. Isaac Mossman was a member of the "Miller Train" that arrived in Oregon in October 1853. He joined the Oregon Mounted Volunteers, then in 1860 started a pony express company that traveled to and from "Nez Perces, Salmon, and John Day's and Powder River Mines." Frank Mossman was a colorful character who was, the story goes, sent around the world for two years by his father. The boy was only fourteen, but his father arranged the trip so that he could avoid the consequences of stealing a horse. If all the stories about him (or written by him) are true, he may have single-handedly rid Oyster Bay of bear and cougar in the late 1800s. However, Mossman had a gift for hyperbole. In a newspaper column he wrote, he said of a bear he killed at the head of the bay, "His head was three feet long from the ears to the nose; from tip of tail to nose he was ten feet, three feet and a half inches . . . the claws of his forefeet were five inches in length and as sharp as a knife." This American black bear would rank up there with the largest of its species ever seen in the wild.

3. L. K. Cogswell to Washington Territorial Governor Semple, January 20, 1888, regarding women's suffrage, Semple Papers, accession no. 6532-1, box 11/7, Pacific Northwest Historical Documents, Special Collections, University of Washington Libraries, Seattle.

4. Prescott, "Why She Didn't Marry Him."

5. *Siwash* is a term derived from Chinook Jargon and adapted from the French *sauvage*. It is considered to be a derogatory term and certainly was used as such in this context.

6. Howard, "Archaeological Site Survey of Southwestern Puget Sound."

7. These include Dick Jackson, who received his patent for his Oyster Bay homestead in 1886. He had filed in 1879. In his application he was required to swear that he was an Indian "formerly of the Squaxon tribe" and that he had "abandoned my relations with that tribe, and adopted the habits and pursuits of civilized life." Jackson land entry file, National Archives, Washington DC. Jackson's witnesses when he proved his homestead included Harry Weatherall, John Smith, and James Tobin. The government required such statements from anyone filing under the Indian Homestead Act.

8. A full discussion of issues of landownership and citizenship in this period require a discussion far beyond the scope of this book. See Asher, *Beyond the Reservation*, 76–79, for more.

9. Barnett, *Indian Shakers*; and Castile, "'Half-Catholic' Movement."

10. Barnett, *Indian Shakers*.

11. Castile, "Indian Connection," 122.

12. The Shakers may not have known what others of their European American neighbors were up to. The Walter family's activities would have made interesting fodder for conversation in the local Indian community if they were let in on their lives. Catherine and William Walter, at the very least, dabbled in spiritualism. Spiritualism was popular during the first half of the nineteenth century. William Walter records a visit he made with his wife to the infamous Dr. Slade during Slade's visit to Olympia in 1879: "We (wife and myself) had a sitting with the world wide known Dr. Slade. Had several communications from my brother John from the other world. Saw the lid of an instrument fly in a circle or from under the table to the top of the table and other wonderful things that are not in accordance with nature, as far as nature is known by former philosophers." Catherine and William Walter diary.

For a fascinating account of Dr. Slade's work, see *Preliminary Report of the Commission*, 7–13, 51–77. Slade traveled widely and was notoriously prosecuted in 1877, before the Olympia trip, under the Vagrant Act while in London. He was accused of using "subtle craft, means, or devices." His conviction was discharged on a technicality, according to the *New York Times*, January 30, 1877.

18. TURN AROUND

1. This first child disappears from the record after the age of six and is mentioned by Joseph Gale in a court document as having died.

19. JOSEPH'S COMPLAINTS

1. Harris, *Alaska and the Klondike Gold Fields*, 50.
2. Harris, *Alaska and the Klondike Gold Fields*.

20. THE OYSTER BAY SCHOOL

1. The account of the May 1898 program at Oyster Bay School is drawn from contemporary newspaper accounts and the printed program handed out at the event. All performances are listed on the archived program. I had some photographs of the school at the time and accounts of other local schools and their activities during the same period to help fill in the "story" of the day. Obviously, I have imagined much about this day.
2. See Hunt, *Bold Spirit*.

21. KATIE GALE DIED UNDER A FULL MOON

1. Information for this section is paraphrased or quoted directly from *Wheeler's Handbook of Medicine*, by William Jack, first published and available to physicians in 1894.
2. Troy later became vice president of Olympia National Bank. He died in May 1929, missing the stock market crash by a few months.
3. The will excerpts are from the original, signed by Katie Gale, in the Record of Wills, Superior Court of the State of Washington, Mason County. The description of the signing is in part based on the story of Ellen Sam's will as described in probate papers by her attorney, E. N. Steele, June 1917. "Jennie" is the spelling Krise used when signing the will, although her name also appears in historical records as "Jenny"; I have used the latter spelling in this book.
4. The 1895 Bush Act categorized oyster land. First-class land was considered prime culturing area and hence the most valuable.

22. A "BROAD AND LIBERAL MAN" MEETS HIS DEATH

1. Long-distance telephone connections between major cities were available by 1884. Gale apparently could place calls to Shelton and Olympia with his.
2. Shelton Lodge AOUW no. 51. It was a two-story building, thirty feet by ninety feet, at the corner of Third and Railroad. Built in 1889.

3. Red Men are said to have been among those who dressed as Indians during the Boston Tea Party, disguising themselves as Natives as they carried forth patriotic aims. The Red Men continue to use the appellation even today, for The Improved Order of Red Men is still an active organization, headquartered in Waco, Texas, with a women's auxiliary group called The Degree of Pocahontas.

Fraternal societies in the late nineteenth century served to bond men one to the other, even implicitly obligating them to serve and support each other in their endeavors. Membership in the organizations distanced them from women and rough society. Their meetings, with their vows and rituals, served to underscore and bolster certain economic and cultural values that privileged white men and capitalists. These associations were so valued that some men in southern Puget Sound, a story goes, rowed through the rain to get to meetings of their brotherhoods and rowed back, probably still tipsy, early in the morning to get home in time for milking.

The association may have worked in other ways in the still-growing communities of white men around the United States. Fred Barkey notes in "Red Men and Rednecks," "The little work which has been done to date on the impact of the fraternal lodge in working class communities suggests that they were an important vehicle in helping to socialize the workers to the discipline and ethics of the new industrial order." He adds that a "recent study of the Odd Fellows [another fraternal group] stresses that this lodge . . . reduced alienation by bringing together men from different classes in an atmosphere and ritual which stressed diligence, discipline, sobriety, and success by individual effort." See also "Improved Order of Red Men"; and Barkey, "Red Men and Rednecks."

23. THE END OF AN ERA

1. The spelling of the names Maud/Maude and Fanchier varies in public records. The most common variation of Fanchier is Fanshier.

2. For a biography of John R. Chaplain and a brief description of People's University, see Prosser, *History of Puget Sound Country*, 412–41. *Directory of Olympia City* contains a full-page photograph of the school and an advertisement for its various departments. Also see Stevenson, *Lacey, Olympia, and Tumwater*.

3. Prosser, *History of Puget Sound Country*, 413.

4. James Tobin and Steve Lundin, personal communications with the author.

5. Waterman and Greiner, "Notes and Writings," frames 142–79. Louisa Tobin, Dick Jackson, and others gave notes on locations on Squaxin Island, Olympia and Budd Inlets, Mud Bay, and Oyster Bay.

6. Older Indians like "Auntie Slocum" were treated by members of the press as walking anachronisms, quaint holdovers from another era. Alexandra Harmon writes, "The myth of Indians' imminent extinction, along with nostalgia about the past, explains the attention lavished on individual aged Indians during this era." Chief Seattle's daughter Angeline received this kind of attention. Lucy Gerard on Vashon Island did as well. Comments made about them were superficial, and "sightings" of them were reported in such a way as to emphasize details that would seem silly or pathetic to white readers; that is, popular representations of Indians reinforced race and class and, in many cases, gender hierarchies of the time. Use of endearing kinship terms such as "Auntie" were part of this kind of representation. Harmon, *Indians in the Making*, 148.

7. Steele, *Immigrant Oyster*, 1.

8. Dick Jackson testimony taken March 1, 1927, in *Duwamish et al. v. United States of America*, 222–24.

9. For more information on Japanese in the oyster industry, see Ito, *Issei*.

10. For details on the Japanese on Oyster Bay, see De Danaan, "Mountain of Shell."

11. "Most Beautiful Oyster."

24. WINTER SISTER

1. A tip of the hat to *Winter Brothers: A Season at the Edge of America*, by Ivan Doig. This book was an early inspiration to me. Doig uses archival manuscripts to reconstruct the life of James Swan in the mid-to-late nineteenth-century Pacific Northwest.

2. Foucault, *Discipline and Punish*, 26.

3. W. H. Auden, "At Last the Secret Is Out," in Keillor, *Good Poems*.

POSTSCRIPT

1. Ballard, depositions in *Puyallup Tribe v. United States of America*, copy at Pacific Northwest Collection, University of Washington Libraries, Seattle.

2. Katie Gale and Kitty Gail are one. Katie is a common nickname for Katherine or Catherine, apparently Katie's given name. The name Kitty appears in other documents, including a newspaper article about the reading of her will.

3. Cora writes that Frank sold his oyster bed to J. Y. Waldrip for seventy-five dollars and bought a printing press. He published a weekly paper to spread his populist view that only land held for speculation should be taxed, thus

preventing the rich from accumulating more wealth and stopping the exploitation of those without.

Kloshe tillicum means "good friend" or "friendly relations" in Chinook Jargon. Some Chinook Jargon was used on Oyster Bay, but the European American men seemed not to know much. Joseph complained of its use and the use of other "Indian" languages he didn't understand.

4. Until 1909 it was legal in Washington State to bring a woman's virtue into question in a public context. Joseph Gale made a number of statements that defamed his wife, and in the 1898 proceedings Katie's defenders, among them Frank Gingrich, came forward to speak of her "virtue." State Senator Jeanne Kohl-Wells introduced a bill, Senate Bill 5148, in the 2005 Washington State legislature that would repeal the 1909 act that protects women from verbal assaults on their virtue and make them subject to the same slander laws as men. The *New York Times* reported on February 17, 2005, "The State Senate voted 47 to 1 to repeal a 1909 law that had made it illegal to impugn the virtue and chastity of women. The bill's sponsor, Senator Jeanne E. Kohl-Wells, a Democrat, had said that while insults to women's chastity — including calling them hussies or strumpets or publicly bringing their purity into question — were not welcome, the law was an outdated relic of sexism. The bill now heads to the House of Representatives. Eight other states have similar laws on their books, according to the National Conference of State Legislatures." The bill was passed, repealing the 1909 law.

Bibliography

ARCHIVAL AND UNPUBLISHED SOURCES

Aginsky, Ethel. "Puyallup Texts." Typescript. Boas Collection. American Philosophical Society, Philadelphia.

Ballard, Arthur C. Depositions in *Puyallup Tribe v. United States of America*, Indian Claims Commission, docket 203, 1952. Copy on file at Pacific Northwest Collection, University of Washington Libraries, Seattle.

Blackwell, Alice, and Ruby. Miscellaneous writings and speech, 1911. Blackwell Collection. Puyallup Tribe of Indians Archives, Tacoma, Washington.

Campbell, John. Papers, 1869–1894. Manuscript no. 0013. Special Collections, University of Washington Libraries, Seattle.

Collins, A. M. "Historical Sketch of Mason County." Including transcriptions of letters to his brother James, 1853. Mason County Historical Society, Shelton, Washington.

Conte, Kenan R. "The Disposition of Tidelands and Shorelands: Washington State Policy 1889–1982." MPA thesis, Evergreen State College, 1982.

Cross, Hattie Allen. Statement. Transcript of original produced August 30, 1993. Puyallup Tribe of Indians Archives, Tacoma, Washington.

De Danaan, LLyn. "City of University Place Transit Center Cultural Resource Report." October 31, 2005. Unpublished.

———. Notes from interview with Maiselle Bridges, August 1, 2000.

———. "Preliminary Catalogue of Documents Containing Information on Hunting." Prepared for the Puyallup Tribe of Indians, September 1999. Unpublished.

———. "Report on the Occupancy and Use of Vashon Island and Surrounding Waters by Puyallup and Puyallup Predecessor Bands." Prepared for the Puyallup Tribe of Indians, August 26, 1998. Unpublished.

———. "Use of Trails re: Access to Shellfish Beds." Prepared for the Puyallup Tribe of Indians. Unpublished.

Foster, Rhonda, Larry Ross, and Margaret Henry. "Ethno-History of Mason County." Squaxin Island Tribe, 2010. On file with Mason County Historic Preservation Commission, Shelton, Washington.

Gale, Joseph Marion. "Notes concerning Joseph Marion Gale, an Oregon pioneer of 1853," and copies of two newspaper articles written by him. 921, GA vertical files. Lane County Historical Society, Eugene, Oregon.

Howard, Florence. "An Archaeological Site Survey of Southwestern Puget Sound." 1949. Unpublished. Courtesy of Florence Howard, copy in the author's possession.

Johnson, Kriste. "Bridging the Gastronomic Gap: A Method for Preserving the Olympia Oyster as Foodstuff." MA thesis, University of Washington, 2002.

Jones, Richard. "Kamilche: Being Some Account of the History of Kamilche, Washington, with Particular Reference to the Activity of the Frederick Wallace Taylor Family in the Years 1885–1905." 1959. Unpublished. Vertical files. Mason County Historical Society, Shelton, Washington.

Lane, Barbara. "Anthropological Report on the Identity, Treaty Status and Fisheries of the Puyallup Tribe of Indians." May 1973. Unpublished. Washington State Library, Olympia.

Lost Wagon Train. Various notes and unpublished recollections from the Joseph Leonard family and others; with cover letter dated November 12, 1903. Lane County Historical Society, Eugene, Oregon.

Mason County Death Records, 1891–1906. Mason County Historical Society, Shelton, Washington.

Mason County Probate. Joseph Gale. Box 2, record 142. Washington State Archives, Southwest Regional Archives, Olympia.

McDonald store ledgers. Mason County Historical Society, Shelton, Washington (years 1876, 1884, 1885) and in the possession of McDonald descendants.

Meeker, Jerry (Puyallup). Biographical notes in Alfred J. Smith notebooks, circa 1948. Ms. collection no. 4815, accession no. 4815-001. Author's transcription. Special Collections, University of Washington Libraries, Seattle.

National Archives, Washington DC

Isaac, Henry. Land Entry File, Serial Patent Number WADAA 094241.

Jackson, Dick. Land Entry File, Serial Patent Number WADAA 094268.
Korter, Adam. Land Entry File, Serial Patent Number WADAA 094174.
RG 75, CCF, 1907–1939, Cushman-350, box 39, Probates.
File 1126-1914, Jack.
File 1128-1914, Mud Bay George.
File 1129-1914, Oldman Slocum.
File 1154-1914, John or Sealth.
File 1155-1914, Henry or Chilawit.
File 1156-1914, Dr. Jim.
File 1157-1914, Old Man Sindam.
File 1158-1914, Johnny or Senalesub.
File 2990-1914, Julia or Quastadia.
File 3374-1914, Oldman Sandy.
File 3974-1914, Olympia Jim.
File 106481-1913, Mud Bay Sam.
File 11127-1911, Tobilitza.
RG 75, CCF, 1907–1939, Cushman-350, box 42, Probates.
File 74451-1914, Mud Bay Charley.
RG 75, CCF, 1907–1939, Cushman-350, box 45, Probates.
File 591-1919, Peter Klabash.
File 4045-1919, Julia Ann.
File 9880-1919, Elizabeth John.
Sutton, Nellie M. Land Entry File, Serial Patent Number WADAA 094199.

Rabbeson, Capt. A. B. "Report of Battle Connell's Prairie 10 March 1856." Files 91–98. Mason County Historical Society, Shelton, Washington.

Record of Shaker or Tchaddaub Church, 1892. Indian Shaker Church, MS 29, box 5/11. Washington State Historical Society, Tacoma.

Semple, Eugene. Papers. Pacific Northwest Historical Documents, Special Collections, University of Washington Libraries, Seattle.

Shoecraft, Ross P. "Transcript of Field Notes of the Survey of the Squaxin Indian Reserve in Towns 19." 1874. Microfilm. Washington State Library, Olympia.

Smith, Marian Wesley. Collection, 1907–1961. MS-2794, microfilm (pos.), ca. 1922–1958. 35 mm, 7 reels [AO1736-AO1742]. Royal British Columbia Museum, British Columbia Archives, Victoria. Filmed on behalf of the National Archives of Canada with permission of the Royal Anthropological Institute, London, England, which holds the originals (their reference GB1446 MS 268).

Student Boarder Account Book, vol. 1, 1881–1903. Providence St. Amable Academy, Olympia, Washington. Providence Health System Archives, Seattle.

Thurston County Board of Tide Land Appraisers, 1894. Department of Natural Resources Archives, Commissioner of Public Lands. Washington State Archives, Olympia.

Tolmie, William F. "Journal of Wm. Fraser Tolmie, 1833–1834, 1835, 1836, at F. Nisqually Ft. McLouglin, at Nassriver, Ft. Vancouver." William Frasier Tolmie Papers, accession no. 45 771, box 2, folder 6. Special Collections, University of Washington Libraries, Seattle.

Walter, Catherine, and William Walter. Diary. James Tilton Pickett Collection. Washington State Historical Society Research Center, Tacoma.

Washington Territorial District Court Records. Washington State Archives, Olympia.

Benjamin Madison v. Lucy Madison. Civil files. Case no. 169. 1859. Jefferson County.

Territory v. Alexander Hemphill. Case no. 53. 1878. Whatcom County.

Territory v. Charles Beale. Case no. 52. 1878. Whatcom County.

Territory v. David Whitehill. Case no. 55. 1878. Whatcom County.

Territory v. Enoch Compton. Case no. 57. 1878. Whatcom County.

Territory v. Henry Barkhousen. Case no. 51. 1878. Whatcom County.

Territory v. Henry Fisk. Case nos. 1187 and 1249. 1874. Thurston County.

Territory v. James Taylor. Case no. 59. 1878. Whatcom County.

Territory v. Richard Wooten. Case no. 54. 1878. Whatcom County.

Territory v. Shadrick Wooten. Case no. 56. 1878. Whatcom County.

Waterman, T. T. Catalogue. National Museum of the American Indian, Washington DC.

———. "Puget Sound Geography." 1920. Bureau of American Ethnology Manuscript Collection, no. 1864. Smithsonian Office of Anthropology, Washington DC. Microfilm copies available at Washington State Library, Olympia, and University of Washington Library, Seattle. Published with editing and additional material from Vi Hilbert, Jay Miller, and Zalmai Zahir as *Puget Sound Geography* (Federal Way WA: Lushootseed Press, 2001).

Waterman, T. T., and Ruth Greiner. "Notes and Writings Collected from Others." Fieldnotes of T. T. Waterman and Ruth Greiner on Puget Sound Ethnogeography. Microfilm reel no. 30, frames 142–79. J. P. Harrington Papers. University of Washington Libraries, Seattle.

Weatherall v. Weatherall. 56 Wash. 344 (1909). Nos. 8250, 8251. Washington State Archives, Olympia. See also 105 P. 822.

Weatherall v. Weatherall. 63 Wash. 526 (1911). Nos. 9580, 9581. Washington State Archives, Olympia.

Wessen, Gary C. "Archaeological Perspectives on the Traditional Use of Shellfish Resources in Western Washington." Report prepared for Evergreen Legal Services, April 1993.

Whitener memoir (unpublished memoir with "Whitener" in cursive at the top). N.d. Standing files. Squaxin Island Museum, Library, and Research Center, Shelton, Washington.

Wickersham, James. Collection. Alaska State Library, Juneau.

Winterhouse, John. "A Report of an Archaeological Survey on Lower Puget Sound." 1948. Unpublished. Copy in author's possession.

PUBLISHED SOURCES

"An Act to aid in the construction of a railroad and *telegraph line* from the Missouri river to the Pacific ocean, and to secure to the government the use of the same for postal, military, and other purposes." *U.S. Statutes at Large* 12 (July 1, 1862): 489.

"An Act to create the Office of Surveyor-General of the Public Lands in Oregon, and to provide for the Survey, and to make Donations to Settlers of the said Public Lands." (Donation Land Claim Act.) *U.S. Statutes at Large* 11 (September 27, 1850): 496. Available at Center for Columbia River History, http://www.ccrh.org/comm/cottage/primary/claim.htm.

"An Act to provide for the allotment of lands in severalty to Indians on the various reservations, and to extend the protection of the laws of the United States and the Territories over the Indians, and for other purposes." (General Allotment Act, or Dawes Act.) *U.S. Statutes at Large* 24 (February 8, 1887): 388–91.

"An Act to secure Homesteads to actual Settlers on the Public Domain." (Homestead Act.) *U.S. Statutes at Large* 12 (May 20, 1862): 392. Amended by act of March 3, 1875. (Indian Homestead Act.) *U.S. Statutes at Large* 18 (1875): 420, sec. 15.

Adamson, Thelma, ed. *Folk-Tales of the Coast Salish*. Memoirs of the American Folk-lore Society 27. New York: G. E. Stecheert, 1934. Reprint, New York: Kraus Reprint, 1969.

Anderson, Bern, ed. "The Vancouver Expedition: Peter Puget's Journal of the Exploration of Puget Sound, May 7–June 11, 1792." *Pacific Northwest Quarterly* 30, no. 2 (April 1939): 177–217.

Angle, Grant C., and William D. Welsh. *A Brief History of Shelton, Washington*. Shelton WA: Mason County Historical Society, 1940.

Asher, Brad. *Beyond the Reservation: Indians, Settlers, and the Law in Washington Territory, 1853–1889*. Norman: University of Oklahoma Press, 1999.

———. "A Shaman Killing Case on Puget Sound, 1873–1874." *Pacific Northwest Quarterly* 86 (Winter 1994/95): 17–24.

Ballard, Arthur C. "Calendric Terms of the Southern Puget Sound Salish." *Southwestern Journal of Anthropology* 6, no. 1 (1950): 77–99.

———. "Mythology of Southern Puget Sound." *University of Washington Publications in Anthropology* 3, no. 2 (December 1929): 31–150.

———. "Some Tales of the Southern Puget Sound Salish." *University of Washington Publications in Anthropology* 2, no. 3 (December 1927): 57–81.

Barkey, Fred. "Red Men and Rednecks: The Fraternal Lodge in the Coal Fields." *West Virginia Historical Society Quarterly* 17, no. 1 (January 2003). http://www.wvculture.org/History/wvhs1701.html.

Barnett, Homer Garner. *Indian Shakers: A Messianic Cult of the Pacific Northwest*. Carbondale: Southern Illinois University Press, 1957.

Bates, Dawn, Thom Hess, and Vi Hilbert. *Lushootseed Dictionary*. Seattle: University of Washington Press, 1994.

Beck, David R. M. *Seeking Recognition: The Termination and Restoration of the Coos, Lower Umpqua, and Siuslaw Indians, 1855–1984*. Lincoln: University of Nebraska Press, 2009.

Beckham, Stephen Dow. *Requiem for a People: The Rogue Indians and the Frontiersmen*. Northwest Reprints. Corvallis: Oregon State University Press, 1996.

Bell, Edward, William B. Walker, and Edward S. Meany, eds. *A New Vancouver Journal on the Discovery of Puget Sound*. Seattle: 1915.

Bishop, Frank. *History of Little Skookum Shellfish Growers Tideland from Abraham Lincoln to George W. Bush*. Rochester WA: Gorham Printing, 2005.

Boyd, Robert. *The Coming of the Spirit of Pestilence: Introduced Infectious Diseases and Population Decline among Northwest Coast Indians, 1774–1874*. Seattle: University of Washington Press, 1999.

Castile, George P. "The 'Half-Catholic' Movement: Edwin and Myron Eells and the Rise of the Indian Shaker Church." *Pacific Northwest Quarterly* 73, no. 4 (1982): 165–74.

———. "The Indian Connection: Judge James Wickersham and the Indian Shakers." *Pacific Northwest Quarterly* 81, no. 4 (October 1990): 122–29.

Chase, Cora G. *The Oyster Was Our World: Life on Oyster Bay 1898–1914*. Seattle: Shorey Book Store, 1976.

City of Olympia. "Community Profile." In *2012 Adopted Operating Budget*, appendix. http://www.olympiawa.gov/city-government/budget-financial reports/~/media/Files/AdminServices/Budget/2012%20Adopted%2-Budget/Appendix%202.pdf.

Couch, David, and Thomas J. Hassler. "'Olympia Oyster' Species Profiles: Life Histories and Environmental Requirements of Coastal Fishes and Invertebrates." U.S. Fish and Wildlife Service, biological report 82(11.124). U.S. Army Corps of Engineers, TR EL-82-4. 1989. http://www.nwrc.usgs.gov/wdb/pub/species_profiles/82_11-124.pdf.

Crooks, Drew W. "Governor Isaac I. Stevens and the Medicine Creek Treaty: Prelude to the War in Southern Puget Sound." *Pacific Northwest Forum* 10 (Summer–Fall 1985): 23–35.

De Danaan, LLyn. "Ethnographic Background." In *Vashon Island Archaeology: A View from Burton Acres Shell Midden*, edited by Julie K. Stein and Laura S. Phillips, 17–31. Burke Museum of Natural History and Culture, Research Report 8. Seattle: Burke Museum, 2002.

———. "Mountain of Shell: The Poetry of Miyoko Sato and Yukiko Abo." *Columbia* 25, no. 4 (Winter 2011–12): 3–8.

Directory of Olympia City and Thurston County, Washington. Seattle: R. L. Polk, 1906.

Duwamish et al. v. United States of America. F275. Evidence for the Plaintiff and Defendant. Washington DC: U.S. Court of Claims, 1927.

Eells, Myron. "The Puget Sound Indians." *American Antiquarian* 9, no. 4 (July 1887).

Elmendorf, William W. *Twana Narratives: Native Historical Accounts of a Coast Salish Culture*. Seattle: University of Washington Press, 1993.

Emerson, Michael O., and Christian Smith. *Divided by Faith: Evangelical Religion and the Problem of Race in America*. New York: Oxford University Press, 2001.

"The Family History of Raymond & Corinne Blakeslee." http://calvinlawson.files.wordpress.com/2008/12/history.pdf.

"Fatal Accident of Joseph Gale." *Mason County Journal*, September 27, 1901.

Fisher, Andrew H. *Shadow Tribe: The Making of Columbia River Indian Identity*. Seattle: Center for the Study of the Pacific Northwest in association with University of Washington Press, 2010.

Ford, Sidney S., Sr. "Report to M. T. Simmons, Chehalis Special Indian Agency, W.T., June 30, 1859." In *Report of the Commissioner of Indian Affairs*, 400–401. Washington DC: Office of the Commissioner of Indian Affairs, 1859. Digital Archives, University of Washington Libraries, Seattle. http://content.lib.washington.edu/u?/lctext,2065.

Foucault, Michael. *Discipline and Punish: The Birth of the Prison*. Translated by Alan Sheridan. New York: Random House, 1979.

Fritz, Henry E. "The Making of Grant's 'Peace Policy.'" *Chronicles of Oklahoma* 37 (Winter 1959–60): 411–31.

Furtwangler, Albert. *Answering Chief Seattle*. Seattle: University of Washington Press, 2011.

Gay, E. Jane. *With the Nez Perces: Alice Fletcher in the Field, 1889–92*. Lincoln: University of Nebraska Press, 1987.

Gibbs, George. "Tribes of Western Washington and Northwestern Oregon." In *Contributions to North American Ethnology*, vol. 1, pt. 2, 157–241. Washington DC: Government Printing Office, 1877.

Gorsline, Jeremiah, ed. *Shadows of Our Ancestors: Readings in the History of Klallam-White Relations*. Port Townsend WA: Empty Bowl, 1992.

Griffin, Susan. *Woman and Nature: The Roaring Inside Her*. New York: Harper Colophon, 1980.

Haeberlin, Hermann, and Erna Gunther. *The Indians of Puget Sound*. Seattle: University of Washington Press, 1975. Originally published in *University of Washington Publications in Anthropology* 4, no. 1 (1930).

Harmon, Alexandra. *Indians in the Making: Ethnic Relations and Indian Identities around Puget Sound*. Berkeley: University of California Press, 1998.

———. "Lines in Sand: Shifting Boundaries between Indians and Non-Indians in the Puget Sound Region." *Western Historical Quarterly* 26, no. 4 (Winter 1995): 429–53.

Harris, A. C. *Alaska and the Klondike Gold Fields*. New York[?]: J. R. Jones, 1897. Available at Library4History—American History, http://america.library4history.org/Harris-Discovery-Women/contents.html.

Hunt, Herbert. *Tacoma, Its History and Its Builders*. Vol. 1. Chicago: Clarke, 1916.

Hunt, Linda Lawrence. *Bold Spirit: Helga Estby's Forgotten Walk across Victorian America*. New York: Anchor, 2005.

"Improved Order of Red Men." Phoenixmasonry Masonic Museum. http://www.phoenixmasonry.org/masonicmuseum/fraternalism/red_men.htm.

In the Matter of the Estate of Katie Gale. Creditor's Claim and Record of Wills. Superior Court of the State of Washington, Mason County, 1899.

Ito, Kazuo. *Issei: A History of Japanese Immigrants in North America*. Seattle: Japanese Community Service, 1973.

Jamison, David W. "Plainfin Midshipman (South Sound Marine Life)." *Olympian* (Olympia WA), July 30, 2007. http://www.theolympian.com/624/story/176197.html.

Johnson, Adolph. "White-Indian Marriages Recalled by Old-Timer." *Mason County Journal*, December 1, 1977.

Johnson, Kevin R. *Mixed Race America and the Law: A Reader*. New York: New York University Press, 2003.

Joseph A. Gale v. Katie Gale. Case 534. Affidavits of John Leslie, Joseph Kullrich, William Krise, and C. C. Simmons. Superior Court of the State of Washington, Mason County, 1898.

Kane, Peyton. "The Whatcom County Nine: Legal and Political Ramifications of Metis Family Life in Washington." *Columbia* 14, no. 2 (Summer 2000): 39–44.

Kappler, Charles J., comp. and ed. *Indian Affairs: Laws and Treaties*. Vol. 2, *Treaties, 1778–1883*. Washington DC: Government Printing Office, 1904.

Katie Gale v. J. A. Gale. Case 255. Superior Court of the State of Washington, Mason County, 1893.

Keillor, Garrison, ed. *Good Poems*. New York: Viking Press, 2002.

Kincaid, Harrison. *James Newton Gale: Pioneer of 1853*. Cottage Grove OR: Sentinel Print Shop, 1971. Originally published in *Oregon State Journal*, May 1889.

Kluger, Richard. *The Bitter Waters of Medicine Creek: A Tragic Clash between White and Native American*. New York: Vintage Press, 2011.

Landis, Barbara. "Carlisle Indian Industrial School History." 1996. http://home.epix.net/~landis/histry.html.

Laws of the Washington Territory, Enacted by the Legislative Assembly in the Year 1879. Olympia WA: C. B. Bagley, 1879.

Leavitt, Judith Walzer. "Under the Shadow of Maternity: American Women's Responses to Death and Debility Fear in Nineteenth-Century Childbirth." *Feminist Studies* 12, no. 1 (Spring 1986): 129–54.

"Living Pioneer — Mrs. Charlotte Koontz Simmons." *Mason County Journal*, April 2, 1920.

"The Lost Wagon Train and Oregon Trail Cutoff Fever." Online exhibit. Lane County Historical Society, Eugene, Oregon. http://www.lanecountyhistoricalsociety.org/resources-lost_wagon_train.html.

Mapes, Lynda V. *Breaking Ground: The Lower Elwha Klallam Tribe and the Unearthing of Tse-whit-zen Village*. Seattle: University of Washington Press, 2009.

———. "Winter Visit Pays for the Pipers: Mud Flats Provide Feast for Lively Dunlins." *Seattle Times*, December 2, 2000. http://community.seattletimes.nwsource.com/archive/?date=20021202&slug=dunlin02m.

Mark, Joan T. *A Stranger in Her Native Land: Alice Fletcher and the American Indians*. Women in the West. Lincoln: University of Nebraska Press, 1989.

McBride, Delbert J. "Viewpoints and Visions in 1792: The Vancouver Expedition Encounters Indians of Western Washington." *Columbia* 4, no. 2 (Summer 1990): 22–23.

Meany, Edmund S. "Newspapers of Washington Territory." *Washington Historical Quarterly* 13, no. 4 (October 1922): 251–68.

———. *Vancouver's Discovery of Puget Sound: Portraits and Biographies of the Men Honored in the Naming of Geographic Features of Northwestern America*. New York: Macmillian, 1907.

Meeker, Ezra Pioneer. *Reminiscences of Puget Sound: The Tragedy of Leschi*. Seattle: Lowman and Hanford, 1905.

Menefee, Leah C. "The William Gale Family." *Lane County Historian* 10, no. 3 (December 1965): 51–55.

Menzies, Archibald. *Journal of Vancouver's Voyage*. Edited by Charles Newcombe. Victoria BC: W. H. Collin, 1923.

Miller, Bruce Granville, ed. *Be of Good Mind: Essays on the Coast Salish*. Vancouver BC: UBC Press, 2007.

Miller, Jay. *Lushootseed Culture and the Shamanic Odyssey: An Anchored Radiance*. Lincoln: University of Nebraska Press, 1999.

———. *Shamanic Odyssey: The Lushootseed Salish Journey to the Land of the Dead*. Menlo Park CA: Ballena Press, 1988.

Morgan, Murray. *Peter Puget On Puget's Sound*. Seattle: University of Washington Press, 1979.

Mossman, Isaac V. "Crossing the Plains." *Oregon Native Son Historical Magazine* 2, no. 6 (November 1900): 299–305.

"The Most Beautiful Oyster." *Longlines* (newsletter of the Pacific Shellfish Growers Association) 5, no. 3 (May/June 2002). http://www.salishseafoods.com/.

"Muster Roll of Captain C. W. Swindal, Company F. of the Second Regiment of Washington Territory Volunteers, Army of the United States, from 1st day of February, 1856, to the 31st day of July 1856." In *Biennial Report of the Adjutant General, 1891–92*. Olympia WA: State Printer, 1893.

"Muster Roll of Captain George B. Goudy, Company C. of the First Regiment of Washington Territory Volunteers, Army of the United States, from the 23d day of October, 1855, to the 24th day of January, 1856." In *Biennial Report of the Adjutant General, 1891–92*. Olympia WA: State Printer, 1893.

Nelson, Humphrey. *The Little Man and the Little Oyster*. Belfair WA: Mason County Historical Society, 1990.

Newell, Gordon R. *Ships of the Inland Sea: The Story of the Puget Sound Steamboats*. Portland OR: Binford and Mort, 1960.

Oregon State Archives. "Half-Breed Citizenship Bill, 1957." *Echoes of Oregon History Learning Guide*. http://arcweb.sos.state.or.us/echoes/link22.html.

Pascoe, Peggy. *Relations of Rescue: The Search for Female Moral Authority in the American West, 1874–1939*. New York: Oxford University Press, 1990.

———. *What Comes Naturally: Miscegenation Law and the Making of Race in America*. Oxford: Oxford University Press, 2009.

Pierce, J. Kingston. "Panic of 1893: Seattle's First Great Depression." November 24, 1999. HistoryLink.org. http://www.historylink.org/essays/output.cfm?file_id=2030.

Preliminary Report of the Commission Appointed by the University of Pennsylvania to Investigate Modern Spiritualism. Philadelphia: J. B. Lippincott, 1887.

Prescott, Cynthia Culver. "'Why She Didn't Marry Him': Love, Power, and Marital Choice on the Far Western Frontier." *Western Historical Quarterly* 38, no. 1 (Spring 2007): 25–45.

Prosser, Col. William Farrand. *A History of Puget Sound Country: Its Resources, Its Commerce and Its People*. New York: Lewis, 1903.

Prucha, Francis Paul. *American Indian Policy in Crisis: Christian Reformers and the Indian, 1865–1900*. Norman: University of Oklahoma Press, 1976.

Raibmon, Paige. *Authentic Indians: Episodes of Encounter from the Late-Nineteenth-Century Northwest Coast*. Durham NC: Duke University Press, 2005.

Redway, Jacque, and Russell Hinman. *Natural School Geography*. New York: American Book Company, 1898.

Richards, Kent. "The Stevens Treaties of 1854–1855: An Introduction." *Oregon Historical Quarterly* 106, no. 3 (Fall 2005): 342–50.

Session Laws of the State of Washington, Session of 1895. Olympia WA: O. C. White, 1895.

"Simpson Investment Company History." http://www.fundinguniverse.com/company-histories/Simpson-Investment-Company-Company-History.html. Citing *International Directory of Company Histories*. Vol. 17. Chicago: St. James Press, 1997.

Smith, Marian W. "The Coast Salish of Puget Sound." *American Anthropologist* 43, no. 2 (April–June 1941): 197–211.

———. *The Puyallup-Nisqually*. Columbia University Contributions to Anthropology 32. New York: Columbia University Press, 1940.

Spier, Leslie. *Tribal Distribution in Washington*. General Series in Anthropology 3. Menasha WI: George Banta, 1936.

Squaxin Reservation. 38th Cong., 1st sess., 1863. House Executive Document, serial no. 1182.

Stannard, David E. "Disease and Infertility: A New Look at the Demographic Collapse of Native Populations in the Wake of Western Contact." *Journal of American Studies* 24, no. 3 (December 1990): 325–50.

Starna, William A. "The Biological Encounter: Disease and the Ideological Domain." In "Shamans and Preachers, Color Symbolism and Commercial Evangelism: Reflections on Early Mid-Atlantic Religious Encounter in Light of the Columbian Quincentennial," special issue, *American Indian Quarterly* 16, no. 4 (Autumn 1992): 511–19.

Statutes of the Territory of Washington, Made and Passed at a Session of the Legislative Assembly Begun and Held at Olympia on the Fourth Day of October, 1869, and Ended on the Second Day of December, 1896. Olympia WA: James Rodgers, 1869.

Steele, E. N. *The Immigrant Oyster*. N.p.: Pacific Coast Oyster Growers Association, 1962.

———. *The Rise and Decline of the Olympia Oyster*. Elma WA: Fulco, 1957.

Stevenson, Shanna. *Lacey, Olympia, and Tumwater: A Pictorial History*. Norfolk VA: Donning, 1985.

———. *Superior Shipping Service: A History of the Port of Olympia*. Olympia WA: Port of Olympia, 1989.

Sturtevant, William C., ed. *Handbook of North American Indians*. Vol. 7, *Northwest Coast*, edited by Wayne Suttles. Washington DC: Smithsonian Institution, 1990.

Swanson, Jack. "Bainbridge Island: Old Is New Again." *Kitsap (WA) Sun*, February 15, 2001. http://m.kitsapsun.com/news/2001/Feb/15/bainbridge-island-old-is-new-again/.

Swanton, John R. *The Indian Tribes of North America*. Smithsonian Institution, Bureau of American Ethnology, Bulletin 145. Washington DC: U.S. Government Printing Office, 1952.

Taylor, Marian. "Seam-Itza." In *Shadows of Our Ancestors: Readings in the History of Klallam-White Relations*, edited by Jerry Gorsline, 200–201. Port Townsend WA: Empty Bowl Press, 1992.

Thornton, Russell. *American Indian Holocaust and Survival: A Population History since 1492*. Norman: University of Oklahoma Press, 1987.

Thrush, Coll-Peter. *Native Seattle: Histories from the Crossing-Over Place*. Seattle: University of Washington Press, 2007.

Thrush, Coll-Peter, and Robert H. Keller Jr. "'I See What I Have Done': The Life and Murder Trial of Xwelas, a S'Klallam Woman." *Western Historical Quarterly* 26, no. 29 (Summer 1995): 168–83.

"Treaty with Nisquallys &c Dec. 26, 1854." In *Statutes at Large and Treaties of the United States of America from December 1, 1851 to March 3, 1855*, edited by George Minot, 1132–37. Boston: Little, Brown, 1855.

Ulrich, Laurel Thatcher. *A Midwife's Tale: The Life of Martha Ballard, Based on Her Diary, 1785–1812*. New York: Vintage Press, 1991.

United States v. State of Washington. 873 F.Supp. 1422 (W.D. Wash. 1994).

United States v. Washington. 384 F.Supp. 312 (W.D. Wash. 1974).

Vancouver, George. *A Voyage of Discovery and to the North Pacific Ocean and Round the World*. London: J. Stockdale, 1801.

Van Kirk, Sylvia. *Many Tender Ties: Women in Fur-Trade Society*. Norman: University of Oklahoma Press, 1983.

Vowell, Sarah. *The Wordy Shipmates*. New York: Riverhead Books, 2008.

Walzer, Judith Leavitt. "Under the Shadow of Maternity: American Women's Responses to Death and Debility Fear in Nineteenth-Century Childbirth." *Feminist Studies* 12, no. 1 (Spring 1986): 129–54.

Washington State Department of Ecology. "DNR Bush Callow Act Handout and Available Maps." Shorelands and Environmental Assistance Program. Shellfish Aquaculture Regularory Committee meetings materials. August 27, 2007. http://www.ecy.wa.gov/programs/sea/shellfishcommittee/mtg2/5%20DNR%20Bush%20Callow%20Act%20Handout%20and%20Available%20Maps.pdf.

Waterman, T. T. "The Geographical Names Used by the Indians of the Pacific Coast." *Geographical Review* 12, no. 2 (April 1922): 175–94.

———. *Notes on the Ethnology of the Indians of Puget Sound*. Indian Notes and Monographs, Miscellaneous Series 59. New York: Museum of the American Indian, Heye Foundation, 1973.

Whaley, Gray H. *Oregon and the Collapse of Illahee: U.S. Empire and the Transformation of an Indigenous World, 1792–1859*. Chapel Hill: University of North Carolina Press, 2010.

White, Richard. *"It's Your Misfortune and None of My Own": A New History of the American West*. Norman: University of Oklahoma Press, 1991.

Williams, Phil, and Vivian Williams. *Pioneer Dance Tunes of the Far West*. CD. Seattle: Voyager Recordings, 2006.

Winthrop, Theodore. *The Canoe and the Saddle*. Portland OR: Franklin-Ward, 1913.

Work, John. "Journal of John Work, June 21–Sept. 6, 1825." *Washington Historical Quarterly* 5, no. 2 (1914): 83–115.

Wray, Jacilee, ed. *Native Peoples of the Olympic Peninsula: Who We Are*. Norman: University of Oklahoma Press, 2002.

Wright, E. W., ed. *Lewis and Dryden's Marine History of the Pacific Northwest: An Illustrated Review of the Growth and Development of the Maritime Industry*. Portland OR: Lewis and Dryden, 1895.